DreamBIG
OVERDeliver
BeUNDENIABLE

Jason Glass

© Jason Glass 2022

All rights reserved. No part of this publication may be reproduced, distributed, or transmitted in any form or by any means, including photocopying, recording, or other electronic or mechanical methods, without the prior written permission of the author, except in the case of brief quotations embodied in critical reviews and certain other non-commercial uses permitted by copyright law.

ISBN 9798843047801 (Paperback)

ACKNOWLEDGMENTS

This book is dedicated to my wife Julie, daughter Emily and son Jamie for supporting my mission to Inspire Others to Greatness and not letting me take myself too seriously in the process.

Big hugs to my family and friends for making me the man I am today. Thanks to my athletes for pushing my abilities as a coach and trusting me with their bodies, minds and competitive spirits; my Mentorship Graduates for allowing me to inspire them to DreamBIG, OverDeliver and BeUndeniable; my teammates Lance Gill and Mark Blackburn for their friendship, support and all the fun we shared together travelling the globe; and Greg Rose, Dave Phillips and Chris Poirier for providing me with a stage to live out my dreams.

Thank you to Jeff Karon for "polishing the turd" and making this book a reality, and Adam Stevenson for pushing me through the writer's block and encouraging me to continue.

And finally a huge thank-you to all Glisteners of the Coach Glass Podcast for giving me a reason to switch on the mic each week.

If you enjoyed this book, please gift it to someone who needs a little nudge toward their DreamBIG. It could be the best gift you ever give. I wrote this book for them!

FOREWORD:
BY MIKE WEIR

The book you are about to read is like a training manual to not only accomplish your goals, but your *dreams*. Reading it has allowed me to clearly identify the things that made me a champion and provided me with a ton of gems that I now incorporate in my performance plan.

Throughout my career on the PGA Tour, I have had the pleasure of working with some of the best coaches in the world. I've sought their insight to help me understand the mechanics of the game of golf and develop the physical engine needed to perform with consistency, accuracy, and power. A huge part of my success comes from my competitive spirit, ability to create clear goals, and follow up with a ferocious work ethic. Coach Glass refers to this process as *dreaming big, over-delivering* on your dreams, and *being undeniable* in the process.

Over the last couple of years, "J" as I call him, has helped me focus on where I'm at now and not where I wish I was or where I think I should be. Once you know where you are, you can take steps to improve without just hoping or having some unrealistic expectation of what you can do at this moment. Your future self starts here, and it needs to start *now*!

There is so much more to this book than optimizing your mind, body, and daily routine. The lessons you learn from Jason's personal life stories will help you navigate change, embrace struggle, and overcome insecurities by not taking yourself so seriously. *DreamBIG, OVERDeliver, BeUNDENIABLE* is a user manual for all the things we experience in being human and will empower you to rise up to the challenges you face, whether in your career, relationships, or personal life.

PREFACE:
AN OPPORTUNITY

My biggest fear is that you could spend the next five years chasing a dream that leaves you unfulfilled when you accomplish it. Even worse, you could spend those years without any idea of the destination, wandering aimlessly on a path determined solely by others. Your life is built from the thousands of choices you make every day, and the bigger the choices, the bigger the consequences.

You picked up this book because you are about to make a big decision, the kind of decision that will forever change the course of your life. You are looking for inspiration and direction on how to maximize your potential and ensure that you have the skills to execute this dream. It's worth spending some time diving deep into the *Why?* behind your decision before embarking on a plan.

This book will help you answer the *Why?* by uncovering your truly "big" dream, as well as provide the tools you need to make it a reality. That singular dream is what I call your DreamBIG™.

Working toward your DreamBIG will become a way of life. It is like adding jumper cables to the Law of Attraction and living your dreams in real time. Right now, you, like most people, have novel ideas, fantasies, and daydreams of fame and fortune, but they all just briefly spark and fizzle out without producing any lasting results. The only time a spark turns to flame is when that spark is in the presence of fuel—and that fuel is your focus. If you focus your energy into taking action, your spark will become a steady flame.

Your daily inspired actions and habits continually throw logs on the fire, which in turn provides heat for the important aspects of your life. Fire can create a warm, cozy place for you to curl up and read a book, or it can create a life-threatening catastrophe that burns your house down. The difference is where you focus the flame and how you manage the fire. This book is your personal safety guide to building the world's biggest bonfire of greatness: *your life.*

Avoid the Should Haves or Could Haves

This book is going to save you working your ass off for five years to accomplish your "dream" only to find out later that your dream was unfulfilling. So many people make life-altering choices based on epiphanies that happened in the blink of an eye. No background checks, no stepping away to take a breath, no seeing it from a height of 10,000 feet, and never asking, "Is this what I truly want?"

Why must we wait until we are on our death beds to realize that we should have taken life by the horns and made our one shot on earth a memorable one? Years and opportunities fly by at an ever-increasing speed. Are you a passenger or a pilot? A spectator or a player?

A lot of your friends and acquaintances will simply follow the same path their parents walked: Date, get married, get a practice dog, have a baby, and daydream about the day they retire. Others just let life happen to them: Date, baby…oops, marry, divorce, get an emotional support dog.

Professionally, I have seen thousands of coaches and professionals do the exact same thing. Tell me if this describes someone you know: Loved sports, career ended after high school or college, went into fitness because they loved being in the gym and heard that "those who can't, coach!" After years of working as a personal trainer, they had to decide if they should get a "real job" or open their own gym. "If I had my own gym, I would coach my way, on my schedule!"

They invest everything the bank will give them to create their vision. They end up, however, behind a desk at their gym, putting more reps in an Excel spreadsheet than on the gym floor, balancing their budget instead of their clients' diets, and managing their ungrateful staff instead of training. Is this really what they signed up for? I thought they said they wanted to be a coach!

You may know a chiropractor who goes to school for half of their life and racks up a lifetime of debt. Gets a job at someone else's clinic so they can pay off their student loans and save up so they can one day open their own clinic. The new clinic plops them into even deeper debt, which handcuffs them to the treatment table until the day they are treated to a pine box. They wanted to be a Doctor of Chiropractic, not a Doctor of Debt!

A social influencer with a dream of reaching more eyeballs might create content that doesn't match their sensibilities. They began to dislike the "likes" and spends the rest of their life avoiding the judging eyes of those who were categorized as "friends."

All these horror stories could have been avoided if they pursued the curriculum of DreamBIG. This book would be the main text, and the class would reverse-engineer your life, starting with *your* five-year goal, then working back to your three- and one-year goals. You would become crystal clear on exactly what you want out of life, diving deep into the currencies that you value and what you would do in exchange for them. You would mine for your Golden Nugget and find authentic ways to share it with the world. You would develop the skills needed to execute the checkpoints along the road to your DreamBIG and lay a foundation that makes producing your best work possible day in and day out. Finally, you would gain the ability to flawlessly recreate, morph, and adjust your DreamBIG to match your current needs and grow with you.

Focus on the Right Mindset

Over my long career in fitness, I have come to understand a few truths that can be applied to all aspects of your ambitions. If you want to truly make changes in your life, you need to approach the project with the right mindset.

Focusing on the outcome instead of focusing on the process is a recipe for failure. Your goal can be outcome-based, but your daily focus needs to be on the process.

Let's use weight loss as an example to demonstrate this concept. If you want to lose weight, don't buy a scale. The scale measures outcomes and not the process. If you use a scale, you will do one of two things:

1. Reach your goal weight and celebrate by reintroducing the things that got you into this mess in the first place ("I deserve it!").

2. Struggle to reach your goal weight and get frustrated. Frustration leads to you returning to your previous unhealthy coping mechanism ("Just this one, then tomorrow I will start for real!").

The only way you will truly lose the weight is if you change the reason you eat the things you eat and focus on the *why* behind your choice of physical activity. The Dali Lama once said, "Lose weight because you love yourself not because you hate yourself!" Eat what makes you feel good and engage in activities that energize you. Living by the foundations in "The Undeniable Body" chapter you will make you feel better, which in turn will make you want to live this way more often. The more you live using these foundations, the more you will, as a by-product, lose weight. You will continue this lifestyle because you feel amazing and forget about why you started it.

I have taken this same approach to career goals. If your goal is to make money, don't focus on making money. Focusing on money as the destination will send you down a path that will never quench your thirst for more money. Instead, focus on the currencies outlined in the chapter, "The Currency." You will live a life driven by the currencies of life and, as a by-product, become wealthy—and not just financially.

It is time to start the process of designing your DreamBIG and learning the skills needed to OverDeliver on that dream. It will be challenging. Anything worth accomplishing always is! But you will be Undeniable.

The stories and habits I share in this book will inspire you to take on challenges that will take you out of your comfort zone and test your fortitude. You have all the elements in you to accomplish your dreams. This book will shine a light on your unique abilities like a magnifying glass focusing energy that ignites your greatness.

Coach Glass Notebook January 13 Checklist

✓ 6:13 am: Write my first book.

✓ 6:14 am: Get coffee!

✓ 6:20 am: Return to writing my first book.

CONTENTS

ACKNOWLEDGMENTS	I
FOREWORD: BY MIKE WEIR	III
PREFACE: AN OPPORTUNITY	V
INTRODUCTION: MISSION DREAMBIG	1
PART I: Build Your DreamBIG	**5**
CHAPTER ONE: DREAMBIG CURRENCY	7
CHAPTER TWO: FIRST SUCCESSES	11
CHAPTER THREE: THE RULES OF DREAMBIG	17
CHAPTER FOUR: THE BOX	27
CHAPTER FIVE: THE GOLDEN NUGGET	36
CHAPTER SIX: SILENCE ALLOWS US TO TRULY HEAR	46
CHAPTER SEVEN: LIFE PURPOSE	52
CHAPTER EIGHT: THE ENTREPRENEURIAL WARRIOR	69
CHAPTER NINE: THE RESISTANCE	87
CHAPTER TEN: KNOW YOUR ROLE—DON'T SLOW YOUR ROLE	93
CHAPTER ELEVEN: FINDING THE WHY	103
CHAPTER TWELVE: WRITE YOUR FIRST DREAMBIG	115
PART II: OverDeliver	**119**
CHAPTER THIRTEEN: FLIP THE SCRIPT	121

CHAPTER FOURTEEN: PERSPECTIVE IS A CHOICE   125

CHAPTER FIFTEEN: INTENTION AND OVERDELIVERING   135

CHAPTER SIXTEEN: THE GAME PLAN   143

CHAPTER SEVENTEEN: SPEAKING SKILLS   157

CHAPTER EIGHTEEN: POLISH THE TURD   177

CHAPTER NINETEEN: THE SET-UP PUNCH METHOD   181

CHAPTER TWENTY: STAY FRESH   187

CHAPTER TWENTY-ONE: PROBLEMS AND SOLUTIONS   191

CHAPTER TWENTY-TWO: TIME TO OVERDELIVER   201

Part III: Be Undeniable   **205**

CHAPTER TWENTY-THREE: NO HOLDS BARRED   207

CHAPTER TWENTY-FOUR: UNDENIABLE BODY   227

CHAPTER TWENTY-FIVE: THE INJURY OBSTACLE   249

CHAPTER TWENTY-SIX: HOW TO BE A ROAD WARRIOR   257

CHAPTER TWENTY-SEVEN: THE UNDENIABLE MIND   263

CHAPTER TWENTY-EIGHT: PRESENT–FORMER–FUTURE SELF   279

CHAPTER TWENTY-NINE: CREATING CHANGE   287

CHAPTER THIRTY: SETTING THE UNDENIABLE STAGE   293

CHAPTER THIRTY-ONE: FACTORY RESET YOUR HARD DRIVE   299

CHAPTER THIRTY-THREE CLOSER TO THE DANGER ZONE   305

CHAPTER THIRTY-FOUR: SURFING FAILURE   317

Part IV: Balance Your Life   325

CHAPTER THIRTY-FIVE: COMPARTMENTALIZATION   327

CHAPTER THIRTY-SIX: THE MIDDLE-AGED ATHLETE   333

CHAPTER THIRTY-EIGHT: SELF CONFIDENCE AND SELF BELIEF   339

CHAPTER THIRTY-NINE: THE YIN–YANG OF LIFE   351

CHAPTER FORTY: TIME TO RECONNECT   359

Part V: You Have Reached Your Destination.   365

AFTERWORD: A LETTER FROM ME TO YOU   369

INTRODUCTION:
MISSION DREAMBIG

My mission in life is the following: Inspire others to greatness. This book will help you develop a similarly focused mission that will become clearer and more concise as you follow the lessons, rituals, and stories and complete the prescribed tasks.

I have lived by this life mission for the past ten years, and it has guided my daily actions, decision-making process, interactions with others, and how I view the world around me. When faced with an opportunity or decision in life, I keep coming back to the question, "Does this help me inspire others to greatness?" If it does, I do it. If it distracts me from my mission, I say no to it. It's that simple.

Will starting a podcast help me inspire others to greatness? Yes! I started the Coach Glass Podcast in 2013 and created a platform that changed my life as well as the lives of others. As of 2021, I have inspired and entertained more than one million listeners who call themselves the Glisteners, which is shorthand for Glass Listeners.

Should I start a junior golf academy to help high school aged kids grow into highly productive members of our community through fitness and the game of golf? Will it help me inspire others to greatness? Yes! I created the Tour

Performance LAB with my business partner and golf coach, Matt Palsenbarg, in 2010.

Should I train professional athletes? Will it help me inspire others to greatness? Yes! I have worked with athletes from the NHL, NFL, NBA, LPGA, the PGA Tour, and extreme sports. I have helped major championship winners, tour winners, Super Bowl competitors and Hall of Famers. Through their success, they have inspired countless other athletes to pursue their dreams.

Should I travel around the globe lecturing and mentoring coaches to help countless coaches accomplish their DreamBIGs so they can inspire greatness in others? The answer should be clear by now.

We will get to the task of you writing your life mission later in the book, but if you are that eager person who is itching to get started, you can attempt a first draft now. I guarantee it will evolve and morph as we get closer to what truly drives you and your DreamBIG.

To start a journey like the one you are about to embark on, you need to know the destination. You need to see the end result so you can draw a straight line in your mind from the person you are now to the person you will be at the end of this book. I think it was Nickelback that sang, "Started from the bottom now we here, started from the bottom now the whole team here!" Maybe it wasn't Nickelback, but the message is the same. I don't know where your "bottom" is, and I don't know what "here" means to you, but I do know what the most direct and authentic way to reach your destination is.

The "here" is really where you are at in your life right now. It is the present and the only thing that you have control over. You can't change the place you just were six months ago, but the actions you take in the "here" directly affect your future. What you do now will lead you to an unbelievable "there" if you take the right approach. "There" is what you are working towards, the place you want to get to. It is your DreamBIG.

I know you have heard before about being the author of your own life, but what we are about to do is not just write it, but actually live it. Imagine buying a ticket and watching a movie about a young boy with a dream of flying. The first scene shows him lying on his bed, looking up at the glow-in-the-dark, stick-on stars on his ceiling, dreaming of one day taking flight and exploring the universe. Over the next three hours, you watch him play on his smartphone, grow old, procrastinate, and float through an uninspiring life of blah. The movie ends with the main character living in the basement of his mom's house, depressed, looking at his outdated iPhone, wishing he had gotten off his ass and made the first step toward his dream of being a pilot.

You would be pissed! You just wasted three hours of your life watching that? Now replace the dream of flying with your dream and switch out the depressed slob of a character from the movie with yourself. How angry would you be if this movie was about you? At the end of your life, you looked back and wished you could get a refund for the movie you wrote, you directed, and you starred in.

That ain't happening on my watch! We are getting off the proverbial couch *now*, and we are burning it to the ground. We are taking a step forward that will build up so much momentum that it will take a nation of millions to hold us back.

Members of the public are average and mediocre, and you are Public Enemy Number 1. You are relentless, a bulldog, and there is no stopping you on your path to your dreams.

But I forgot to ask you the following:

What is your dream?

PART I: BUILD YOUR DREAMBIG

Before we start designing and planning out your goal or redefining an existing goal you have neglected to act upon, let's set out some ground rules. No dream is too small if it leads you toward bigger dreams. The only dreams that are too big are ones that defy the laws of science. "I want to levitate!" Okay, when you are done levitating, we will give you a couple of days for the magic mushrooms to leave your system, and then we will get to work on a realistic dream.

DreamBIGs should involve more than just financial or fame-based outcomes. Money rules the world—I get it—but you need to have other nonmaterialistic outcomes to go with your pile of money if that is your dream. If you dream of fame, it needs to be side-saddled with an outcome that will cushion the fall from grace, which is inevitable due to the yin-yang nature of fame. So let us discuss the currencies of a DreamBIG worth pursuing.

CHAPTER ONE:
DREAMBIG CURRENCY

There are many currencies in life: the currency of money, time, fame, freedom, and love are the most coveted. I'm not bragging, but I am wealthier than anyone I know. Money slowly accumulated over time as I became more sought after in my professional life. Financially, I became a millionaire at the age of 40, but that is only a drop in the bucket when it comes to the wealth I have created in my life.

My currency of love, freedom, and time took me from a millionaire on paper to a kazillionaire in life. I have a modest house, drive a modest car, and shop at Costco like everyone else. My true wealth is wrapped up in a mutual fund I created the day I met my wife. It is comprised of blue-chip stocks named Julie, Emily, and Jamie. It is a balanced portfolio with bonds of love, equities of freedom to make my own schedule, real estate holdings that give me a natural playground to run in each morning, and diversified security holdings of time to explore what it means to be me.

I wake up each morning at 6 am, grab a coffee, and sit at my computer with the Wi-Fi off and write. I then take my kids to school and get ready for either hot yoga, a kettlebell workout, or a run in the forest that surrounds my home. Then I come home, shower, have breakfast with my wife, and get in my home office/studio at around 11 am. I write my to-do list for the day to get me closer to my most recent project or DreamBIG. The Wi-Fi gets turned on, and the world now has access to me. After a late lunch and more work, I pick up the kids from school. I finish up any loose ends by 4:30 and then shut the door to my office, change my clothes, and turn into a dad, husband, and Chef Jay. I love to cook for my family and watch them enjoy my creations while we sit and eat together each night. Service to others is my love language, so I carve out opportunities to serve my loved ones daily.

How good does that sound? This may not be your cup of tea, but for me it is a DreamBIG come true. I created this world that I live in, and it is built on hard work, determination, and a deep understanding of what will bring me joy in my life.

It didn't just happen. I wrote out what I wanted and put together a plan that would make it a reality. I used the same techniques I share in this book to accomplish my DreamBIG.

I shared my story with you to help you dive deeper into the design of your DreamBIG. It can't be all about money and fame. If you focus on the accumulation of the other currencies of life, money and fame will become a garnish on the side of your plate instead of the main course for your happiness. We will dive deeper into this topic in a few chapters.

Throughout this book, I will provide you with strategies and systems to help you accomplish unimaginable things in your life. I will also be sharing stories about various DreamBIG experiences I have had and those dreams I have helped my athletes and mentorship graduates accomplish. I will share the hardships I have fought through to become Undeniable and how I Overdelivered time and time again. I will also share stories about my clients, friends, and colleagues who have created lives that dreams are made of and how they inspired me to Dream Bigger. If you want stories about historical dreamers like Columbus finding North America or modern-day dreamers like Jim Carey writing a postdated ten-million-dollar cheque to himself for "Acting Services Rendered" only to find ten years later that he was going to be paid ten million dollars for *Dumb and Dumber,* such stories are only a click away on the internet. The stories I am going to share have never been written down. These true stories are going to sink into your subliminal mind and feed your appetite for dreaming bigger.

I am going to share with you a secret: Back in the 1990s, a movie came out that swept through society, one DVD player at a time. It was called *The Secret,* which was clever because the goal of the movie was quite the opposite. The basic premise is that if you think it, feel it, taste it, and dream it, the universe will manifest it. If you want a Ferrari, all you need to do is think about a Ferrari and picture yourself driving the Ferrari with the wind in your hair and your hands on the wheel, and the universe will find a way to get you that Ferrari.

I kind of agree with this way of thinking except they were missing one key element: getting off your ass, working every day, and saving enough money to buy your Ferrari! If you just work, like the rest of us, you probably won't own a Ferrari. But if you went to bed every night and woke each morning dreaming of owning a Ferrari and worked each day saving your lunch money and every penny you have, you could own a Ferrari one day.

Spending every dime you ever earned on a car doesn't make financial sense and will probably bankrupt you. A better system would involve you dreaming about a plan that would create enough wealth and security that would make buying a Ferrari a responsible purchase, then working on that plan every day until it is realized.

I am all about dreaming *Big*. But the realization of that dream is based on hard work. This may sound cliché, but the true joy in accomplishing your dreams is actually in the journey. Every time I have reached a major DreamBIG in my life, I feel an incredible sense of accomplishment, followed instantly by a gut-wrenching feeling of emptiness. As you accomplish a dream, you lose the journey.

CHAPTER TWO:

FIRST SUCCESSES

I will never forget the day my first DreamBIG came true: I stood on the grandest stage, presenting my own material in front of hundreds of my peers, who were on their feet, clapping and cheering in response to my presentation. I had been a public speaker for a few years before I developed the DreamBIG vision. I was doodling in my notebook while passing time on a flight about eight months before the World Golf Fitness Summit. I drew a picture of myself from behind, looking out at the crowd with the lights in my face and my arms up in triumph. I looked down at the paper and started to stream tears of joy.

I can still see each stroke of this rough sketch I put on the page. It was burned into my mind from that day forward. I pictured it each night before I went to sleep and woke each day with a burning desire to get to work on my presentation and find new opportunities to work on my craft. This is inspired focus and not just putting in the work. Work just for the sake of work will yield different results.

I was pretty green and had only presented a few little workshops of my own and taught maybe a dozen seminars for the Titleist Performance Institute. I was by no means a world class presenter. Without opportunities to get on stage, I had to visualize it, feel it, and live it in my mind.

Fast forward to the 2008 World Golf Fitness Summit. I had the last spot on the final day of the Summit. I opened by running up through the crowd while wearing a lab coat and toward the stage with my entrance music blasting out the loudspeakers as though I was a cage fighter entering the ring. This had never done before at such an event and caught the audience and the organizers off guard.

I hit every beat and every note that I had choreographed in my mind each night before I went to sleep. I did my show exactly the way I envisioned, it and the place erupted. Friends and attendees rushed the stage afterwards to congratulate me and celebrate the finish to what was a magical event. The CEO of Perform Better, which is one of the largest distributers of fitness equipment and the world leader in fitness education, came up to me. "Can you do what you just did there for Perform Better minus the golf stuff?" Of course I could! My dream of one day becoming a Perform Better speaker and getting a standing ovation from my peers all came true in one slow-motion, dream-like moment.

After taking pictures and enjoying the accolades, I went up to my hotel room to call my wife and tell her how it went. As soon as I heard her voice, I felt an incredible emptiness and sadness come over me. Through my tears, I squeaked out, "I did it." Why the emptiness and the sadness? I had spent the previous eight months of my life thinking about nothing other than that image that I drew on that flight. I had climbed my Mount Everest. Standing on that peak, I came to the realization that I thought so much about getting up to the top I never prepared a plan for coming back down.

Where would I go? What would I do? I couldn't see the next peak that I needed to summit. The journey was over, and I felt like I had lost a friend who was in my conscious thoughts each day and was in my dreams when I slept. My friend was gone—the journey was over.

From Ferraris to Porsches

As a personal trainer, I worked with some of the most successful businesspeople in Vancouver. One of my clients was an entrepreneur who took massive chances which yielded incredible rewards and equally impressive failures. He pulled up for his workout late one day, and I was waiting at the entrance to the gym to let him know that I had been waiting. He parked his new Porsche 911 convertible and grabbed his gym bag from the back seat. I said, "Nice car!" He replied, "Yeah, it's my second Porsche, but this one is special."

We went for a warmup run through the neighbourhood while he shared with me the story of how he bought this car, and why it was so special to him. He said he had always dreamed of owning a Porsche. When he was in college, he pictured himself sitting in his Porsche, cruising the streets of Vancouver with a hot babe on his arm. The first

Porsche he bought was used and cost him every dollar he had from his inheritance he received from his grandfather. It wasn't much, but enough to get him his dream car. He drove the car for two years and never truly felt any joy from the realization of his dream.

The Porsche he envisioned in his dreams was a symbol of his success. He knew that if he worked hard and accomplished his dream of being a successful entrepreneur, he would be able to afford a Porsche. Due to the unfortunate passing of his grandfather, he had acquired the symbol of success without the actual success. As you can imagine, he went on to build numerous businesses and create incredible wealth. He drove a modest car, lived in a modest home, and put everything he had into his businesses. The purchase of his second Porsche represented the true realization of his DreamBIG. Years later, he still enjoyed his accomplishments when he fired up that engine that fuelled his future successes.

Mushroom Carpet

It doesn't matter where you are in life: It is all about the mindset. Whether you grew up in middle-class suburbia or on the streets of a slum, it is your mindset that will determine your future. It's not where you are at that matters; it is all about where you see yourself in the future that dictates your final destination.

When I was in college, I had one mindset: to graduate with my human kinetics degree and start working with athletes. I lived in the basement of a house with my stoner roommates who all worked at West Beach Skate and Snowboard Shop. I was the only student in the bunch. The basement was old and showed the wear and tear from the previous generations of basement dwellers. It flooded each raining season, which in Vancouver is three out of the four seasons. The shag carpet would change colours, and at one point, we had mushrooms growing in it. The shower had black mold, and we sublet our cupboards to a family of rats.

I know that all this sounds disgusting, but the funny thing is that I didn't notice. I was so determined to get what I wanted that my surroundings became a temporary place to inhabit while I chased my dreams.

I ran into an old roommate years later while I was in the park having a picnic with my wife and three-month-old daughter, Emily. This was a beautiful family moment with blankets, stroller, and belly time for the baby. "Jay Glass? Is that you?" my old roommate yelled as he cut across the field. "The last time I saw you I was in your dungeon smoking a bong and watching skate videos. What are you doing now? Married with a kid? What a trip!"

I told him I was working as a strength coach and living in the suburbs. "How the hell did you do that? Did you go to school or something?" What he didn't realize was that I was going to school for the entire five years I lived in the house. He was too stoned to realize that I wasn't home during the day—I was working toward my future.

15

It's not until you go back and see where you came from that you appreciate where you are today.

The future can seem like walking across a foggy field at night: You can see the light in the distance but have no idea how many cow pies you will step in along the way. No one can predict your final destination in detail. Instead, the final destination is determined by the decisions you make, the focused and inspired work you put in, plus a bit of luck. The most important thing you can do is take the first step toward the light and see where it gets you.

With each step, the fog will clear, and you will start to see an outline of the house that the light is coming from. As you get closer, you will see more and more detail until your destination is in high definition.

But   first   you   have   to   start.

CHAPTER THREE:

THE RULES OF DREAMBIG

T he Rules of DreamBIG establish a road map and rules of the road to help you navigate the journey toward your dreams. You will see these rules and recommendations pop up throughout each chapter. Here is a brief breakdown of the fundamentals.

Mine Your Golden Nugget

Everyone has something that is unique or special. You may not know what yours is, but I assure you that your friends and loved ones can see it in you. It is that little thing that makes them want to be a part of your life. Once I learned that I had the ability to inspire others and accepted that comedy was an integral part of everything I do, I finally found success.

Maybe you possess leadership qualities or empathy. Maybe you are a great listener or have an incredible work ethic. Maybe you are particularly creative or are very organized. Maybe you are good at lifting heavy shit up and putting it back down again. Whatever it is, it must be a part of your DreamBIG.

Set the Stage

Create an environment that is conducive to big-picture thinking. When creating a DreamBIG, some people find it helpful to locate a special coffee shop, park bench on the ocean, or a family cabin in the woods. You want to create the big-picture concepts in places that inspire you.

Imagine coming up with your DreamBIG, the thing that is going to change your life, while sitting on the toilet in your underwear. Now picture sitting in the lounge of a beautiful hotel with marble floors, comfy seats, and a view of the skyline. For the cost of an overpriced coffee, you can feel like you are actually staying at the hotel. Doesn't your DreamBIG deserve a little pampering?

Be Extremely Clear on the Destination

A big chunk of this book is dedicated to finding the DreamBIG that will truly fulfill you in all aspects of your life. This is an important step that many fail to take the time to work through. What happens to those who neglect this important stage of their journey is that they lose momentum along the road to their destination because they were never really into reaching it. It would be like you sitting on your couch while friend says, "You know what we should do? We should get a McDonalds ice cream cone from the drive-through." Once you get there, the line is so long you that realize it's not worth waiting 30 minutes for an ice cream cone, and you bail.

Your DreamBIG is not an ice cream cone—it is *every-thing.* James Clear, author of *Atomic Habits,* says, "You need to have a rigid destination but be flexible on the journey you take to get there. Start with magic and then work backwards!" This book will help you explore your magic.

Map Out Your Journey Before Embarking

Make sure that your DreamBIG destination will take you on a path that will be enjoyable. Don't pick a horrific path to an awesome payoff. You will fail. The journey is the destination. It is the journey toward your DreamBIG that gets you up each day and energizes you to keep putting one foot in front of the next.

Pick your destination and draw a line that connects where you are yo where you want to be. If the entire road is filled with tar pits, quicksand, and pastures covered in cow pies, you may want to find alternate route. You aren't looking for an easy path—in fact, you want challenging mountain ranges, rivers to cross, and snowdrifts to slide down. Each obstacle is like a classroom that will teach you about yourself and give depth to your accomplishments.

Routine

Create a routine that can resist distractions. Studies show that being distracted while performing a focused task will take you 23 minutes and 15 seconds to return to the workflow you were in before the distraction.

I wake up at 6 am every day and write before the kids and the rest of the world wake. I keep my Wi-Fi off until I decide I want the world to have access to me. I have coffee, water, and a light snack on hand. I even went as far to install an "On Air" sign like the ones at a radio station or film studio. If the light is on, leave me alone!

Accountability Partner

Share your DreamBIG with an accountability partner. You don't want someone asking you if you made your bed, flossed, and washed behind your ears. But you do want someone who can be excited about your journey and check in with you from time to time to see how it's going.

I have a friend who was once a mentee of mine who became a mentor. When he came to my yearly Mentorship, he said he wanted to be an author. Now three books deep, he was the perfect person for me to tell that I was writing a book. Every month or so he checks in and asks how the book is coming along and shares some insight into the roadblocks and triumphs he faced when writing his first book (thank you, Adam!).

Notebook It

Get a notebook or notepad. Your DreamBIG notebook is a place for you to journal your journey and plan your next move. When you reach your destination, you will be able to look back and see all the steps, setbacks, obstacles you overcame, and victories you had along the way.

Create an Overdeliver Mindset

An Overdeliver Mindset is like buying your lover the perfect gift. Is that enough? *Nope.* You need to wrap it in beautiful wrapping paper. Is that enough? Can you do more? Of course, you can! How about you OverDeliver and put a bow on it and deliver that personally-made mix while wearing a string of Christmas lights around your nether regions? Now that's OverDelivering.

Be Undeniable

You will need a strong mind and strong body to get to the end of this journey. You will need to incorporate life-style changes to increase your capacity to work through the hard times and overcome any obstacles that obstruct your path.

It's quite simple. Set your mind to being the best version of yourself and hold yourself accountable to that ideal. You don't have to have an eight-pack that reaches your pubes or biceps that is so big you can't scratch your nose. You just need to respect your body by eating clean, committing to being hydrated, sleeping like it's your job, and finding a way to move beautifully every day.

Start

The most important thing you can do right now is START. Whenever you are thinking, *Should I or shouldn't I?* just START. Let's go....

You are going to need a notebook or notepad, preferably a fresh one. Go get one right now — we will wait for you.

Now write on the top of the first page "DreamBIG." Flip five pages forward and write today's date. This is the start of your checklist.

Checklist Item #1:

✓ Start your DreamBIG notebook. (You just accomplished your first checkmark.)

Place the notebook off to the side. We need to add some context to the journey you are about to embark on. I had you flip forward five pages to start your checklist because the first five pages are reserved for your DreamBIG and any alterations you may make to it along the way.

The DreamBIG will be formulated over the coming week while you dive into the DreamBIG section of the book. This section is designed to spark ideas and open your mind to the possibilities that await you upon this journey. I share personal stories and stories from my mentors, colleagues, and inspirational figures that will help you define your DreamBIG and ensure that it is a journey worth embarking on.

This notebook will be a roadmap, journal, and an accountability partner for you. I have kept every notebook from every DreamBIG I have accomplished in my career. One day my wife was clearing out the office and came across my pile of notebooks. To an outsider, they look like dog-eared scribble pads with checkmarks, crossed out items, and random thoughts. I shouted, "Don't throw those out! Those are my notebooks. Every DreamBIG I have had are written on those pages." As she flipped through them, she said, "Oh, I remember that: You ended up getting that job. Oh, this is when you wanted to create your lab coat thingy show you did, and this is when—you know, every one of these came true."

She then stopped me in my tracks: "Maybe you should DreamBIGGER!"

My notebooks evolved over time. I was given a beautiful leather-bound notebook for speaking at an event in Beijing, China. I thought, *This is such a beautiful book, a book worthy of my next DreamBIG*. The problem was that it was too nice. I was afraid to make a mistake in it like it was a piece of art. I much prefer to think of the notebook as workbook of sorts. Coffee mug stains, different coloured pens, doodles, and anything else that was on my mind that day made it on those pages. No judgement, just the blood, sweat, and tears that combined to create the greatest accomplishments of my career.

At first, I would draw a little box beside each item so I could check it off when it was completed. Each checkmark represented my getting one step closer to accomplishing my dream. One day, I had a particular line item that had stared at me for three weeks. I put it off each day and would have to transfer it to the next page. I put it at the top of the next page in the hopes that I would make it a priority and finally knock it off my list. After three weeks, I had enough. I woke up and went to work at typing out the written description for each of my 16 weeks of LoadXplode workouts, a daunting task that took me the entire day. When I pressed "Save" for the final time, I grabbed a pen and scratched a deep line across the item. No checklist for this one: Oh no, this one deserved being literally scratched off my list. It felt incredibly liberating.

From that day forward, I draw a line through each item on my list. No more checkmarks, but for some strange reason, I still draw the little boxes. Like giving your BBQ tongs three test clicks every time you pick them up, there are some things you just do.

This isn't rocket science—we are just breaking down the steps into digestible morsels. If this was the secret to success, this book would be over at the end of this page. It is, however, one of the most important habits for accomplishing your DreamBIG. Each page can represent a day or a week. Make sure you put the date on each page so you can refer back to when each element was completed. You can do it any way you like. Checked boxes, scratch-throughs, or little happy faces, I don't care. You just need to ensure that every day you have a list of actionable items that will get you one step closer to your dream.

I want you to have a pile of success stories in your office one day. When you need a confidence boost, you can flip through the old notebooks and see how this process helped you in the past. But before we focus on creating a pile of notebooks, let's start with the first one, which is the most important, the one that creates the habits for the others to be built upon.

At the end of this book, your notepad will be filled with some amazing accomplishments and hundreds of completed tasks. It is exciting to think that your journey is about to begin. Get fired up. This is a big deal.

Before we begin checking off boxes, we need to define our DreamBIG. Read through the rest of this section and learn the techniques needed to pick the right DreamBIG for where you are in your career or life stage. If you have something in mind, jot it down on a separate piece of paper. Place it in your notebook and see if it holds up after reading the DreamBIG section.

It's like getting a tattoo. I always tell people to draw what they want for their tattoo on their skin with a Sharpie first. After three weeks, if there isn't anything you would change, then get it done. Inevitably, most people will change the font, size, or colour of the tattoo. Unlike a tattoo, your DreamBIG will evolve through this process, but I do want the first rendition of it to be legit. If you don't have any clue what you are capable of accomplishing, enjoy the stories and perform the tasks on the coming pages and get to work. Start.

CHAPTER FOUR:

THE BOX

So many of you live your life through the lens through which others see you. You become the person that the people around you expect you to be. You are confined by the box that you allowed others to put you in. This book will help you escape or redefine that box. It will help you create a box that *you* designed. When you do that, it changes the way others interact with you and the way you interact with the world.

I want you to live your life from a new perspective. I want you to view the world from inside the box looking out and not from the outside world looking in. There is a massive difference between these two perspectives, and we will dive deep into them later in this book.

My life mission is "Inspire others to greatness," but it also has a sidebar: "Express your creativity without boundaries." This mission helps me with my main life mission by encouraging me to express myself without worrying about what others may think.

Imagine how many people you could inspire if you didn't have to worry about the repercussions from speaking truthfully from your heart. This mission statement allows me to express myself in ways that may not fit inside the box that others want me to fit in. I am a husband, a father, an entrepreneur, a strength coach, and a lecturer. If you read those descriptors without knowing me, you might expect to meet a pretty serious dude. What doesn't fit in that box is what makes me the person I am: a silly goose, a stand-up comic who goes to hot yoga classes and loves to cook. I was once described as "The Stoic Buddha" based on how I approach life and help others break through their personal barriers. Well, how the hell are you supposed to fit all that in the box that your mind previously built for me based on what I do for a living?

I will never forget a mind-altering experience I had when I was 18. No, it wasn't LSD. The summer of my 18th year, I went on a solo journey to Greece. It wasn't really the travel thing that many high school grads do before they start "real life." It really was more of a "Oh shit—I don't know what to do with my life, so travelling sounds like fun" thing.

As I jumped from island to island, I met many unique people from different countries, ethnic backgrounds, and contrasting cultures. The best part was that none of them knew me. No one I met had a preconceived idea of who I was based on the box that my family and friends built around me over the previous 18 years. In my last two years of high school, I was awarded Athlete of the Year. I was a skateboarder with divorced parents, a brother and stepbrother, an ex-boyfriend, and a class clown. But to these island-hopping wanderers, I was Jay, the Canadian. For the first time in my life, I didn't have to be the life of the party, the leader, the one to bring your problems to. I was able to shed the roles that I felt others had put on me. I arrived at each island with a blank slate. I was a quiet loner who wanted to experience the world on his terms. There was no one to say, "Nah, I hate vineyards. Let's go to the beach instead."

As I spent time with people I met along the way, I was shocked at how quickly I fell back into my role as an entertainer, leader, and confidant. These strangers saw me as the same person that the others back home saw, but somehow it was different. This time it was on my terms. It took a while to sink in, but the reaction of others to me without any idea of who I was back home confirmed who I really was: *me*. The contents inside the box resembled the labels that others had put on the outside.

TODAY'S TASK: Take a piece of paper and draw a vertical line down the middle dividing the paper into two halves. On the left hand side of the page, I want you to write down all the labels or descriptors you feel those around you would use to describe you. Once you have taken some time to compile this list, I want you to write a list of who you are on the inside of the box on the right side of the page. The inner box person is the one that you see when you truly look in the mirror, the person you are when no one is watching, the inner you.

This exercise can be an extremely valuable and nice way to start your journey to understanding who you really are, and it will help create a life mission that fits. This exercise can also be challenging, especially if there are descriptors on either side of the list that trigger you. Read each descriptor and take note of how it makes you feel on an emotional level. If an item on your list angers you or maybe never even made it on the page in the fear of someone else reading it, you need to dive headfirst into it. It is a part of you and probably the way others around you see the outside of your box. You can change it. But only if the person inside the box has changed.

We all hate to admit it, but we live our lives through the lens of how others see us. You do things a certain way and say things that receive a favourable response. More importantly, we avoid saying things that will produce a negative reaction from those around us. You put on a Hawaiian shirt with a lizard surfing on it because it makes you feel like you are on vacation. As soon as your wife sees it, she instantly rejects it and has it off your back and into the Goodwill donation bag faster than you can say, "Aloha." You show up at your homie's BBQ with a six pack of Zima and vegan garden burger patties and never get invited back. The people you surround yourself with shape your identity.

What if they got you all wrong? What if the person they think you are or should be is not the same as the person you truly are inside? I have faced this personally my entire life and could write a three-part miniseries on just this topic. I will share a few examples to help you connect with some of the dissonance or internal struggles in the person you present yourself to the world as.

When I was 12, one morning during my summer holidays I watched a movie that came on one of the 5 channels we had access to back then. The movie was about a young man who finds his true self through tap dancing. Gregory Hines gave the performance of a lifetime. I didn't understand the feelings that were brewing inside, but one thing was for sure: I had to tap. I took two bottle caps and stepped on them as hard as I could. I practiced a few moves and thought, *I am a natural.* I looked out the window at my neighbourhood crew who were out on the street kicking rocks. I ran outside on my heels to avoid losing my tap caps, excited to share my new discovery.

"Hey guys. Check this out." I must have tapped my little feet off they were moving so fast. The sound of the caps hitting the asphalt was like hail on a tin roof. I flailed my arms like Michael Jackson on the Pepsi commercial set when his hair caught on fire. I finished with a spin, jumped up, and landed in a showbiz *ta-da!* stance while shaking my "jazz" fingers. I held my pose and looked up at my buddies who had their arms crossed and looks on their faces like they just saw someone having a seizure.

"What the hell was that, Glass? That was whack."

In one instant, my dreams of being a world-class tap sensation were dashed by some kid whose name I don't even remember. Just imagine the life I would have had tapping my way around the globe, inspiring the next generation of tap dancers. Obviously, that wasn't going to be my destiny, but the lesson was clear: Don't share your dreams with others or you will be ridiculed. But this is a horrible way to live: Suppressing your dreams is a recipe for a life unfulfilled.

I didn't realize it at the time, but the movie really wasn't about tap dancing at all. It was about a man with a dream and the journey he took to see it come true regardless of the obstacles the world put in his path.

Have you ever had one of these moments? One morning you are daydreaming in bed and an idea is sparked in your mind that will change your life forever. You excitedly run downstairs to tell your significant other your incredible revelation. As you fumble through trying to describe your rough draft of an idea, you clearly see that they are not as jacked up about this concept as you seem to be. You started the conversation with the energy of a tornado and it tapered off at the end like a light breeze that wouldn't blow out a candle. Why is it that something so profound can be doused by others with one look of disbelief?

The problem is that the people around us put us in a box that makes us easily identifiable. Any time we step outside of that box, it disrupts this visual they have of us, and they try to rectify it. My neighbourhood friends saw me as the funny skater kid. Why can't I be the funny skater kid that tap dances? In high school, the preppy girls couldn't accept that I had long hair and wore surf shorts and skate shirts in the winter. They said I would look super cute with a flat-top haircut and wanted me to wear polo shirts and khakis like everyone else in our group. My college football teammates didn't understand why I shaved a line in my hair and listened to the Beastie Boys instead of AC/DC before games. When I was a personal trainer, my colleagues wouldn't accept that I was married and wouldn't sleep with my clients.

When I was lecturing, my co-presenters struggled to accept my inability to keep inappropriate innuendos to myself instead of sharing them with the audience. I couldn't help it—I was also a stand-up comic. I needed an outlet, so I took the stage at night as my alter ego, JJ Murphie. Why did I have to change my name to do comedy? What would my colleagues and seminar attendees think if they found out I did stand-up? I might lose my job.

But this is who I am.

I never took tap dancing lessons but ended up in a breakdancing crew, trading my taps shoes for shell-toe Adidas. I cut my hair and wore preppy clothes to impress the girls and never got a date. I still have a shaved head and think the Beastie Boys are the best band ever. I have been 100% faithful to my wife and didn't lose any clients over it. I now jump on comedy stages as Jason Glass and integrate my humour into my lectures.

Now who are you?

34

CHAPTER FIVE:

THE GOLDEN NUGGET

You are an individual. You are unique. You are one in a million.

You probably read the previous statements and said to yourself, "Of course I am." Many of you may have had a cheeky little smile growing inside of you as you read them. It feels good to be different, to be noticed, to be appreciated, to stand out from the pack. The need to be noticed is built into our DNA. "Look Mom. Over here—watch this."

Society, however, likes to organize us in groups. First, we divide you into male, female, or other; separate you by skin colour, age, weight, and any other initial physical first impression we can make about you. After that, we need to get to know you a little deeper and have a conversation about your beliefs and personal preferences to see if you are one of "us" or one of "them" and subdivide you even further. This subculture could be based on your religion, sexual preference, job, where you live, who you support, or your financial status. "I am a bald, nondenominational, middle-class, heterosexual, white, male strength coach." "I am a tall, college-age, Islamic, upper-class, bisexual, Asian, transgender, Midwestern police officer."

As you read these descriptors, you started to build a Mr. Potato Head in your mind of what that person looked like. Many of you, unfortunately, also made some judgments about this person without having the information needed to validate these assumptions. Are they nice people? Are they skilled? Could they contribute to the team? Are they one of "us" or one of "them"? As much as society wants to put you in a category, you have an inner desire to be unique.

Once you get a large group of people together, the group will start to subdivide. Each of these subsets will have smaller subsets inside of them. Looking at the group from an altitude of 10,000 feet, the members all look uniform. But the closer you look at the group, the more you will see that each and every person that makes up that group is an individual.

If you look at a military group, for instance, you can tell the difference between a member of the US Armed Forces and the Viet Cong. They wear different uniforms, different headgear, and are of noticeably different ethnicity. It is easy to create an "us" and "them." But inside the US Armed Forces, there is the Army, Air Force, Navy, Marine Corp, Coast Guard, and National Guard. The Army thinks the Navy is lazy, the Air Force looks down on the Army, and the Marines hate them all. Inside the Navy, you can subdivide them even further. "Oh, I am different. I'm not like those guys. I am special. I am a Navy Seal." It even goes further: "Yes, I am a Navy Seal, but I'm not like these muscle-head assassin teammates of mine. Oh no. I have a PhD in Engineering and specialize in ballistics. I have a family waiting for me back home in Toledo and play drums in a garage band that covers Rush songs. I am no Neil Peart, but one day I hope to stand beyond the gilded stage. You may not understand that reference because you are not one of us." You are an individual? You are unique to everyone else in your Seal Team, in the Navy, in the US Armed Forces? But to the Viet Cong, you are all the same: the enemy.

> *All the world's indeed a stage*
> *And we are merely players*
> *Performers and portrayers*
> *Each another's audience*
> *Outside the gilded cage*
> *Living in the limelight*
> *The universal dream*
> *For those who wish to seem*
> *Those who wish to be*
> *Must put aside the alienation*
> *Get on with the fascination*
> *The real relation*
> *The underlying theme*

(Lyrics from Rush's "Limelight," *Moving Pictures*)

What the hell does all of this have to do with selling more boxes, getting more clients, or creating an audience? *Everything.* Understanding that everyone seeks individuality and uniqueness and has a deep desire to be noticed can be an incredibly powerful tool. Not only do they want to be unique, but they also seek out others who are unique—just like them.

On my first day of high school, I saw a kid wearing a Bones Powell Peralta shirt. I instantly knew he was a skater, and we were going to be friends. *He is different but different like me.* The secret is to find what makes you different and dive deep into it. Once you do that, you will attract more people who are different and appreciate your unique qualities.

In an organization or subculture, there are certain norms you must adhere to. In the golf industry, you are expected to wear a golf shirt and khakis and have Lego hair (hair that you can take off one person and plop on another person, and they look the same). Just walk through the PGA Show in Orlando, and you will see 10,000 Lego-haired clones. "But I'm a Titleist guy, not one of those Taylor Made wannabes. Oh, here comes one of those Ping guys—they are so weird."

You are all the same. Want to be unique? Tell me what you are into when you aren't golfing. What are your other passions? "You like to cook? Cool. I love to cook as well, but I do all my cooking in a plastic bag. Maybe we should start a club. The Lego-Haired Sous Vide Assassins." See what we did there? We just took two people from what seemed like a common group and made them a unique subsect.

What Is Your Golden Nugget?

The Golden Nugget is the unique thing that describes you that can't be visually detected. Its deeper than your job title, what you wear, how you do your hair, and the car you drive. Suppose a close friend of yours told you about this guy they recently met: "You got to see this dude. When he steps in the room, the place lights up with energy. He has the ability to fill a room with laughter, and two minutes later, go so deep that the audience is holding back tears. He inspires people to maximize their potential in life both physically and mentally."

Are you interested in meeting this guy? Suppose this same person was described in this way: "I met this guy who is a bald, nondenominational, middle-class, hetero-sexual, white, male strength coach." Uh, no thank you. I'm sure there are thousands of those, he is not worth my time or energy. But the first guy you described? I am all in.

The difference between these descriptions of the same person is the Golden Nugget.

I have a friend and colleague, Dave Phillips, who is one of the world's most renowned golf-teaching professionals and often called the co-creator of golf fitness. Dave's Golden Nugget is storytelling. If you have ever had the pleasure of having dinner with Dave, you would be in awe of his ability to hold a room's attention through his gift of story. The first time I witnessed this talent was at a Titleist dinner where Dave was at the head of the boardroom-like table filled with a dozen of the region's top golf pros. Dave told story after story, and each one made the audience demand more.

Later that evening while leaving the restaurant, I told Dave we should travel the world hosting events called Dinner with Dave and sell tickets. Dave realized his Golden Nugget early in his career and uses his natural storytelling ability to propel him up the ranks in his profession. Here is how this example will help you. If I were Dave's business manager, we would both make millions. To maximize his performance as a leader, business developer, and salesman, I would set up meeting rooms akin to how a kindergarten teacher sets up story time. I would have Dave at the front of the room or head of the table and the customers (audience) in a semicircle around him. Dave's only job that week would be to curate a story that coincides with the product or action we want the customers to take. I would then let loose the storytelling maestro and watch for the perfect opportunity to send in my closer to seal the deal. For the deal closer, I would need someone with a Golden Nugget that was able to coolly calculate, adjust on the fly, and thrive on getting a "W" (that is, a win).

Utilizing your Golden Nugget and understanding your teammate's strengths and weaknesses allows you to get the most out every opportunity.

At my yearly Mentorship event, I have the opportunity to help each mentee find their Golden Nugget and then build a plan to turn it into their DreamBIG. One of them was a physiotherapist who was struggling to find that special little something that separates him from the rest of the pack. I asked him, "What makes you different from all the other Physio in Canada? If I lined you up against a wall with every other physio, what would make you stand out?"

He struggled to find that unique thing. I prodded him to think of what brought him to the profession. "I just want to help people." I replied, "Great. Step back in line with everyone else. Every Physio wants to help people. What makes you different? What do you do when you aren't physioing?"

He grinned. "I love drumming. I used to be in a punk band in college, and any time my wife leaves the house with the kids, I run into my basement and jump behind my drum set. I bang away until I hear the front door open, then wipe the sweat from my brow and go back to being a dad."

I told him he needed to combine his two passions. "Do drummers ever need soft-tissue treatments or physio visits? Why don't you write a blog post or start a website that is aimed at drummers looking for information on drum-related overuse injuries?"

He took my advice. It was slow at first, but soon enough the drumming community got behind his unique content. He said that he would race home each day after work to write articles on proper warm-up techniques and how to adjust your posture and drum ergonomics to reduce fatigue. He was alive. A year later, he received an email from a legendary rocker who wanted him to stop writing his blog posts. He was asking him to put down the pen and come on the road as the head physio on their upcoming world tour. He is now travelling the globe sharing his greatness.

What is your Golden Nugget?

TODAY'S TASK: Explore your Golden Nugget. Think about what separates you from the pack. What is that thing that you do that makes the people around you pay attention and take action? I want you to describe yourself without using any descriptors that would allow someone to put you in a subsect. Once we have defined your Golden Nugget, we will amplify it and use it as the superpower that makes you Undeniable.

We are all artists with a gift. For some of you, the gift may be musical, athletic, mathematical, visual, social, or like me, the gift of gab. The key is acknowledging your gift and then freeing yourself to express your gift and share it with the world.

To truly express your gift, you need to consciously decide to not care what others think. You need to make this a way of life when you are in the act of creation. Thoughts of what others may think about what you are creating will stifle the creative process. Creating with regard for the approval of others is like colouring in a colouring book. You can choose the colour of crayon you use and how hard you press on the paper, but you are still colouring inside the lines of someone else's creation. This is safe and can be enjoyable for a short period of time, but to truly express your art, you need to start with a blank canvas and create your own lines.

If you are working from your heart and being honest to your inner artist, you will be free to create truly unique pieces that represent a little piece of you. Share your gift without any monetary expectations, adulation from your peers, approval from your loved ones, or future benefit and you will truly be free to create personal excellence.

Creation for the sake of renumeration will shape the creation process. Don't get me wrong: It is great when you can earn money and adulation doing the thing you love, but don't make monetization the starting point.

Once you find your Golden Nugget, it is time to share it with the world and create a community of people who appreciate its shimmer. Usually, these people have similar passions, values, and beliefs, and live a similar way of life. If you are opening a small boutique-style gym, for instance, picture in your mind what the perfect client would be who would satisfy your needs so you could feel fulfilled in your daily work. Envision ten of these curated clients all together at a social event. What are they talking about? What kind of activity would they all want to enjoy together?

If your goal is to make obscene amounts of money, surround yourself with money people in a position of power. If your goal is to create a more caring and spiritually enlightening environment, find people with a more altruistic character and create charitable events you can all get behind. Write out in detail what this group would look like and detail the characteristics of the individuals who make up this community.

Now here is the kicker: Share this detailed ensemble with your closest friends and colleagues. They should read it and instantly respond with, "Oh hell, yes. This is so you." That's when you know you nailed it.

The next step is to go out and market yourself to this community. You will find great marketing techniques and insight in the Greatest Salesman chapter, but we aren't done dreaming.

CHAPTER SIX:

SILENCE ALLOWS US TO TRULY HEAR

Have you ever sat behind a great DJ and watched them endlessly loop record after record, seamlessly matching beats and tempos to create new organic music from records that were created long before? If the DJ does their job, they can change the mood and energy in the room, making people sway together with their hands in the air like they just don't care, then the next moment making them jump around, jump up, and get down. What sounds like a smooth, beautifully-orchestrated execution of a thought-out plan through the speakers is actually organic chaos behind the turntables. The DJ is so busy focusing on what comes next that they rarely get a chance to listen to the music they are currently playing.

This is a great metaphor of the way we live our lives. The fast-paced world we live in has us reaching into the crate and putting the next record on before we even had a chance to enjoy the one that's under the needle. We try to find the next matching beat before the song ends to avoid leaving a gap of silence. Occasionally we look up to see how the audience is responding to the beats we are pumping out, then back into the crate to find the next banger.

In 2020, the Covid 19 virus forced us to lift the needle from the record during an unprecedented worldwide shutdown. Planes stopped flying, businesses shut their doors, borders closed, kids were home from school, parents were laid off, and people performed social distancing to curb the ferocious spread of the virus. In the absence of the world's relentless spinning turntable, a few things happened. People had the time to dig in their crates, unearth records that had been neglected, and dust off some rare gems. We also had the time to examine grooves that had been over-played and become aware of missing pieces in our box of beats that could use some freshening up. New grooves were explored, old grooves were made new again.

Every great DJ has a set list that they roll out for weddings and another for a late-night club gig. They know what will get the crowd bumping. Often there is a disconnect between what we think the audience wants to hear and the groove that our inner DJ wants to spin. We are constantly pumping out the same product, message, energy, and content. The product we play through the speakers to our audience gets played so many times that we start to believe that it's our anthem.

What drives us to put our playlist on a continual loop is the response from our community in the form of a like, a thumbs-up, increased sales, and high-fives. Take this time to analyze whether the music you have been playing matches the backbeat of your DreamBIG.

You have goals, DreamBIGs, and final destinations that push you to get up each morning and put in the work. For some people, the driver of this movement forward is fame, money, accolades, and respect from peers. There is nothing wrong with this type of ambition. You will be successful once you *reach 100K followers, get that vacation home, open a second location for your business*, or *gain a spot on the main stage*. You have been playing this playlist for so long that it becomes background music. Sometimes you don't even it hear it playing. What happens to all these goals when you lift the needle from the record?

Silence allows us to truly hear.

In the absence of noise, you can hear your heartbeat. Your heart has been beating this whole time—you just couldn't hear it. Your heartbeat, metaphorically speaking, is the true essence of who you are and what you have to offer the world. We mask the sound of our hearts with our day jobs, daily routines, hobbies, and interests that act as an ever-looping track in our headphones. We are constantly distracting ourselves with YouTube videos, Netflix series, and social media, distracting ourselves from dealing with what we really need—anything to keep the turntables turning and drown out the sounds that really matter.

Stop.

What you really need is to connect to the rhythm of your heartbeat. If you listen hard enough, your heart will find some neglected records you put in the crate a long time ago. You put them in there for a reason: They resonated with your soul. They may have been overlooked and left out of your usual mix because the melody seemed be too slow, mellow, or off beat. Put them back in the rotation. You may rediscover the underlying groove that is truly your jam: for example, a desire to belong, to be a part of something bigger than yourself, to contribute, or to express yourself creatively. Tap into that groove. Make note of each track that makes you really move.

Once the turntable of life starts up again, you will need these records to keep you dancing to the correct beat. This is the beat that drives your true DreamBIG.

Take this time to be in silence. Spend quality time with the ones you love. Walk in nature without headphones. Paint, write, renovate, cook, and feel. Create for the sake of creating and not for the sake of financial reward. Do something for someone else because its the right thing to do and not for what it will do for you.

Actively being in silence could be one of the most important elements you add to your daily routine. When I talk about silence, I don't mean the world around you has to be silent. Your mind does, however. Sometimes I find my deepest silence in a world of chaos. I will dive deep into strategic planning or programming for my athletes with hip hop backbeats in the background or plan out my month in the buzzing hum at a busy coffee shop.

External noise isn't the distraction you are seeking to avoid—it is the internal noise you want to quiet. You need to switch off the task-orientated parts of the mind to activate the creative ones. Dreams are created by the creative mind. The task-oriented mind takes the executable tasks that make up your dreams and feeds off the fuel from scratching each item off the list.

CHAPTER SEVEN:

LIFE PURPOSE

It is way too early in this book for you to clearly identify your life purpose. To do that, you need to sit with your feet deep in the murky waters of our DreamBIG discovery. At this point, we have barely dipped our toes in. I do, however, want to plant the seed. I would hate for you to get through all the work and self discovery in this book and not understand that gurgling feeling in your gut, screaming to get out and be acknowledged.

Your life purpose isn't something you decide. It's not a goal—it's what drives you toward your goals. It's not your DreamBIG. It's what your DreamBIG will satisfy.

Your life purpose is the driver of everything you do. As Confucius once wrote, "He who rides on dolphin does so on porpoise." You would think if it was so present in your day-to-day life, you would know what it is. I thought the same thing until a mentor of mine asked me what my life purpose was. I told him that I was born to be a coach. He replied that being a coach is what you do. A coach is a job, a thing, while your life purpose can't be a thing. If you lost all your clients and had no ability to express yourself as a coach, would you still have purpose?

My Uncle Norm was an amazing musician. He played lead guitar in numerous rock bands in the 1970s and went on to do a solo career in the 1980s and 90s. He developed a debilitating form of arthritis that caused his hands to curl up to the point that he could barely hold a knife and fork, let alone a guitar.

When the music stopped, so did his passion for life. He became understandably irritated, frustrated, and depressed. He felt as though his life purpose had been taken from him. He attached his life purpose to being a guitar-wielding rock star. Take away his ability to play, and his life was taken away as well.

I used to think I would be fulfilled once I found love, had kids, worked with pro athletes, was recognized as the top of my industry, created DVDs and online programs, and made some serious money. I was able to check each item off the list but still felt unfulfilled. Then I would add some more boxes and check those off. I kept adding to the list, searching for something that was already there.

My life purpose was driving all of these dreams, goals, and aspirations. I was chasing things (outcomes) while not aware of what was driving them. What drove me to accomplish my goals and fuelled my ambition was my life purpose.

Stoic philosophers and followers of the Stoic principles play a game of What If? What if I lost the things I think give me purpose? What am I left with? They felt that you would appreciate your loved ones more if from time to time you meditated on their loss.

53

Imagine your spouse and kids didn't exist. Then daydream about what life would be like. By the way, if this thought brings you joy you may want to get couples therapy! The Stoics would create a *What would I do without them?* plan. They felt that preparing for the worst would make them appreciate their family more while, at the same time, knowing they could survive without them gave them a sense of strength and resiliency.

I tried this Stoic exercise on my own life. I imagined myself with no status, no accolades, no clients, no followers, no family. When I removed all the things I had worked so hard to acquire in my life, I was faced with a question: What am I left with? Who am I in the absence of everything I thought made me who I thought I was? As this empty vessel, what do I want to accomplish for my life's work?

I wouldn't allow my mind to fill this void with things. I forced myself to go deeper. I still had a drive. I still had a hunger and a sense of an unfulfilled life. I needed to define what my purpose for being on this earth was. Take away everything and then ask, "What am I here for?" I boiled it down to four words:

Inspire Others to Greatness

If those four words drive everything I do and I get to execute on it, the successes and failures in daily life have little effect on my happiness. If I make an online program and it fails, I ask myself, "Did I work today on inspiring others to greatness in building this program?" *Yes.* "Was it received the way I wanted?" *No.* But I can't control that. I satisfied what I had control over, which was doing the work of Inspiring Others to Greatness.

A Buddhist monk can spend his entire life in a temple in the Himalayas, completely disconnected from the world with no possessions, no accolades, and nothing to show that he existed. But, somehow, he feels complete. He completed his life purpose. On the other hand, you can live in Manhattan and be the most successful person on Wall Street and die empty inside. It's not what is left in your final will that defines you. It's whether or not you fulfilled your life purpose.

If you focus on your life purpose and not relationships, jobs, accolades, money, fame, and other things outside of your control, you will find joy in your job. Again, I can fail in my day when it comes to outcomes in my business, but if I expressed my ability to inspire others to greatness, I feel satisfaction, fulfillment, and joy.

As you work through this book, you will have some powerful moments that will tap into your life purpose. It may be unclear, and you may not be able to write it out formally just yet, but awareness of its presence will help you get closer to the answer.

Find your purpose. Execute each day on that purpose. Push away the frustration through the work of executing your purpose. Enjoy the joy. You can do it through sport,

55

business, or any other pursuit in life. Just find joy in doing the work, and do it with purpose.

Currency

Before you decide what you want to achieve, you need to clarify what you will receive in exchange for what you are delivering. Western society has placed money and fame as the primary currencies of life. Listen to any modern music or watch popular media, and it's all about the Benz and the Benjamins. But when you sit down and have a real conversation with people, you realize that there is more depth to the currencies of life than boats, hoes, and blowing snow up your nose.

Your goal is to identify the currency of life that you value the most and build a DreamBIG that will reward you with the commodities you desire.

Money

When I question my mentorship students (mentorees) on what it is they want to get out of their DreamBIG, the most common answer is money. We were brought up to think that money brings security, power, freedom, and happiness. As you will see in the following sections, this is not only a false statement, but the belief in this notion can lead to emptiness and frustration.

You definitely need money, and yes money can provide you with a comfortable lifestyle. Thomas Plumber once said, "People who say money can't buy happiness are just buying the wrong shit." Princeton economists stated that Americans' threshold for wellbeing is $80,000 per year per family. If you have children, you will need more. Make less and you will stress about money. Make more and your happiness will not vastly improve whether you make $95,000 or $250,000.

My wife and I used to play What if? What if we won the ten million in the lottery that week—what would we do? Sure, we could upgrade our home, buy a vacation spot, but on a daily basis, how would it change our lives? I thought and I thought about it some more, and all I could come up with was that I would probably play more golf. My wife reminded me that I have a golf academy at one of Vancouver's best courses where I can play for free anytime I want, and yet I still played only a few times a year.

Would I retire? I would still want to do my podcast, train my athletes, and hop onstage at the comedy club. Well shit, that's what I already did. I asked her what she would change. All she came up with was she would like to get her nails done every once in a while. I told her that she could get them done every week right then if she wanted. We realized that more money wouldn't mean more happiness. For that, we would have to look elsewhere.

Any DreamBIG worth doing needs to be rewarded. I want you to dream of a world where you are free from debt, own your home, and have saved enough for a comfortable retirement with some money to enjoy your time with family and friends. Past that, you will need some different forms of currency to drive your fulfillment.

Time

Money means nothing if you don't have the time to enjoy it. I have met many miserable millionaires who work from dawn till dusk eight days a week. They have created a business that they think can't run without them. They have become shackled to their own creations.

The currency of time is about freedom to do what you want when you want. It is not about creating time off. If you want fulfillment in life, you need to fill your time with things that bring you joy. Writing this book is bringing me enormous amounts of joy. If I was worried about keeping the lights on and feeding my family from pay check to pay check, I certainly wouldn't be sitting at this computer right now writing a book. I would be on the streets earning a buck. I would dig ditches from 6 am to 8 am, work a sales job from 9 am to 5 pm, and go straight to the restaurant to wash dishes before I would ever let my family struggle.

Fortunately, I have been able to create a world through successful DreamBIGs that affords me the freedom of time to work on projects that bring me joy. The time currency is an illusion as we cannot control time. No matter how hard you try, you cannot stop the sun from rising or setting each day. What you do while the sun is in the sky is up to you.

Fame

When I graduated from college, I worked at a boutique personal training facility that serviced Vancouver's rich and famous. My manager asked me whether I preferred fame or money, and I chose fame. I said that, if I had fame for something positive, the money would come. The manager added that you can either be rich and no one knows who you are or be famous and broke. I still took fame.

I knew early on in my life that the black hole inside me that could never be filled required constant affirmation. I used to line up two hours before the comedy club opened to sign up for a five-minute open mic spot so I could tell jokes to complete strangers. This is not a normal behaviour for most people. Once I realized that admiration from others was worth more than money, I knew I had to design a world where I could create unique content that would entertain and inspire the masses.

Fame can come in many forms. I don't want to be famous for negative acts like OJ Simpson or David Koresh. I don't want fame in the form of glitz glamour and paparazzi like a Kardashian either. I just want my work to be recognized and valued by my community, peers, friends, and family, but I want to do it with some pizzazz.

How would you answer the question? Money or fame?

Respect

Respect from your peers and clients is a different commodity than fame. Respect is a valuable commodity for me in my professional life. I want my athletes to value and respect my skills. I feel pride when my colleagues and peers congratulate me on my successes. Usually, I deflect their accolades or minimize the accomplishments to make them sound less impressive. Compliments and pats on the back negatively serve the grinder in me. I value respect from my peers but quickly squish it deep down inside and go back to being the underdog who is hungry for a win.

How important is it that you are respected in your industry? How important is that Emmy, Grammy, Golden Globe, or salesman of the year award? I would rather be respected by my small inner circle of mentors, family, friends, and clients than awarded trainer of the year by *Men's Health* magazine. That might seem counterintuitive for someone who values fame but being trainer of the year is not what I want to be famous for.

Respect is something you earn. You are what you constantly do. If you consistently do things that earn the respect of those you cherish, you will be respected. Look at the values you respect in others and reflect them upon yourself. How do you rank? Would you respect you?

Health

Health is a commodity, but I was reluctant to discuss it here as it is often out of our control. I train every day and eat healthily. That doesn't stop me from throwing my back out every two to three years or save me from the flu.

Health can be the most valuable commodity you can have. The problem is you can't save it, hoard it, or lock it away. We are all vulnerable and susceptible to illness, injury, and disease. What we can control we will. A big part of the Undeniable chapter of this book is doing what you can control to optimize your performance. Optimizing is one thing, becoming bulletproof is another, but nothing can guarantee that your long-term health will be there for you in the end.

Security

Many of you walk around with an uneasy feeling that metaphorically forces you to constantly be looking over your shoulder. You hug your bank account like your teddy bear that your sibling is threatening to drown in the toilet. You insure your car, home, and life. You barricade your home and have a Glock under your pillow while you sleep. (Others sleep with the doors unlocked and share their passwords and PIN numbers with family members and their BFF.)

If security is a primary currency for you, you will need to focus on the long game. Your DreamBIG will be based on squirrelling away money into your holding company, selling long term contracts to your clients, paying off your mortgage, and investing in blue chip stocks. Playing the safe game has its drawbacks and may keep you from truly dreaming big, but I'd rather you be comfortable and dream small than live a life of anxiety and fear.

Creative Freedom

Creative freedom is a commodity that allows you to express yourself without external restrictions. Imagine if your dream was to have your own talk show like David Letterman or Jimmy Kimmel. You work your whole life to get it, and once you sign the deal with CBS, you find out that you are only allowed to read from the teleprompter and speak the words written by the producers. You want to be a rock star, but aren't allowed to play your own songs. You want a podcast but can only have guests on that your sponsors approve.

Creative freedom is something I value more than money, fame, and security. I have turned down sponsors, cancelled speaking gigs, and refused podcast guests because of this currency. The thing that made me who I am today is my ability to speak my mind, be 100% authentic, and share my vulnerability in everything I do. Once I started to get some attention and fame, those who helped me rise to the top attempted to control me. "We love what you are doing, Jay, but can you tone it down a bit, change your look, say this, don't say that, and try and do it this way?" It would be like trying to make hot sauce less spicy, make Motorhead play quieter, or Tom Brady less competitive. You will take away the true essence of why we love it.

Some of you may not care about creative freedom. Maybe your DreamBIG is less artistically driven or involves less of your creative input. This should give you the green light to chase the other currencies like fame, time, and money with reckless abandonment. The important thing is that you recognize this early so you don't have regrets later when your creative input isn't valued or considered by your team or organization.

> **TODAY'S TASK:** What is your currency combination? What are the top three currencies in your portfolio? The goal is to create a world where not only will you be able to acquire these currencies but also enjoy true fulfillment when you finally posses them. Write them in your notebook in BIG CAPITAL LETTERS. Now check your DreamBIG. Will accomplishing your DreamBIG provide you with the currencies you value?

Choose Your Own Adventure

Success comes from consistent daily actions toward a defined destination. Sometimes the end seems so far away that we lose focus or the motivation to continue. I can assure you that anything that is worth pursuing in life requires the practice of patience, resilience, grit, and determination. You will face crossroads along your journey, and

63

you will need to rely on your gut for the answers to the question "Which way is the right way?" Your gut always knows best.

Life is universally hard, so don't take it personally. I wish I knew the following when I was younger. You will have heartache, failure, hardship, pain, and loss, and you will die one day. These are probably the most important and beautiful parts of life. Knowing this and accepting it makes every day, in the absence of these events, a blessing. It is the yin that contrasts with the yang. It's the light that shines in the dark, the sour that makes the rest sweet.

You need both. The secret is how you perceive it and how you react to it. It's going to happen regardless, so you might as well enjoy the ride. Complaining about it makes life dark, sour, and miserable. Celebrating it makes life a beautiful miracle to be experienced to the max.

When I was a preteen, I use to read the *Choose Your Own Adventure* books that allowed you to alter the direction of the story by presenting various options every few pages. Each choice you made sent you to a different part of the book for a new adventure, which allowed you to read the same book multiple times and enjoy completely different outcomes based on your choices. One of my favourites was *The Cave of Time*. When the story got to the cave, it asked, "Want to enter the cave? Go to page 43. Want to go around the cave? Go to page 78." Once inside the cave, you found a treasure chest with a skull on the front and the words "Do Not Open" written in blood. Once again, you were faced with a decision that would alter the story from that moment forward. "Open it? Go to page 132 or leave it be and go to page 97." I always went in the cave and always opened the treasure chest. I couldn't help myself—I wanted adventure.

As much as I loved *The Cave of Time*, there was one *Choose Your Own Adventure Book* that changed my life forever: *You're Going to Die*. It had picture of an innocent-looking child on the front with a tear coming from his eye. What was he crying about? He was going to die, I presumed. I read that book a thousand times, and no matter what I did, the kid always died.

Once I realized that his fate was inevitable, I was freed up to take chances. Should he eat the purple mushroom? Should he go behind the barn with his Uncle Willie? What's the worse thing that can happen? He's going to die anyways, so let's do it.

I experienced some amazing journeys in that book that I'll never forget. I quickly realized that life is a choose-your-own-adventure book with the same ending that this poor boy inevitably encountered each time I read it. In your real-life story, you may never come across a cave or treasure chest, but I can assure you that you will be presented with crossroads and life-changing decisions to make. These decisions will have life-altering consequences as well as set you off on some amazing adventures.

My advice is to go in the cave. Open the treasure chest. Live the greatest adventure you can. You get one shot at your own story. Make it a great one.

Unlike a *Choose Your Own* adventure book, the decisions you make in real life have real consequences. You can't respawn like in a video game after you irresponsibly bungee jumped into the hotel pool after your buddies assured you that they measured the cord length twice. In the real world, you need to follow your gut.

I have never had a decision go wrong when I followed my gut. The bigger the decision, the more I felt it in my gut. There is actually a biological answer to this feeling. The enteric nervous system that enervates the entire digestive system is often called the second brain. I don't know about you, but when I get upset or nervous, my bowels turn over like day two on a Mexican all-inclusive. I used to go to the bathroom up to five times before teaching seminars and still feel the urge before a big comedy night.

But it's what your gut says when you are in the throws of a tough decision that interests me the most. Instead of inducing diarrhea, it guides us to make the correct decision. If you go against its better judgement and things go negatively, you will regret it for the rest of your life. If you go with your gut and for some reason it doesn't work out, at least you know you did what you thought was right.

TODAY'S TASK: Choose your own adventure and follow your gut. It is the only way to truly DreamBIG. By the way, you are getting closer to your DreamBIG every chapter. Each lesson is guiding you toward making it something truly special. What is your gut telling you? What thoughts are popping up in your mind and how does your gut respond to that thought? Journal it.

CHAPTER EIGHT:

THE ENTREPRENEURIAL WARRIOR

If you are going to dream of owning your own business, you better figure out if you have what it takes to be an entrepreneur. It's not for everyone. If you read this chapter and decide it's not for you, it doesn't mean you should stop dreaming. It just means you should dream about things that fit your mindset and won't put you into a situation that you aren't suited for. You may need to hitch a ride on someone else's dream. For me, there wasn't any option. I was born an Entrepreneurial Warrior.

I wake up frustrated, am discontented throughout the day and restless in the evenings. This frustration or restlessness is coming from my unquenchable thirst for achievement and accomplishment. The only thing that reduces the torturous twisting and turning of my soul is work. Every day that I work I take one step closer toward my DreamBIG.

When daily life gets in the way or menial tasks take me away from the "work," I feel the frustration or resistance build. I am not a workaholic—I am an "achieve-a-holic."

Work to me is not the time you spend returning emails, working with clients, or performing the mundane administrative tasks that keep the office lights on. The work is checking off the list of actionable items staring me in the face each day on my notepad that I have beside my keyboard. It is an endless list of steps broken into manageable chucks, doled out each week like ladles of gruel, to culminate one day in the greater whole. Each check gets me one step closer to reaching my final destination: success.

The bigger the goal, the longer the process. The longer the process, the more obstacles and distractions I will face along the path to my dream. The bigger the project, the longer I live in a state of restless discontent. I feel relief only when I reach milestones or benchmarks I have set for myself along the way.

These moments are brief. The arrival at one benchmark creates the need to achieve the next. Achievement is infectious and builds as you get closer and closer to your goal. My wife will often say to me, "You have been off with the fairies for weeks. What's on your mind?"

Work.

I have always been wired this way. When I was younger, my DreamBIGs were sports-based. I wanted to be a pro skateboarder. I would get up each day, get on my board, and hit every curb, jump ramp, 1/4 pipe, bank, or rail I could find. At the end of the day, I would be covered in bruises, raspberries, and scabs. I would go to bed with the images from Transworld or Thrasher and dream of the new Jason Glass pro model deck coming out or my own signature wheels.

I was living in Toronto at the time, so I felt the inner resistance most when the winter came and my ability to

70

work toward my dreams was under three feet of snow. The frustration would build and build week by week. My thirst was still there, but there was no nectar to sip from. When the first indoor skatepark with a 20-foot halfpipe opened in Toronto, I would walk 30 minutes through the snow to catch a bus then take the subway and another bus, and two hours later I would arrive.

I would make that trek countless times on school nights, falling asleep on the bus on my way home and missing my stop, then backtracking on the next bus and trudging head down, following the streetlights' glow in the snow to finally arrive at my destination: my pillow where I would finally fall asleep with that restless, gnawing feeling in my gut being quenched. "I took one step closer today toward being rad" was my last thought before night took me from the conscious to the unconscious world, the world where my dreams lived, a world where I had already become the pro skater I knew I was destined to be.

As I evolved through the years, that restless frustration took many forms. I worked toward my dream of becoming the starting running back for the Washington Huskies, and then the Seattle Seahawks, becoming the winningest high school football coach in history, owning my own business, owning my own gym, working with professional athletes, becoming a Perform Better Speaker, seeing my first book on the rack in the airport magazine shop and performing on stage at the Comedy Store as a paid regular. The goal or DreamBIG changes as I journey through the various phases of life, but the inner drive for accomplishment has never dimmed. This is the life of the Entrepreneurial Warrior.

My wife is a Scottish Unionist and wouldn't have it any other way. Fair pay, equality, benefits, paid holidays, and a pension. Safe, predictable, and reliable. There is a definite attractiveness to this lifestyle. Knowing what your paycheck is every two weeks, the number of vacation days you will get each year, your exact retirement date, and what your pension will be is comforting. What isn't comforting for me is knowing that no matter how hard I work or how I master my skillset, I will be paid the same and given the same benefits as the lazy slouch who schemes to avoid doing any work throughout the day.

I had union jobs in the summers while I was in college and worked alongside the "lifers" who would say, "Slow down, Glass. You are making us look bad. You'll be back at school in a month, and the boss will expect us to keep up the same workload when you leave." But my inner Entrepreneurial Warrior was clawing at my insides, trying to break free. "There, there my precious. This is a step we need to take to get us closer to becoming the person we want to be. We need money for school so we can get a degree so we can become the number one strength coach in the world. Have patience—our time will come."

The Entrepreneurial Warrior fears comfort and conformity and thrives on the chaos of the unknown and the need to control it, as well as knowing that success or failure is on your own shoulders, and that the success you have can be taken away at any moment and any failures can be erased by your next successful venture.

Win big? Take your winnings and squirrel it away while you play with house money. Tough times? Just put your ante in each hand and wait for your time to go all in. You know only one way, and it's never the easy way. The easy path doesn't quench your thirst for achievement and success. The easy way is an appetizer that never satisfies the hunger for the main course. The problem is that if you eat enough of the easy way appetizers you can prolong the need for the main course, and in doing so you put off success for yet another day.

By the way, success never comes. It is like trying to find the end of the rainbow: The closer you get to it, the further away it becomes. The end goal you envision today becomes a pebble in the big pile of boulders that becomes your life's work.

Did I ever play running back for the Huskies and Seahawks? Nope. But the steps I took and the work I put in toward that dream landed me in the Jr CFL and a spot on the University of British Columbia Thunderbirds football team. Number one high school football coach? Nope. I did, however, create a junior golf academy and coached countless high school golfers, helping them develop into great players and even better people.

Train professional athletes and become a Perform Better Speaker? Yes. I have worked with athletes from the NFL, MLB, PGA, LPGA, NBA, and extreme sports world, as well as becoming a regular on the Perform Better and TPI speaking circuit for over a decade.

Book? You are reading it.

Being a paid regular at the Comedy Store, I know that my drive toward that goal will lead me to success in my local comedy scene. If I set my goal to have local success and underachieved, I would achieve nothing. The point is that you may not achieve all your dreams, but the journey toward them will yield incredible life experiences and unlock skills and knowledge you didn't think you had. This alone will drive you to do the work.

Warning to the Future Warrior

Most entrepreneurs start a business because they want freedom. The problem is they end up shackling themselves to their own expectations. They become the CEO of their company and expect the most out of their top employees. They won't take any bullshit, give any slack, or get too hyped off this employee's work. They will work that employee to the ground in the process of chasing success. This employee will never meet their expectations because that employee is the entrepreneur.

I remember one of my Coach Glass Mentorship Alumni who came up to Vancouver in the hope that we could help him turn his business around. His five-year goal included making enough money to allow him to take a day off each week. He wanted to take his family on a vacation for the first time in seven years. He told us that the three days he was spending with us at the Mentorship were the first three days he had been away from his clinic in years.

Doesn't that sound crazy? He opened a physiotherapy clinic that provided jobs for ten therapists and fitness staff, but he couldn't take a day off. His initial dream didn't include being shackled to his facility every waking minute. He was stuck with big overhead and a staff that he felt personally responsible for. He did everything for his working family. He justified the long hours with the thought that he was a provider to his wife and kids at home. Unfortunately, he wasn't providing his family with the one thing they really needed: him.

I have seen this time and again. That is why I push everyone away from owning their own business. Anyone who comes to my mentorship with the dream of owning their own gym or clinic gets an ear beating. Am I a dream killer? No. I am a dream definer. If someone really wants it, they will get it. Try telling me not to get on stage, don't work with that athlete that no one else will touch, don't take chances on your podcast or write a book. I dare you.

If it is truly your dream, no one—and I mean no one— will talk you out of it. I push my mentees till they break. One of two things will happen. They either agree that owning their own business is a bad idea, or they look me right in the eye: "I don't care what you say, Coach. I am going to open my own gym if it kills me."

They are now ready.

Hard Work

Looking back at my shackled mentee, no one could argue that he didn't work hard. Being an entrepreneur is hard work, hard work is like a magnet. The harder you work, the stronger the magnet becomes. Opportunity and creativity are like metal filings. They are attracted to the magnet. The problem with our shackled friend is he kept the magnet in the same place too long. The metal filings built up so much that he was smothered in his own work.

You must take the time to clear the magnet of its metal filings from time to time and redirect it in the direction you desire. There are times in my year when the workload wanes, and I get a chance to peek my head out of the minutiae. This is when I get creative. I write, create videos, journal, and DreamBIG. It is this type of work that truly creates opportunity. Knowing this, I work extremely hard in the mundane to create opportunities that will free up time so I can be creative and create bigger opportunities to free up more time. I work hard at *not working*.

One of the most successful filmmakers and producers in the world of comedy is Judd Apatow. At any given time, he can be found creating a major motion picture while simultaneously developing and producing two sitcoms. How can one man do all these things at the same time with such quality? There are times that he is writing a current season of a sitcom when it gets picked up for another season. He now has to create a story arc that will bridge the two seasons together with a cliff-hanger to keep the audience at the edge of their seats during the hiatus between the two seasons.

A TV show writers' room is like a frat house compressed into a boardroom filled with discarded bottles and energy drink cans, sugary snacks, and worn-out writers sprawled all over the floor trying to catch an hour of sleep. Some rooms will write for 12 hours a day, stretching into the early hours like a girl's night out in Vegas: late nights, no sleep, bad nutrition, and zero exercise. This goes against everything I stand for and breaks every peak performance rule in this book.

How can you possibly be as productive and successful as Judd in this environment? Judd realized early in his career that he needed to have his finger on every detail of his creations for them to be successful, but he didn't have to be in the process of creation the entire time—that's why he hired writers. What he needed to do was be the level-headed creative person who directed and guided the writers down the right path. To do this, he needed a clear mind.

Judd gets up each day and follows the performance guidelines that you will read in Part III. He sleeps like it's his job, eats clean, moves beautifully every day, and meditates. He then enters the writers' room with a clear vision of what he wants to create, replenishes the Twizzler bowl, restocks the Red Bull fridge, and delivers the notes for the writers to work on that day or night. He then steps out of the room, compartmentalizes that part of his day, and moves to the next project.

You need to take the oxygen mask and put it on yourself first so that you are capable of helping others.

I used this story with my mentee, and with the support of the other nine people in the room, we convinced him that the only way he was going to free himself from the prison that he created was to change the way he did business. I called some of my mentors who were once my mentees and asked for their assistance. As a group, we were able to come up with a plan that would provide valuable time with his family and allow for some time by himself.

The time designated for himself was not for selfish reasons. It was designed to help him recharge and see the big picture regarding his business and life. He pressed PLAY on the plan and got to work on working less. Not only was he able to take weekends off, but he finally got that family vacation he and his family deserved.

He called me with the great news, and all I could say was, "Time to get back to work." Time to create a business that will allow you to work four days in the clinic, one day on strategy and big project creation, and two free days without dragging the shackles along on your family outing. Then create the next business structure that needs you even less.

Success.

Are You a Warrior or an Employee?

You are either a warrior, or you are an employee. Employees can do the same job as the warrior, but they do it with a different mindset. Employees say they do it because they love it. They are passionate about their craft and work their butt off to maximize their contribution to the team. They look for opportunities to climb the ladder or increase their value inside the organization. Once they punch the clock, they go home and enjoy the other parts of their life, the nonworking parts.

Entrepreneurial warriors don't have a choice. They work when they are at work and think about work when they are "off." They are the work, and the work is them. They would do it for free they love it so much. It's personal. They will wake up each day with one thing on their mind: Curb that hunger for success through work. Douse that burning desire to step on someone's throat who gets in the way of their dreams.

It's not something they can turn off and on when they need it. It doesn't follow a schedule. There is no schedule. Someone once asked the great author, Somerset Maugham, "Do you write on a schedule or only when inspiration strikes?" "Only when inspiration strikes," he replied. "Fortunately, inspiration strikes at 9 am sharp each morning." They are disciplined and consistent with their actions and cadence.

The path of the employee and the warrior are both noble. You just need to know which one you are on. If you are an employee at heart and take on an entrepreneurial venture, you will hate your life. If you are a warrior and choose to work in an organization, you will resent the leadership and take actions that will lead to your demise.

The Grass Is Always Greener

When you sign up to DreamBIG, you are signing up for a marathon. Anything worth dreaming about will take considerable effort and time to complete. That is why it is so important to make sure that your DreamBIG is coming from the right place. The driver of your DreamBIG needs to be coming from your soul. That way, when you hit an inevitable obstacle, you can be Undeniable.

The following is a story and analogy that will take you from the start of a DreamBIG all the way to its completion. It is a lesson on why your DreamBIG needs to be carefully thought out before you embark on the journey. It helps you navigate the twists and turns you may find along the way. Sometimes you need to feel the sand under your feet from your DreamBIG destination to help you envision what is possible.

Starting your journey without a clear destination is like treading water in the middle of the ocean. Sure, you are expending energy and making a splash ("Look, Mom!"), but you're not getting anywhere. I prefer to pick my DreamBIG destination from the shore while looking out at the ocean. The end of the journey is an island on the horizon that you can barely make out with your naked eye.

Once you have confirmed the destination and worked out the coordinates, you are ready for your first decision. You can either stand on the shoreline and wait for a boat to take you there, or you can take a run down the beach, cannonball, and begin to swim. At first, you will flail around and feel like you aren't moving, but soon enough you get your stroke down, and you are on your way to the island of your dreams.

As my dreams get bigger, the distance between the mainland and the island gets so expansive that I often lose track of why I started the journey in the first place. I do find myself occasionally treading water midway through a DreamBIG. This is why it is so important to write down your DreamBIG and even better share it with an accountability partner. If I ever find myself treading, I stop, go back to the front of my notebook where my DreamBIG started, and study it. I think of the person who wrote it and how it resonates with the person I am today and hope to be tomorrow.

This is a nautical map which needs to be reviewed from time to time so that you don't get blown off course. There have been times that I had to make some amendments to the original dream, but the underlying theme is always constant. I like to think of it as though my initial destination was Maui, but after a year of swimming, I switched to Kona. It's still Hawaii. I didn't go from DreamBIG Hawaii to a DreamBIG polar expedition. Same direction but a different port of call.

In 2016, I had a DreamBIG to start up an online marketplace for all my video-based content, a pay-to-play portal for everything Coach Glass. This would provide me with passive income to free me up to pursue bigger projects and provide training to people who don't have access to me in person. It took two years of paddling to build the website and e-commerce interface and develop our first consumer-based, follow-along, 16 Week LoadXplode training program.

Right before the launch of the website, I could see my final destination. I swam as hard as I could to get to shore. I pulled myself up on the beach. I was on dry land for the first time in 24 months. I had made it.

Or had I?

I always envisioned pulling myself up onto the sand, rolling over, and basking in the sun for a while. Some locals in grass skirts and coconut infused bras would offer me a tropical drink with an umbrella in it. I would take the time to enjoy the fruits of my labor. A voice in the back of my mind said, "Nope." *But I don't have to tread water anymore. I've made it. I've done it. I did the task, and the task is complete.* Once again, "Nope."

The problem was that I had been treading water for so long that I didn't even know where I had landed. I was too deep for too long, and even though I had my feet planted on solid ground, I couldn't help but still feel lost. Was this really the place I envisioned two years before? It didn't feel like a success. It was however, even better than my initial dream. I just couldn't appreciate it for what it really was.

The problem was that it took me so long to reach my destination that I had started to dream of bigger, better islands along the way. After catching my breath and seeing the results of the initial launch, I decided to pivot. I could see a bigger opportunity for my online content. I instantly started to look back out on the horizon for a bigger island. My mind started to fantasize about the next island having bigger coconuts, better Wi-Fi, and a sports bar. I fell victim to the grass is greener on the other side fable.

I had to remind myself that my feet are planted on *this* island. I can't be bothered about what could be on the next island. I knew that at some point I would jump back in the water and set off on the next great adventure, but for now it was time to heal my chaffed nipples and rest my sore muscles from the journey I just endured. It was time to get to work on making this island the best island possible: Build a shelter, start a fire, and find a fresh source of water. The hardest part of the journey has been completed. Now it's time to make the most of all my hard work and time for some short-term goals. Soon I will have a home with a view of the ocean, a front lawn, and a place to call my own, I thought.

It is human nature to want what you don't have. Others' lives may look shinier and more fun, especially in the modern world of social media where you can scroll through someone's highlight reel, which cumulatively makes you feel like everyone else, but you are living their best life.

My challenge for you is to take care of your island or lawn before you start looking at your neighbors' lawn and wondering what it would be like to sip a mint julep in their hammock while receiving a foot rub.

Take a good look around and what you might see is that there's a little bit of neglect of your lawn. You spent so much time looking over the fence that you didn't notice the brown patches, crabgrass, and dandelions growing on your side. It's time to invest in your lawn. Buy some quality seed and fertilizer. You think your neighbor's significant other is hotter than yours? Have you looked at yourself lately? They have a nicer car. When is the last time you washed your car?

While you are bitching and complaining about what you don't have, someone else is looking at your life: "Man, they really got it made. I don't even have a lawn—I live in an apartment.'

You may not think it, but I can guarantee that someone out there is scrolling through your Instagram feed and wishing they could be you. This life is yours—now take care of it. Make it good. There's a lot of value in that lawn that you're standing on, if you just cultivate it and make the most out of it.

I'm not saying you need to stay where you are right now for the rest of your life, but sometimes you spend so much time looking at that next destination that you neglect to acknowledge where you've come from and where you are today.

You did not make that trip across the ocean for nothing. Don't let that treading water go in vain. Enjoy it. Kick your feet up and take it all in, then ask yourself, "How can I make what I've got right now the best possible destination?"

And then do it.

TODAY'S TASK: Take an honest look at where you are at before you start dreaming of where you want to get to. Are you ready to jump in the water and swim toward your DreamBIG, or should you take care of what you currently have first? If you don't take care of your Nissan Versa, you will probably also neglect that BMW that you are planning on working toward. Make a list of things that you currently neglect in your business and life and ask yourself if the DreamBIG you envision will flourish with these habits you currently posses.

CHAPTER NINE:

THE RESISTANCE

Before I sat down to write this section of the book, I made breakfast, watched 3/4 of a show on Netflix, made my second cup of coffee, came to the computer, and spent five minutes picking out the right music mix for this writing session. What was meant to start at 6:30 am has commenced at 9:30 am. What held me back from accomplishing the goal that I set out at 11 pm last night when I set my alarm?

"Tomorrow I will write about the resistance." It is exactly that: the Resistance.

The Resistance is the space that lives between where we are and where we want to be. It is a barrier that makes us comfortable in our current state and fogs up the window into what we really want to accomplish. Steven Pressfield wrote about this in his book *The War of Art*. He eloquently breaks down the various forms of resistance that creative people will face when they are embarking on the art of creation. It is this barrier of resistance that holds talented people from ever creating their life's work. If it was easy, everyone would be an author, actor, sculptor, comedian, painter, or content creator.

Think about how many people you know who have come to you with grandiose ideas of starting a podcast, auditioning for a play, writing their first book, or getting on stage for the first time at an open mic. How many actually saw it through? How many of those who saw it through truly allowed themselves to express what was really in their soul? Many will dip a toe in, but only a select few will create what they had envisioned in the truest form.

The resistance is what makes us come up with excuses or allows distractions to pull us away from acting on our dreams. If you go half-assed and fail, you have an excuse for why you didn't fully execute your dream. If you give it 100% of everything you got and fail, you must face the hard truth that you just weren't good enough. The fear of that realization strengthens the resistance.

The worst representation of the resistance is when the resistance keeps you from allowing yourself to DreamBIG. You have a ceiling to what your brain will allow you to dream. If I said you could fly like Superman if you set your goals, build your checklists, and execute each day, you would say I was crazy. If I replaced flying like Superman with running a 10-kilometer race as your goal, you would think I'm not dreaming big enough. Somewhere between Superman and an attainable physical feat is this barrier. The job of this section of the book is to help you raise that ceiling or push that barrier forward.

TODAY'S TASK: Let's play One UP. You probably have a friend who one-ups everything you say. I saw the Beastie Boys at Lollapalooza in 1992. "Yeah, I was backstage and smoked a joint with Cypress Hill." Really? I want you to play One Up with your DreamBIG. Think of your DreamBIG and think of a way to One Up on your dream. Keep playing One Up until you feel you hit the Resistance ceiling, and you know you are truly dreaming BIG. Write it out and live with it for a few days. Think about it when you go to bed and upon waking, and revisit it a few times throughout the day. If after four days it still feels crazy, you probably need to dial it back a little. If it feels too comfortable, you can play another round of One Up.

Dreaming big is one thing, but taking your first step to making it a reality takes balls. (Ladies, you have balls too.) The first step is the hardest as it breaks the resistance. But like most barriers, once it is broken, there is no looking back. Every night the barrier will try to rebuild itself, forcing you to grab yourself by the nut sack and break through it again and again.

Once you accept that the resistance will never go away, you will strengthen your ability to chip away at it. If you woke up each day in your mother's womb and had to break out to start your day, you would get pretty good at it. For some of you, the warmth of your bed is a form of womb. The resistance loves comfort. Were you put on this earth to be comfy in between the sheets or were you meant for greater things?

Acting on your DreamBIG is hard work. It requires dedication and discipline. You need to structure your day and set your work environment to minimize the resistance. I write at 6:30 each morning because I know that I won't be distracted by the rest of the world asking for my time. I turn off my Wi-Fi and remove any sources of distraction that may draw me away from writing. I structure an end-point to my writing as well. I take my son to school at 8:15 am, so I stop typing at 8. Some days, I am constantly glancing at the clock, struggling to get to 8, while other days my son is yelling at me, "Daaaad—we are going to be late."

I have always said that if you want a kid to love golf, drag them away from the range kicking and screaming. Take them to the driving range, hit half of a bucket, and leave just when you see them having fun. Buy them an ice cream on the way home and wait for them to say those precious words: "Dad? Can we do that again next weekend? That was fun."

The other option is to buy three buckets and have them begging you to leave before the first bucket is empty. "Dad, can we go now? This is boring."

I never want to feel bored when writing. I always want to go to bed while looking forward to the opportunity to finish the last page I started.

You are setting yourself up for success—it's like tantric writing. How often do you go to bed excited about tomorrow's work? If the answer is never, you need to dive into a DreamBIG that will get you excited enough to wake up early for it. The resistance is strong when you are doing something you hate. I am not saying every workday has to be like running through the tall grass naked, but it should give you a tickle somewhere special.

You set tomorrow's resiliency for fighting the Resistance when you close your eyes each night. "Tomorrow, I get to check off some boxes on my notepad." You need to speak to yourself like you are trying to convince a child that going to the dentist is fun. "Tomorrow we get to see Dr. Drillbit. Ooh, it is going to be so much fun. He is going to give you a needle that will make you talk like Grandpa after a few whiskeys. On the way out, you get to pick out a plastic toy made in China by another child with bad teeth."

It's all in the way you speak to yourself. Your desire to accomplish your DreamBIG should be enough for you to overcome the Resistance. If the tasks on your checklist don't excite you, then you will need to go to bed while thinking of the bigger picture. Daydream about what your life will be like once you accomplish your DreamBIG.

When I went to bed last night, I spent 20 minutes envisioning renting an RV next summer and touring my book across America, having my podcast Glistners show up in Portland at a hipster bookstore, buying Coach Glass merch, drinking coffee, hearing stories about how this book changed readers' lives, and finally finishing off the evening running through the tall grass naked.

TODAY'S TASK: Make a list of all the forms of Resistance in your life. For each one, create a strategy to overcome it. You need a plan, and you need to stick to it if you are going to win. As soon as you are aware of the Resistance, you need to take immediate action before it gains momentum. Once defeated, give yourself a Tiger Woods fist pump to emotionally reinforce your power over the resistance.

CHAPTER TEN:

KNOW YOUR ROLE—DON'T SLOW YOUR ROLE

Whether you are an entrepreneur or an employee, you need to DreamBIG. As an entrepreneur, the sky is the limit to what you can dream. As an employee, you are bound by the structure of the organization you belong to. I have seen many of my Coach Glass Mentorship attendees either climb the corporate ladder or create new positions and opportunities inside an organization. Either way, you need to understand where you are at and where you want to go.

The fact is that you have a job. You show up each day and perform the tasks associated with the job you were hired to do. Even if you are an entrepreneur, you built a business that requires specific tasks that need to be accomplished each day. If you are your own boss, you can track the employee that you give the tasks to each day in your business: you.

Being your own boss doesn't just involve sitting back smoking cigars and counting money. It also requires you to perform the roles of delivering your service or product to your customers and all the little things that keep the lights on and pay the rent. If you are an employee in an organization or corporation, the following will resonate deeply and help you define your role.

93

Inside the Lines

The lines in which you must color inside of are determined by the roles and responsibilities you were given. You do your job. Let's pull out the cassette player and rewind the mix tape of how you got here all the way back to the day that you decided to drop off your resume for the job you have today. If you are hearing Duran Duran right now, you have rewound too far.

Who were you? Maybe you were just in between jobs and needed some quick cash so you could get new brakes on your Volvo 760 so you could take Jenny to the laser U2 show at the planetarium. You had no idea you would spend the next 20 years climbing the corporate ladder in a company that makes a product that is now obsolete. Sure, selling fax machines was sexy when you were hired, but now the fax/facts are that you hate your life.

Obviously, this is an extreme example, but I'm sure there is some truth to how this relates to your current work situation. You took the job because you had to, or the job was the right fit for the person you were and the place in life that you were at. The problem is that the person who took the job has now become the job.

What roles are you responsible for in your job or business based on your job title? What are the daily tasks that you are required to do to justify your salary or commission? And not what you want to be doing but what your bosses or clients require you to do to get your job requirements met.

Many of you just made that face you make when you are unsure whether it was a fart or a shart. What are your roles? It should be a simple question to answer — you perform them every day. This will be a very valuable exercise for you. Stop what you are doing and complete the next task.

> **TODAY'S TASK, PART 1**: Write down on a piece of paper or in your notes a list of roles or responsibilities you have in your current job. Be general and don't spend too much time with it. What first comes to mind is probably a more accurate representation of what you do than what you come up with after three days of trying to convince yourself you are more important to the world than you really are (we will get to fixing that later).
>
> Number each role or responsibility for future reference, like this: #4. *I am responsible for making sure my clients leave with a smile on their face and sweat on their back.*
>
> Go. Now. Write down your roles.

The roles you just wrote down define you. "But I am so much more than just a customer support agent, morning meeting coffee jockey, or new-gym-member orientation facilitator." I agree. But these are the roles you have been given, roles that have been bestowed upon you for a few reasons: They are important, they are necessary, and everyone around you thinks you are perfect for those tasks.

You have been given those jobs based on your perceived skill set, position in the company's seniority pecking order, or maybe because someone just has to do them.

Has this exercise created a little fire in your belly? Maybe you feel a little under-appreciated and that you have so much more to offer—*good*. The exercise should make you feel this way. Now what are you going to do about it? Wait until they hire a newbie who can take over the coffee manager role?

Instead, why not redefine your role?

What Is Your Superpower?

Redefining your role can completely change the way you approach your daily tasks and transform the mundane into the extraordinary. Superheroes wear their emblems on their chests. When Superman walks in the room, you know it's Superman. He has a specific set of skills that are unique to him. Need someone to jump a tall building in a single bound? He's your guy. But if you want someone to haul all the kryptonite that has been piling up in your office closet to the dumpster, you may want to call the janitor.

When you walk in the room, what do your coworkers see? What does your boss see as your superpower? If you can define your roles, you can redefine the way you approach them and in turn redefine the way you are perceived by those around you.

Let's cut to the chase, shall we? I recently had a conversation with a mentee after he completed the task of defin-

96

ing his roles. One of the roles he came up with was customer service and, to be more specific, customer care for those who struggle with the product his company was selling. I asked him, "How does that make you feel?"

"I hate it. All I get is complaints about the product not working, the app not synching, or the shipment being late. I want to help them because I truly care for my clients, but I am more than a customer service/technical support guy. I have more to offer."

I told him that we must redefine his role. He agreed that the job of customer care has to be done. It was important, necessary, and an integral part of the business. He also agreed that he was the best person for the job because of his people skills, advanced communication skills, and ability to problem solve and connect with the customer.

We experimented with role reversal. "Let's look at your job from the customers' point of view. You are saving them from a frustrating and overwhelming problem that they cannot solve on their own. You are diffusing their anger, removing their fears, and helping them enjoy the product the way it was intended. In many ways, you are an advocate for the customer to create a bridge between them and the product. How do you think the customer feels after you have helped them get this purchase back up and running? How do you think they see you?"

He replied, "They always thank me and appreciate the time and care I give them. You can actually hear them smiling on the other end of the phone."

"You are not a customer service rep/technical support agent. You are a customer advocate when you jump on a call or meet a client in person," I continued. "Wear that on your chest like it's a superpower: 'I am a customer advocate.' Own it. Do you think if you walked in a room with that emblem under your shirt that you might approach the client in a different manner? Instead of thinking, *Oh, what's wrong with them this time?* you could think, *Wait until I unleash my super advocate powers on this guy and blow him away with how much I can help him.* Wouldn't that make your approach to the situation and the reaction of the customer different?"

"I hate getting my coworkers coffee. Do I look like a hipster barista to you?" now becomes "How can I fuel my team with something they love and create an environment that is conducive to creative problem solving?"

"I have a degree in social science. Can't someone else check the final order before shipping?" now becomes "I am the only person in this firm who has the analytical mind needed to ensure there are no fuck-ups on this order, and we can avoid an angry customer call or returned shipment."

Customer Support	=	Customer Advocate
Coffee Jockey	=	Creative Team Fuel Facilitator
Completed Order Inspector	=	No-Fuck-Ups-on-My-

Watch Manager

You may be rolling your eyes right now. "Come on, Coach. This is silly. You can't take my shitty task, paint it with a positivity rainbow brush made from straightened Swedish unicorn pubes, and make me love cleaning the gym at the end of a long day." I know it sounds corny, and I am aware that cleaning the gym or any other menial task sucks. But does the job need to get done? Is it necessary and important for the company to function? Are you currently in the position at your company that carries out this duty?

If so, find a way to get 'er done with purpose, and actually make it make a difference for your organization. I know a successful gym owner who still cleans his own gym at the end of each day once the staff leave. He decided that his gym being "surgically clean" was his priority and a cornerstone to the success of his business. He won't leave that responsibility to anyone else because it is that important. (And secretly, between you and me, I think he likes sniffing cleaning supplies.)

TODAY'S TASK, PART 2: Take each item you previously listed as your roles and redefine them. Make them as sexy and powerful as possible. Be creative. Try each role on as your superpower and walk around with it on your chest. How does it feel? If you approached that specific task with your newly redefined role, would it make you better at your job? Try wearing your new role when you take your next customer call, meet a client, or interact with a team member. If it feels good and you are getting a positive response, hang it in the closet and put it on the next time you need to fill that role.

Still feeling belittled and that you have more to offer the company? You were put in the position you are currently in based on how others see you. If you want to change your position in the company, you need to change how others see you, and that starts with changing how you see yourself.

If you want a promotion, show them you are the right person for the job by being the best version of yourself in the job you have right now. Stop wondering why you keep getting passed over and start creating a world where they will have no other option. Create a world where they either need to move you up or lose you to a competitor without saying a word. Threaten them through your actions. Create a problem that you are the solution for.

Out of the Fryer

My first job in high school was at Wendy's fast-food restaurant. During my first shift, I was given my uniform and put under the supervision of a young man who was also still in high school but had a mystical power that came from a magical name badge with these words: Shift Manager.

After a lengthy orientation process, the manager taught me how to run the french-fry station. An order would come in and a screen over my head would ping with how many orders of fries I was to put in the fryer. A timer on the fryer would tell me when they were perfectly golden brown and ready for the salting tray. There were constant dings, pings, and flashing lights that drowned out my teenage manager when he yelled at me for undercooking, overcooking, or not adhering to the quality control guidelines on the laminated pictograph above the fryer.

I was stressed and hot, and had enough of cooking fries after 30 minutes. I looked longingly at the burger flipper who was calm as a father posted up on his BBQ grill, beer in hand, on a summery Sunday, flipping pucks for his family and friends. I asked the manager if I could switch over to burgers for a while. He looked at me like I was asking to meet the owner Dave Thomas so I could ask for his red-headed daughter Wendy's hand in marriage.

"Burgers? Oh no, you are not ready for burgers. Maybe in a few months after you master the fry station. After fries, you go to condiments, then shakes, and then maybe, just maybe, you will be ready for the grill." I saw the next year flash in front of my eyes. Before my brain could register the act, I shoved my apron and hairnet in the manager's chest and quit.

It was the shortest job I ever had: two hours of orientation, 30 minutes on the fryer, and I was done. Six months later, I received a letter from the Wendy's Corporation with a vacation pay cheque for three cents. I laughed to myself , but then realized that if I had stuck it out in that job, I would be on shakes right now.

Define and Dream

The key is to define your role. Decide if the role is truly beneath you or is it just where you are at right now. If the fire to move further up the ladder is in you, show your bosses that you are ready. Do your job so well that they can't help but promote you.

If you really despise those above, it may be time for you to move on to greener pastures. Or maybe you need to go solo. You can DreamBIG in an organization, but it is easier as an entrepreneur—that is, easier to dream, but harder to execute.

It's time to decide. Your DreamBIG will be based on this answer, so don't take it lightly.

CHAPTER ELEVEN:

FINDING THE WHY

Choosing your DreamBIG should be easy. It might be a little scary to dream outside of your comfort zone, but the basic premise of the dream should come to you freely if it follows in the direction you are currently traveling. If you are a singer, for instance, it would make sense that your DreamBIG involved musical achievements. If you are a recently divorced 55-year-old and you want to become a lawyer but have nothing more than a GED, you may want to go back to the drawing board and save your money for that red convertible you have your eye on.

The process of developing the detailed plan for your DreamBIG should be arduous. If it was easy, you would have already done it. Before we start the hard work of laying out the roadmap to success, I feel it is imperative that we dive deeper into WHY you chose this particular #DreamBIG to hang your future on.

The WHY is the thing you will come back to time and time again when you hit an obstacle or meet an obstacle that threatens your undeniability. The WHY is the force inside you that will help you overcome seemingly unsurmountable challenges and remind you why you started this journey in the first place. Like the hunger inside a starving lion who stalks the Serengeti every day while looking for a morsel of food and knowing the search for food may use up the last energy reserves it has for survival. It could lie down and save the energy to live out another day or two or use it to feed today and keep this cycle of life moving forward.

The hunger drive inside you is the WHY.

TODAY'S TASK: In your notebook, I want you to draw a vertical line that breaks the page into 2/3 on the left and 1/3 on the right (basically, draw a line down the page with more space on the left side of the page). Write down the three most successful moments you have had in your career in the left column.

This should come easy: the first three big events that come to your mind, ones that involved some form of a decision you had to make to create the opportunities. For example, one could be the decision to go to college and the memory of how proud you felt when you graduated, or perhaps securing the bank loan to open your business based on the business plan you spent sleepless nights developing, or perhaps the day you got hired for the job you knew was a little out of your grasp, but you applied for it nonetheless.

Now write down the three biggest failures you have had in your career below your successes. For some of you, this will be an easier list to come up with if you have a negatively-skewed mindset. It could be the day you got fired from that job you knew was a little out of your grasp, the day that you fired your first employee due to a lack of customers, or the big contract you were in the running for but got out-bid by your closest competitor.

Put the list aside for a minute—we will come back to it once we get an understanding how you got to where you are at based on these life defining moments.

What drives you to be *you*? If I ask you superficially, you may come up with some grandiose combination of words that you think *should* define you: "Its my inner determination and never-give-up attitude to live life to the fullest, bro." The attributes that you think define you are really just the attributes that you want others to see in you.

The actual attributes that drive you are often the subtle underlying things that pop up time and time again in life-defining moments. If you feel you are a courageous person but every time you are faced with an uncomfortable situation you drift into the background and watch others deal with the situation, you are not courageous. The fact that you are attracted to the ideal of being a courageous person is an important thing to note, but acknowledging the fact that you are not courageous at this moment is more important.

If you feel you are an understanding and empathetic person, and every time that your friends and family members have a problem they come to you for help or advice, you are in touch with your true attributes which should drive your DreamBIG.

There are basic drivers that all humans possess. The relationships we have with others and the relationship we have with ourselves are based on how much of each driver we use in our actions and the decisions we make each day. Russel Brand laid out these drivers in his book *Recovery* in such a simple and clear way that it would be silly for me to try to do it better. (Thank you, Russel.)

Here is a list of the drivers that guide our actions and are at the root of our successes and failures. I have put a letter beside each driver so we can easily identify them in today's exercise:

Pride (P)   *What I think you think about me*

Self Esteem (SE)   *What I think about myself*

Personal Relationships (PR)   *The script I give others*

Sexual Relations (SR)   *Pertaining to sex*

Ambitions (A)   *What I want in my life, my overall version of my "perfect" self*

Security (S)   *What I need to survive*

Finances (F)   *Money and how it affects my feelings*

Here is an example of how these drivers can affect our decision-making and guide our actions. The following is a real situation I had to negotiate and the inner dialogue I had with myself through the highs and lows that transpired. I have noted the drivers that were pushing my decisions beside each twist and turn.

I recently was asked to speak at a medical conference in the fall. Instantly I felt a rush of pride (P). My inner dialogue went like this: *Me? You want me to speak at your conference? Gosh, I would be honored, and I appreciate your thinking of me* (P). I returned their email, letting them know that I was interested but needed more details. I sent them my day rate and conditions that I needed met to perform at the conference: How long do you want me to speak? Is there a specific topic you want me to present that would match the overall theme of the conference? How many people are going to be there? 400? 1,000? 3,000?

They came back with the details. My day rate was too high (F, S), there would be approximately 200 professionals at the event, and I could choose any topic, which I read it as, "Talk about what you want since no one is going to be there anyway. And we think you may have accidentally added an extra zero to your day rate because we aren't paying you that number. Who do you think you are, Oprah?"

In reality, it was simply a budget issue for such a small event and had nothing to do with not seeing the value in my speaking abilities. Yet my pride (P) and self esteem (SE) took a hit. I asked myself whether I had built up a vision of being the keynote speaker in front of 3,000 professionals, being treated like royalty, and making a great deal of money. The answer was a clear yes (F, S).

Was my daydream too lofty and anything less than what I pictured in my head would be a letdown? Absolutely. Part of being a #DreamBIG kind of guy is to daydream about opportunities and then work to turn those daydreams into realities, but sometimes there are specific components of your dream that are out of your control. The next email I received from the organizer indicated that the other five speakers he was negotiating with—the top dogs in the industry—agreed to come for one half as much as I was requesting. *You put me in the same category of speaker as these legends? (SE) I would have thought they would demand more money for speaking than little old Jay (P).*

He then shared that he would be meeting with his board of directors to discuss changing the budget to accommodate my day rate (F). They really want me to be a part of the event and would do whatever it took to get me there (SE). He also suggested that he could potentially match my day rate if I was able to lead a daylong workshop, rather than just a presentation (F, S), which would require moving a few other speakers around (SE). *Making special moves just for me? I may be able to make that work, espe-*

108

cially if you had to call a special meeting with all your hoity-toity big-wigs to talk about me. I'm not bragging or anything, but I am kind of a big deal (P, SE, F).

They sent me the dates of the event, and as I looked at my schedule, I realized that I was double-booked. I had already committed to be in San Diego for TPI Fitness Level 3 on Friday and Saturday, and the medical conference organizers wanted me on the other side of the continent speaking Sunday morning. I checked the flights and saw that a late flight out Saturday evening could have me arriving at 2 am Sunday. *I could sleep for 4 hours and get to the conference by 8am and then speak for 8 hours straight. Totally doable, right? Of course, you are a globe-trotting superstar. You are like one of those DJs who do two shows a night every night all around the globe* (SE).

My pride and self-esteem were pumped up like a testosterone-fueled teenager. Was it realistic? *No.* Did my ego and pride want to try to pull it off so I could bring home the big bucks from doing three days of speaking in two cities? *Yes* (P, SE, F, A). The thought of pulling this off tweaked my Ambition driver. I wanted to be the type of person who could pull off the unthinkable (P), the type of person who could execute at the highest level under intense pressure. I would never know if I could or couldn't do it if I never pushed myself to be that person (A).

When we break this real-life example down, you can see some trends. Pride (P) and how I think others see me is my primary driver. I am a people pleaser. I want others to

109

think of me in a positive light. When I felt that others weren't valuing me as I had hoped, it affected my Self Esteem (SE). Financially (F), I was enticed by the money aspect, but my hang-up with my day rate was completely pride-based. The number on the check reflects how I was valued. If I felt that my response to this particular interaction was negative, I would have to focus on my Pride. If I was to ever make a true change in how I would handle a similar interaction in the future, I would have to deal with my Pride. Even after asking my wife if she thought it was possible to pull this off, my Pride was boiling up and pushing me to prove to everyone that I could do it.

TODAY'S TASK (CONTINUED): When you take on the task I outlined earlier (write down three successes and three failures), you will quickly recognize the driver trends you have in your life. Beside each success and failure, I want you to either write out or mentally walk through the events that led to the outcome. Put the corresponding letters beside each event that drove you to the actions you took at that time.

You will quickly see a trend when you acknowledge the number of times each driver pops up in the success section and which ones led to your failures. If you don't get your answers in a list of three life events, try six. If you are being honest with yourself, the answer will reveal itself. So put down this book, grab your notebook, and start the Task. *Now.*

The WHY

Why do we do what we do? Why do we choose to dream what we dream? The task you just completed should shed some light on the answer to this question. When I say shed light, for some of you, it sheds light like a magnifying glass in the hot sun on an unsuspecting ant. You have to reveal the *why* behind your chosen destination—otherwise, you will reach it and not know why you started the journey in the first place.

"We are going for a drive to the beach to get some ice cream." When you get there, you know you arrived when you have an ice cream cone in your hand. If the ice cream shop is closed, you will know *why* you are disappointed because you knew *why* you drove all the way to the beach. You wanted ice cream.

The *why* doesn't have to be a positive reason. It just has to be honest. In the example I shared earlier about being offered a speaking gig, my driver was Pride (P). I care what you think of me, but for my sake not yours. I really don't care what you think when you go home and share your thoughts with your loved ones. I care what you think when I am right in front of you in the moment. It's not about you. It's about me filling a dark hole in my soul with others' recognition that I am making them happy.

This drive is so strong that I will line up for two hours at an open mic and listen to three hours of horrible comedy for the opportunity to sling five minutes of my jokes to complete strangers. That may seem insane to you—and perhaps it is—but at least I know *why* I am doing it.

Do you know why you want to open your own gym, quit your office job and become a freelance photographer, or start an organic mushroom farm? Is it because you crave getting up to your elbows in manure at 6 am each day? Instead, it will come from the list of drivers that we covered earlier. Figure out which one is most dominant in your life and then write your #DreamBIG with that driver in the limelight. If I acknowledge that Pride will need to be in the forefront of my next big project, I better make sure that the end result will satisfy that driver.

> #DreamBIG: Write a book that will inspire others to greatness. Thousands of readers will be so inspired that they will send emails and share on their social media just how honest, funny, and thought-provoking the book is. I will then have to go on a speaking book tour to meet all the #DreamBIGers out there. There will be a Netflix documentary series about the #DreamBIG movement and how it has helped countless people accomplish their dreams.

Do you think this #DreamBIG may just satisfy my Pride driver? You will have to come out to one of my book signings or watch the #DreamBIG documentary to find out.

Sniff Out Disaster

Let's take a closer look at the drivers you found in your failure list. Can you see a trend in the drivers that led you to the decisions that made up the failures you experienced in your life? This part of the exercise is designed to heighten our ability to sniff out disasters before they happen. In my case, my negative driver is the same as my positive driver. I have had three occasions in my life where my gut was saying, "Stand up for yourself and end this business relationship," but my Pride driver that needs me to be seen as a "good guy" prevented me from getting out when I should have.

Who cares what they think of you when they are ripping you off or weighing you down and keeping you from your goal? For many of you, the Financial (F) and Security (S) drivers will be highlighted in this section of the task. It is the (F) and (S) that make you hold on to a stock too long or stop you from investing in an opportunity for the fear of losing money.

Personal Relationships (PR) have always been a weird driver for me. I am really close to a few people whom I trust in my life, while I struggle to connect easily with the rest. People assume I am good with PR because I get into the murky water with them and explore their dreams and deepest desires. But it is usually one-sided: When the conversation comes to how I am doing, I shut down and close up shop.

113

Fear of letting people in is a vulnerability that I am trying to understand in myself. I am vulnerable to myself when I look in the mirror and am comfortable with my insecurities. I shy away from sharing my vulnerability with others unless I think it is for the sake of helping them overcome one of their own obstacles. "No, it's totally normal to dress in lederhosen, eat Cheezies, and masturbate. I do the same thing when I get anxious, minus the lederhosen and Cheezies, of course." I usually cover up my awkward social moments with comedy.

I truly want to get to know people on the deepest level but don't want them to know me. That's right, folks: The Coach has shit to work on as well.

Ambition (A) is what this book is all about: the perfect version of your life as you imagine it. Your ambition is filled with all the other drivers and should feed all their needs. Ambition only becomes an issue when it feeds the negative drivers and snuffs out the positives. For example, suppose you had financial ambition (F, A) to make as much money as possible. In the process, you destroyed all personal and sexual relationships, and you created a false sense of pride that was based on your bank statement. You boosted your self-esteem and met your ambition to be financially secure. You became Scrooge McDuck.

Take some time with this task. This book is not a sprint. It is a journey that when done properly will yield fulfillment of all your drivers. This is a huge step toward clarifying a DreamBIG that will be truly fulfilling.

CHAPTER TWELVE:

WRITE YOUR FIRST DREAMBIG

It's time. You have all the tools and insight needed to write your first DreamBIG. I want you to walk the tightrope between trying to make it perfect while at the same time throwing caution to the wind and just going for it. You can edit, adapt, expand, simplify, and turn it into anything you want it to be. But you need to start with something. This is why we set aside five pages in the front of your notebook for you to make any amendments to what you come up with on the first go.

If you still want more structure perform the following:

Step 1: Write what you want, simply and clearly.

"I want to be the head strength coach for Team Canada." It's that easy. Just say what you want. We will expand on that in the coming steps, but for now you will have a clear and concise destination.

Step 2: Establish if it is possible.

Does your dream defy the physics of the universe as we know it? When I declared that I wanted to be the main man at Team Canada, I had to see what it would take to be "the man." I researched the man who at the time was sitting at my soon-to-be preverbal desk. What background did he have, how did he get there, and what will it take for me to make it a no-brainer for them to replace him with me?

I met with him in Toronto in the guise of seeing how I could be a better at the provincial level where I was currently the S&C coach. He had no idea I was looking for a way to soon step into his shoes. It was possible, and that's all I needed here. Commence DreamBIG.

Step 3: Plot checkpoints to stay on track.

When designing a mission, the Navy Seals set checkpoints to ensure that they are staying on course. "You will come across a church with no door and head north." More importantly, they also set checkpoints that notify them that they are off course. "If your feet feel wet and sandy, you reached the ocean and going in the wrong direction. Build a sandcastle, and then turn around and go back to the base." The same needs to be done with your DreamBIG.

If your dream was to create a political blog that was unapologetically honest, you may have a checkpoint that says, "Reach 4,000 active subscribers." You will know you are off course if all 4,000 subscribers agree with your blog. "No 'Unsubscribe' or a lack of heated debate in the blog comment section indicates that I am catering to the audience and not being 100% honest."

Step 4: Do the work.

Wake up every morning and do the work. I use a separate legal notepad to create my daily checklist. Different from the Checkpoints which are general, the Checklist is a laser-focused task. In the checkpoint example of "Reach 4,000 active subscribers," your checklist may have a box with "Add a subscribe button to the website main page and link it to the email campaign funnel." Each item is either completed or pending. If a box is left unchecked, it is transferred to the top of the next page and attacked first thing the following day. Each item must take you one step closer to accomplishing your DreamBIG.

The second part of this book will take you through the skills you need to OverDeliver on your DreamBIG. It is one thing to accomplish your dream, but to truly realize your dream, you must over-deliver on it.

Before you turn the page, I need you to open your notebook and write your DreamBIG. Define it. It should be one to two sentences long. If you need to write a paragraph, you haven't properly worked through what you really want. Jump to the Set-Up Punch Method chapter for help on how to condense big concepts into powerful, bite-sized pile drives to the face.

Read your DreamBIG out loud. It should give you goosebumps. If you feel no emotion, you haven't dreamt big enough. Rewrite it. It should make you feel like crying with joy at the thought of it becoming a reality.

TODAY'S TASK: Write your DreamBIG.

PART II: OVERDELIVER

OverDelivering is a philosophy I incorporate into everything I do. Execute what is required and then ask yourself, "Is there anything else I can add to make it even better?" If you ask for 10, I will give you 13. Ask for a coffee, and I will make you breakfast. This part is all about OverDelivering in every aspect of your life.

Dreaming big is a big deal. You have established what you want. In the coming chapters, we will look at how to approach accomplishing it. The OverDeliver part of this book will have you rewriting your DreamBIG and rewriting again. Once you see the power of OverDelivering, you will want to OverDeliver on your dream. Let's dive deep into the concept of OverDeliver.

CHAPTER THIRTEEN:

FLIP THE SCRIPT

Nothing gets me more jazzed up than seeing creative people express their genius in bold, nuevo ways, especially when it goes against conformity and challenges the status quo. Take what is considered normal and do the opposite.

There is a phrase used in hip hop culture, *Flip the Script,* which refers to taking what may be a disparaging remark said about you and turning it into something positive. In the story you are seen as the villain, but you flip the script and become the hero. I love the visual of taking a script or book, flipping it over, and looking at it from back to front.

I have always looked for opportunities to flip the script in my career by reengineering something that the rest of my colleagues and peers think is the norm. I love taking elements from other cultures, genres, or fringe groups, making them fresh, and then applying them to my stuffy, conservative fitness community. I mixed my background in hip hop, skateboarding, punk rock, and comedy to deliver health and fitness in a way that had never been done before. Whenever things feel safe or stale in my work, I dive back into music and comedy to find new ways to flip the script.

If you seek to flip the script, you are OverDelivering.

The Story of Chef Jordi Roca

Jordi Roca was the younger brother of two of the most successful restauranteurs in the world. He was the outcast of the family and living like the youngest child in many families, with no responsibility other than to live life to the fullest. His brothers Joan and Josep gave their little brother a job at their three-Michelin-star Spanish restaurant, El Celler de Can Roca, in hopes that he would settle down, stay out of trouble, and finally grow up. They put him to work under pastry chef Damian Allsop, who nine months after starting to train Jordi had an accident that put him out of commission.

Jordi's brothers had a decision to make: Hire a new chef or give their lost-cause brother a chance to step up. Jordi tried to keep up with the recipes set out by Damian but struggled to maintain the same buzz that his famous predecessor created.

Jordi knew that he was on a slippery slope to failure unless he found a way to make his own impact and put his personal stamp on the pastries being offered at El Celler de Can Roca. Jordi was compelled to take a course on the art of making ice cream that was offered by a renowned chef. Jordi learned a lesson that day that changed his way of thinking and his career trajectory took a dramatically different tangent.

"I didn't know it was possible to go that in-depth into ice cream. One day, the teacher talked about how the air is important for an ice cream. It is very important that the air is completely clean so the ice cream does not absorb odours, so it does not add another flavour. I went home and thought the other way around."

Jordi flipped the script and took a rule of ice cream making and turned a common dessert into a culinary masterpiece. If clean air was the key to ensuring no foul odours would affect the flavour of the ice cream, what would happen if he intentionally infused odours into the dessert? He took cigar smoke and infused it into the ice cream to create one of the most famous and interesting desserts in the culinary world, Cigar Ice Cream.

Why would I take you down the path to share a story about a man who created a dessert such that even thinking about it could turn your stomach? You need to study the fringe to push your own boundaries on what is possible in your life.

Every year, I completely reset my computer, which forces me to start my daily work process from a blank slate. We become lazy and stuck in the rut of doing the same thing in the same way and creating the same result.

Every year I perform shows (as I call them) or presentations (as my colleagues call them) on fitness and athletic performance. Every year, my slide show changes and evolves, but the basic elements are consistent. The topic or theme remains the same but each time I perform the slide show I will add slides or take some away. Sometimes entire sections of the show will be cut and rebuilt as my experience and perspective evolves over the years. Every three years, however, I will take my entire presentation and press *delete*. I open up a new blank PowerPoint file and start fresh.

This process forces me to flip the script. Sure, I could just press *replay* on last year's presentation. This year's audience never saw the show I did last year. But that wouldn't force evolution and progression—that wouldn't be OverDelivering.

CHAPTER FOURTEEN:

PERSPECTIVE IS A CHOICE

It is hard to OverDeliver if you are always worried about what others will think. When we take other's opinions into consideration, we tend to under-deliver and play it safe. I want you to live your life from a new perspective. I want you to view the world from inside the box looking out and not from the outside world looking in.

On the PGA Tour, there is enormous pressure placed on every shot. Imagine standing on the first tee of the Ryder Cup in a match between not just you and your competitor but between your country and an entire continent. The stands are stuffed full of chanting, rabid golf fans and loyalists. The entire world is watching. Not a golfer? How about the final penalty shot in the World Cup or a free throw to win the NBA Championship?

You can either see the shot from inside your body looking out or through the eyes of the world looking in. If you are confident and playing well, you will see from the inside out. If you have any question about your ability to rise to the occasion, you will view yourself from the outside in.

This is where your practice of meditation and imagery work comes into play. The more time you spend envisioning yourself on the grandest stage under the enormous

125

pressure of the moment, the more likely you will be able to control your perspective when it counts.

I have worked with players who have had the opposite perspective to what those around them see. The rest of the world saw them as champions, while they saw themselves as people who barely made the cut. This is in stark contrast to people who think they are *the shit* when really they are just shit.

My job with these players is to reframe the way they see themselves from the inside out. They walk alongside legends of the game like Phil Michelson or Tiger or the current hotshots on tour and think, *Wow, I get to play with the Champ today? Cool.* Meanwhile, the champ is looking at them and thinking, *Oh, shit. This guy is pretty green. If I don't beat him, people will be questioning my greatness.*

For these players, we start the process of nightly imagery sessions. It begins with breathing exercises. Once the mind is calm and focussed, the athletes start to see themselves playing their sport. Some will see themselves from a face-on view, while others see from their own perspective of looking down at the ball. The later is the best perspective and the end goal of this session.

Regardless of how they see themselves, I have them look around in their imagined world. I want them to take in as much detail as they possibly can: Hear the crowd shuffling to get a glimpse of the action, notice the smell of the air and the colors of the course and foliage around them. I then get them to go internal and describe the feelings they have inside: the butterflies in their stomachs, the nerves rising to the top, and the jelly-like feeling in their legs. Then I ask them to take a deep breath and *fire away*.

Here is where it gets interesting. Some of the players will describe the ball coming off the club face and flying high with a slight fade, landing, and rolling out in the fairway. Others see the ball flaring out to the right into the hazard. This is where we get into the nitty gritty.

I remember talking to Padraig Harrington after he won his three majors. He said he looked down the fairway from the tee box and could only see the hazards and bunkers. He had no idea where to hit it and where the ball was going to go. He said that, in the two times that he played Sergio Garcia in a playoff to win his majors, his hands were shaking like a leaf, and so were Sergio's. Sergio is like an artist in the way he uses his hands to create enormous power. Since Padraig uses his entire body to hit the ball, he has an easier time hitting the target even if his hands are shaking.

In sports, it is easy to connect the dots between visualization and execution. The more athletes visualize success, the more confidence they feel on game day. It goes deeper than that, however. Studies have shown that there is actually a physiological response by the body when visualizing action. For example, in one study, scientists tested baseline wrist strength. They then divided the group into two subgroups each of which had to immobilize the wrist using a cast for one month. One group would do nothing for a month, while the other group visualized flexing and extending the wrist. The wrist didn't move due to the cast, but they would imagine that it did.

The visualization group was twice as strong compared to the lazy, good-for-nothing control group. This study has been performed in various ways using finger curls, weight training and other tests of strength with visualization, no visualization, exercises plus visualization and just exercises. Time and time again, the test subjects who added visualization to their workouts had the best results.

If you can build muscle through visualization and enhance your performance through mental practice, can you imagine what visualization could do for your DreamBIG?

Applying Visualization to your DreamBIG

How are you going to visualize the success of your DreamBIG? Do you see it from the perspective of your peers, colleagues and loved ones looking at what you have created or through your eyes looking out at the world? If it comes from your perspective, it will deepen the emotional component that goes with visualization. It's not just picturing it happening—it's about feeling it.

It is hard to imagine how others will respond to your work, and, to be frank, it doesn't really matter what they think. Their perspectives aren't layered in emotion and passion. The only way to conjure up the integral parts of dreaming big is to see it from the inside looking out.

To prepare for my stage shows, I would use visualization to practice the timing and cadence of my lecture. When I visualized my keynote speech each night, I pictured myself walking on stage from the audience's perspective. Once they stood up and started to applaud, my perspective switched from them looking at me to me looking out at their smiling faces. I would imagine the butterflies in my gut and the urge to defecate on the podium while I vomited on the microphone.

Yet I always feel that way when I do big shows or stand-up comedy right up until my name is called and I step on stage. Then I feel a calmness roll over me, but I still envision the butterflies and urge to void when I picture myself on stage. I also spend time picturing and feeling what I will be like that evening after the show. I can see myself grinning from ear to ear, with an elevated heart rate and numb body and mind. Success!

The skills of visualization and meditation are integral to any performance you are preparing for. Whether you are picturing yourself signing the paperwork at the bank to pay off your mortgage or seeing yourself on the cover of *Entrepreneur Illustrated* magazine, you should use visualization and deep meditation to walk through the process to get you there.

I lump visualization and meditation together because you can use visualization to help you get into a meditative state, and you can use meditation to calm your mind, which in turn helps you to better visualize what you want to accomplish. They go hand in hand or, more accurately, mind in mind.

Visualization is an art. I work with my clients by starting simply and deepening the experience as they improve their skills. For example, they might begin by visualizing an orange. (You can play along while you read this.)

What does it look like? Describe it.

What color is it? I know it's orange, but provide more detail. Is it ripe? Is there any blemish on it?

Is it perfectly round like a navel or is it more oval like a mandarin?

What does it smell like?

What does it feel like? Heavy? Cold? Sticky?

Now picture yourself holding the orange.

Do you see yourself from the outside while seeing your entire body, face, and hand or from the perspective of looking through your eyes down at your arm and hand holding the orange?

What are you wearing?

We can go on for hours, but I think you get the point. I lead my clients into deeper and deeper details about their visualizations. I always start with something that has little to no emotional connection to them. Not many people have an orange trigger unless they were laughed at by an orange as they pulled it from their lunch bag in grade school.

You are going to have to get good at this. Really good. I want you to go to sleep dreaming big and wake up to the visual of you Overdelivering on that dream.

What if you woke up every day with one thing on your mind?

Pinky: "Gee, Brain, what are we gonna do tonight?"

Brain: "The same thing we do every night: Try to take over the world."

Great accomplishments come from a culmination of work in a focused direction. Here is a quote from Jacob Reils that hangs in the Sacramento Spurs locker room:

When nothing seems to help, I go and look at a stonecutter hammering away at his rock perhaps a hundred times without as much as a crack showing in it. Yet at the hundred and first blow it will split in two, and I know it was not that blow that did it — but all that had gone before.

The act of visualizing your dreams should not feel like work. It should be invigorating. When I am working on a project that I am passionate about, I look forward to going to bed so I can rise and get back to the work. Currently, I am focussed 100% on this book. It is my life's work. I go to bed thinking about getting up early and writing, excited to get a few hours of writing in before the house wakes up. Sometimes during the day, I am like a teenager who has five minutes to spare and sneaks on the computer to get through the next level on a video game. I run up to the office and fire off another page or go on my phone and make some notes that will be added to a chapter tomorrow.

The point is that, if your DreamBIG is worth doing, you have to get excited about it. Even the shitty tasks that are sitting on your daily DreamBIG checklist require your enthusiasm. You know you have to do them anyway, so you might as well get excited about them. If you told me that cleaning the toilet with a toothbrush would help me write this book, I would wake up every morning with my wife's toothbrush in hand, ready to scrub.

Visualize the Obstacles

You will face obstacles along the path to your DreamBIG. It is inevitable, and it is life. I have studied Stoic philosophy for years and incorporate many of its tenets in how I interact with the world. A Stoic mindset starts with accepting that life is going to be hard. You will work from the day you are born until the day you die. You will face obstacles, hardships, heartaches, and perils along your journey. Once you accept this, you can now decide how you want to approach this truth. Are you going to live a life where the world is taking from you, taking shots at you, and shitting on your parade, or are you going to find a way to find fulfillment, peace and joy in this reality? I choose the latter.

If we accept that our journey toward our DreamBIG will face obstacles, don't you think it would be a good idea to include these potential setbacks in our visualizations? Any great general will plan for shit going sideways in battle and have a contingency plan in place for when it does. Formula One race teams have multiple strategies for each race situation that they can employ with a simple message to the driver: "We are switching to Strategy 4, repeat, we will be switching to Strategy 4, box-box." The other option is acting like unprepared teenage lovers on the way to the pharmacist to buy the Plan B pill. I wonder what their Plan A was?

When I visualize performing a keynote speech, I prepare myself for the slideshow not working, my mic cutting out, people walking out in the middle of the show, an earthquake, famine, and Godzilla attacks. Most of these distractions have happened while I was on stage over my ten years of public speaking and performing stand-up. When they inevitably popped up, I never missed a beat.

I was prepared for the worst and hoped for the best. Preparing for the worst and having a plan to execute at the highest level when it does happen makes you Undeniable and leads to OverDelivering.

CHAPTER FIFTEEN:

INTENTION AND OVERDELIVERING

Intension is deliberate. If you intend to Overdeliver and make Overdelivering a way of life, your actions will follow. An intention must be set.

You set an intention by creating a set of rules or boundaries in which you will operate while carrying out an action. If your intension is to OverDeliver, you may set a personal rule: Whenever you are asked to help or deliver a service, you will find a way to do more than what was asked. You ask me to look at your squat mechanics, and I perform a full-body functional screen and send you home with a comprehensive corrective exercise program. You ask me to give you a ride to the bus stop, and I drive you all the way to work. You invite me up to your place for a "coffee" after a successful date, and I make bacon and eggs for you in the morning.

If you have OverDeliver set as your intention, you will OverDeliver. When you OverDeliver and receive the positive feedback from this above-and-beyond action, it reinforces your intention.

If your intention affects everything you do throughout your day, you better be careful what intentions you set.

Intention Is Everything

"I didn't mean to upset you. I thought it would make you happy."

"I thought I was eating right. All those years of Diet Coke and sugar-free this and that. I didn't know it was toxic."

"I thought pushing and grinding through the pain was part of the process. I had no idea the damage I was doing to my knee."

"All those selfies and time wasted making twisted duckface in the mirror wearing nothing but a thong. I really thought I was inspiring others to get in shape."

Intention is everything. If you think you are doing something for the right reason, you are doing it with good intention. If you take action and truly believe it is for the betterment of others or yourself without causing harm, then your intention is justified. Nothing feels better than doing something you believe in with all your heart, and then the results of those actions are positively received.

If you see that your action has negative consequences, you must change the action and understand that, although you set out with good intentions, it was not justifiably received in that light. Once you know better and you continue to do that same negative action, you are an asshole. "It was not my intention to upset Suzy. That was not my in-

136

tention when I slept with Chad. I only intended to show her that she doesn't appreciate him the way she should. I thought it would bring them closer as a couple. Oh well, her loss is my gain."

I am making this point because so many people use intention as a scapegoat for actions they took that backfired. This is not the purpose of this chapter. In fact, it is the exact opposite: True intention requires forethought on the potential result of your action and self reflection on the reason for you taking the action. The next step is to take ownership of that action in the event that your intention is not received the way you intended.

One of the most powerful traits to reflect upon while dealing with the problem of intention is selflessness.

Selflessness

Selflessness is having more concern for others' needs and wishes than your own. If you really dive deep into this topic, you will be a better person for it. Before you post a picture on social media, write an email, take a job opportunity, or share a story at a dinner party, ask yourself this: Is this action for me or for them?

Who is *them*, you ask? Anyone other than you. If you are doing it for you, you are feeding your ego. If you are doing it for others, you are feeding your soul. This is a topic I struggled with in the past and continue to self reflect on from time to time.

In my job, I need to self-promote, which can seem very selfish and egotistical. Putting yourself in the limelight with a big neon sign that screams, "Look at me, look at me!" can feel very soulless. This is where intention comes into play.

Why do I spend an entire day each week recording, producing, and publishing my Coach Glass Podcast? Is it so everyone can listen to my quirky, unique form of Edumatainment and have them pat me on my back and say, "Bravo, good job, aren't you clever?" Follow that up with a social media post each day that promotes my podcast, website, and online training programs and boosts my brand each and every week. "What an egotistical, self promoting, insecure, needy asshole."

But wait: What if my intent is to *Inspire Others to Greatness*? What if all that "putting yourself out there" and looking like a jackass attracted others to listen, watch and engage with what I truly believe helps people overcome their own personal barriers and inspires them to their personal greatness? Same podcast, same selfie in the mirror—just different intent.

I have a close friend who is 13 years in recovery. He invited me to support him one morning at his Alcoholics Anonymous meeting. I found it extremely eye opening. Like a church service, each day they focus on one aspect of their sobriety. That particular day the topic was selflessness.

As participants shared their stories about how selfishness affected their lives, I couldn't help but relate. Selfish behaviour leads to self destruction. I was sitting there feeling like I was living selfishly and felt horrible about myself. We went for breakfast after the meeting, and I shared my thoughts with my pal. I told him that my self promotion was an act of selfishness, and I felt that my entire brand and public image was a farce.

"Stop," he interrupted. "You are one of the most selfless people I know. You coach your athletes with the intention of helping them fulfill their goals. You have never been about the money and always go beyond what is asked to help them achieve their goals. Your social media and podcast are self-deprecating and lighthearted enough to help people take themselves less seriously and brings joy to their lives. When you get deep, you inspire them to be better. You created your online training program to help people who wouldn't normally have access to your coaching. And don't even get me started on what you do for your mentorship family."

"Yeah, but I charge people for those services," I replied.

"That doesn't make you selfish. If you didn't charge them, you wouldn't be able to provide the services that you do. You would have to get a job to pay the bills that would take you away from doing what you are great at. Don't ever feel bad about charging people. If your intention was to just make money, it would come through in everything you do, and people would be turned off."

This brings me to a time in my business when I teamed up with a marketing group. This team loved my brand and my products and felt it was undervalued and needed a bigger audience. I agreed that more eyeballs would allow me to inspire more people to their greatness and would be a win-win.

The problem was that their intention was to make money while my intention was to build my community. The marketing plan they set out involved a sales funnel that would gather a huge pool of potential clients and then aggressively weed out the looky-loos and hard sell interested buyers into a bigger purchase than they were initially interested in. They built an elaborate webinar slideshow that promised the secrets of my training, but it was really a sales pitch to push them through the funnel. My gut was telling me the entire time that this wasn't right. I felt bad for deceiving my community for the sake of making a sale. They assured me that it was all part of the process, and, for every two people we lost, we would gain eight.

Let me be very clear here: I was not upset with this team or their tactics. They were very clear on their intentions, and at the end of the day, I was the one who agreed to it and hired them to launch my product.

After my first webinar, I received some seriously negative backlash. I had emails and texts from peers along the lines of "Seriously Jay? Do you really need money that bad that you had to waste my time and try to trick me? Next time just ask. I have always supported your products but now I'm not so sure." It broke my heart. I shared these messages with the marketing team, who told me that I would have to grow thicker skin if I wanted to play with the big boys.

It tore me up inside because it went against my intention. I wrote every person who complained a personal letter in which I apologized for the approach we took with the product launch. I needed to reconnect them to my original intent.

Since then, I have made my intentions extremely clear to any organization I entrust my brand to or any team member I bring on board. My intention is to *Inspire Others to Greatness*, build a community, and lastly make money to support the mission so we can reach more people.

If you want to sell, you need to sell in a way that matches your intent. In the next chapter, we will go deep into the art of selling yourself while staying true to yourself. If you want to truly OverDeliver, intension is everything.

CHAPTER SIXTEEN:

THE GAME PLAN

You have your DreamBIG destination. Now it is time to roll out the map and create a plan to take you from where you are to where you dream to be. Most of you will want to skip this step and jump right into the execution stage of your journey. This would be a mistake. The following is a quick and effective way to lay out the journey you are about to embark on and will ensure that you pack your bag accordingly.

The Elements of a Plan

To be truly great at anything, you need to have a plan. What the plan looks like depends on what you want to accomplish. There are, however, certain elements that need to be in place if you want the plan to be a success. Your plan is a roadmap that will guide you to your DreamBIG destination.

You also have to be prepared to be flexible and fluid with your plan in the event you need to adjust your route on the fly. I have been guilty myself of creating a plan, seeing it trending downward and being too stubborn to change it in time to save it from failure.

Navy SEALS and special ops create contingency plans for every mission: a plan for everything to go as planned, a plan for every possible alteration, and finally a plan for when shit hits the fan. To see potential disaster before it comes, the SEALs set up checkpoints in their plan. These are points on the map that need to be met before they reach the next marker. If they miss one, they will go back and complete it before moving forward. They also have negative checkpoints that state that, if you see a sign "Warning: Goat Crossing" along the road, you have gone too far and need to double back. In a business plan, this could be a checkpoint stating that if you reach 100,000 sales without hiring more staff, you need to stop and ensure you can handle the capacity.

Start with the perfect plan. Break down the most direct route to your destination with the fewest twists and turns along the road. More checkpoints along this route will ensure you don't accidentally wander off course and end up in a cow pasture.

The checkpoints are clearly defined in your notebook and become little goals that you will chip away at each day on your daily checklist of actionable items. If you are working with a team, you may give an individual or department a checkpoint and let them run with it. The structure looks like the following:

DreamBIG Mission   Overall goal

| **Checkpoints** | Essential elements needed to accomplish DreamBIG |
| **Checklist** | Daily actions to fulfill the essential elements |

My notebook has all the checkpoints laid out in the first few pages. I leave a lot of space between each checkpoint and a few extra pages after the final checkpoint to add the inevitable revisions along the way. I like my daily checklist to be on a separate notepad. The notepad makes it less formal and allows me to doodle, scratch out ideas, and make random notes without judgement.

I used to put all these notes in my DreamBIG notebook but found I was trying to make it look too pretty and was afraid to mess it up with a coffee stain or funny joke premise that pops into my head throughout the day. You may choose to set up your notebook differently, but the important thing is that you have it beside you while you work to keep you on track.

Some business gurus will tell you to write a formal business plan. The business plan becomes your roadmap. I personally see the formal business plan as way too cumbersome and inflexible. Just writing a business plan is a job that will take months to complete. In that time, you could have been immeasurably closer to your destination.

I feel the same about yearly periodization plans for athletes. Coaches lay out these elaborate plans that include macrocycles (DreamBIGs), mesocycles (Checkpoints), and microcycles (Checklists). In my 25 years as a strength coach, I have never seen one yearly periodization plan executed as designed. All it takes is a pulled hamstring, bout of sciatica or three-day bachelorette party, and the whole program goes out the window.

You need an overall plan, but the real work is done daily with the checklist and reviewed monthly or biweekly with your checkpoint list to see if you are still on course.

A DreamBIG Example

Here is an example of one of my DreamBIGs and the road it took with my checkpoints and checklists along the way.

In 2013, I had just started my public speaking career with TPI and Perform Better. It was exciting and new. I was a natural, it seemed from the outside, as I stepped on stage to teach my first two-day seminar. I presented myself as a road-hardened pro who had ten years of public speaking under his belt.

To the outside, it looked like I had landed the ultimate job, and I was on the top of my game. Inside I felt the complete opposite. My guts were churning all morning, my armpits thought I was in a hot yoga class, and my hand trembled as I clicked from slide to slide. I was nervous and stumbled over my words while I tiptoed through the onslaught of questions and criticism that came with lecturing on a topic that at the time was upsetting the apple cart in the fitness world.

I knew that my content was valid, but my delivery needed some sophistication and polish. I watched back some footage after getting home from that first show and was horrified by all my quirks, tells and ticks. I had to get better.

Malcom Gladwell said that if you had 10,000 hours of practice in any endeavour, you could become a master of that skill. After doing the math, I realized that if I spoke two days a month for six hours a day, I would have to perform 833 shows to become a master. I would be over 80 years old. Gladwell's claim was a loose representation of the work performed by Anders Ericsson in his book *Peak*. Ericsson makes it very clear that 10,000 hours of an activity does *not* create world class performances. To create world class skill, you need to put in an enormous number of hours of purposeful practice—practice performed at the brink of failure followed by reflection and adjustment to practice plans based on results.

Performing the same activity at the same intensity and difficulty, day in and day out, will not create great performances. As the class clown all my life I had over 10,000 hours by the time I turned 18. Don't get me wrong: I am really good, but truly world class?

I had to find a way to build speaking skills without having to get on stage. I had to find a way to clarify my messaging and simplify my teaching style to make the complex concepts I was teaching easier to digest. I had to clean up my speaking ticks that I used to bridge thoughts together, like saying, "umm" or "and ahh," which made me sound like an NHL player in a post-game interview. "We played hard and ahh gave it everything we had and ahh worked umm as a team and ahh…." I also had my comedic side rearing its ugly head at the most inappropriate times. I needed an outlet to work my comedy bits before I brought them to the stage. I needed to design a public speaker DreamBIG.

2013 DreamBIG: *Become a world-class public speaker.*

I was doodling in my notebook on a flight and drew a picture: I was standing on a stage with the lights shining down on me, while the auditorium was packed to the brim with fans laughing and hanging on every word. It was a rough sketch, but when I finished it, I felt my eyes well up.

I would travel around the globe lecturing, entertaining, and educating the paying masses. I pictured myself finishing my show with my feet up and looking off the balcony in a tropical locale, with my wife at my side. "Ahh, this is the life." I would arrive home with an inbox full of emails from fans who shared how much my show inspired them and made them laugh and a mailbox full of checks from my previous shows. This is how you DreamBIG.

Checkpoint: *Create opportunities to practice my public speaking to refine my skills.*

I thought, *The best way to get better at speaking is to practice speaking with purpose.* Purposeful practice involves structured practice sessions that push your abilities, challenges your skills, adjusts to match your current skillset, and provides direct feedback on a regular basis. I needed to create a practice environment in which I could explore my speaking skills and find my voice.

I decided to record myself performing a lecture each week on a different topic. This required me to think of an interesting topic, research it, and create a framework that would make logical sense. I would then take that topic and find an interesting, entertaining way to deliver it that would stretch my comfort level.

Speaking into your hairbrush in front of the bathroom mirror isn't purposeful practice—I needed an audience. I realized that if I put these recordings out publicly, I would have to put the hard work in to make sure they were high quality, and recording, publishing, and sending my podcast into the ether would accomplish just that. When I spoke on stage, I had no ability to change or edit what came out of my mouth, so I knew that whatever I was going to put out would have to be raw, off the cuff, and never edited.

Checkpoint #1: *Start a podcast.*

Checklist for Checkpoint #1:

- ✓ Start a podcast.
- ✓ Come up with a catchy name.
- ✓ Create a logo.

✓ Buy recording equipment.
✓ Learn how to produce and upload episodes.
✓ Build a website.
✓ Start recording.

I started the Coach Glass Podcast in 2013. I was obsessed with the new format of "pirate radio" that allowed for anyone to create long-form audio content and publish it to the world. I listened to Jay Mohr, Bill Burr and Joe Rogan religiously. I thought, *I could do this.*

I made a commitment to myself and more importantly to my listeners that I would produce at least one episode each and every week for a long as I felt I was able to produce quality episodes. Each episode would either inspire, entertain, or educate the listeners and keep them engaged. I had no idea that this decision would take me on a decade-long journey that would change my life forever.

If you listen to the Coach Glass Podcast today, you may think, *The production level is very professional, sound bites are added in post-production, and this man is focused and passionate about his subject.* Or you may think, *Jay is on mushrooms, needs to cut back on the #GrassFedBuddah coffee, but for some reason I can't wait to listen to next week's adventure.* This is a far cry from my first episodes that sounded like they were created by an immature, unpolished, stuttering, and distracted amateur.

That's how it was for the first 100 episodes. I clearly remember the first few test episodes that I tried to edit down and turn into a product worthy of your eardrums. I was so nervous. What if they don't like me or even worse, what if no-one listens. I erased them and chalked them up as practice recordings.

I made a pact with myself: I decided that the podcast was for me to develop my speaking skills first and for the benefit of the listener second. To master speaking at the highest level, I decided that the episodes would not be edited. That put enormous pressure on me to speak in clear, thought-out concepts while crafting my next sentence.

While speaking on one topic, I was mentally looking forward to the next topic so I could seamlessly tie it all together. My goal was to make it sound like it was just a casual, off-the-cuff conversation. Jay Mohr shared on his podcast that he loved to go on stage as a comic and start a story with no ending and build his wings on the way down. The image of a baby bird jumping out of the nest and learning to fly on the free fall down to earth energized me. If you don't figure it out soon enough, you will bounce off the forest floor and become a baby bird pancake. Which are delicious BTW!

After almost a decade, I continue to start episode subjects with a general idea of where I want to go and build my wings on the way down. The goal is to finish the episode with an impactful exclamation point on the subject that is created through the process of expressing my passion through the mic.

TODAY'S TASK: For some of you, speaking into a recorder may push you out of your comfort zone. More experienced speakers may benefit from recording scripted, practiced content with the intent to publish. Others need to challenge themselves by turning on the mic with nothing more than a few bullet points, a goal of talking for an hour, and a keyboard full of sound effects to weave into your show.

Take out your phone or set up a camera and record yourself talking about what you are passionate about. Your DreamBIG is a perfect topic. Record yourself and play it back. Don't like what you hear? Do it again. Keep doing it until what you pictured in your head is executed on the screen or in the audio file.

Practice is one thing, but I also had to deal with my on-stage nerves if I was going to be world class. Every time I got on stage, I would feel like my bowels were going to drop out my khakis. I realized that my nerves were a product of not feeling as though my skills matched the challenge. To feel more comfortable on stage, I would have to create a workout that pushed me past the comfort zone and strengthened my ability to handle speaking in front of others.

My old football coach used to say that practice should be so hard that the game should feel like a day off. They say that stand-up comedy is the hardest 15-foot walk—the distance from the edge of the stage to the microphone—in show biz. It's hard because you have to write, produce and perform your own material in front of a crowd of drunken strangers who want to see you fail.

Checkpoint #2: Perform Stand-Up Comedy.

Checklist for Checkpoint#2:

- ✓ Find an open mic.
- ✓ Write jokes.
- ✓ Get the guts to take it to the stage.

I will keep this brief as many of you no doubt wish to get to the skills portion of the book to make your DreamBIG a reality. I have wanted to be a stand-up comic since I was in college. As I started my speaking career, my urge to get on stage became unbearable. The screen saver on my computer was a picture from behind a microphone looking out over an audience in a packed room with two floors of balconies looking down on the stage. I visualized myself each day performing to this sold-out crowd who laughed at my shit and dick jokes.

The first time I stepped on stage at a real live comedy club was in 2014 at YukYuk's Vancouver Open Mic. YukYuk's is the top club in Canada, with locations across the nation. Open Mic is a night where amateurs and first-timers try out their jokes in front of other comics in the hope that they can work on their act, get over the butterflies, and maybe get noticed and put on a real show. Open mic crowds are the worst because you are performing in front of other comics who are either waiting to go up and thinking of their own act or hoping you bomb so their set will look like a success in comparison.

My first set was a success. I got laughs, shit my pants, and as I walked off stage, the host patted me on the back and said quietly, "That was great—don't stop coming. You are a natural. Just keep coming." Of course I was a natural. I had stage presence and timing from years of public speaking, but was I funny?

I continued to go to open mic nights whenever I got the chance. Each week, I would do my act and try to add a new joke or two in the mix. Some nights I would be up late in the order and try new material in front of the sparse, worn-out crowd. Either my expectations had changed or my jokes were getting worse, but I wasn't getting laughs. I would leave the club feeling like a complete failure. Why did I line up at 7 pm for a show that started at 10 pm, then wait until 12:30 am to hear my name called to do my act in front of the five comics left in the crowd? But I kept going.

I performed shows while travelling through the states on work trips. I would get stage time in clubs that I didn't deserve because I was from Vancouver. It looked good for the club to have international "talent" that they didn't have to pay flights and accommodation for. I almost got killed in Houston, bombed in Denver, and fell flat on my face in Chicago. Some of my colleagues got wind that I was doing comedy on our trips and started to show up unannounced at my gigs. The word was out. Jay's doing comedy.

Fast forward to the 2016 World Golf Fitness Summit. The organizers asked if I would open for the band at the social and do my act. The social was at the New Orleans

154

House of Blues. Over 400 of my peers and colleagues would be there. I agreed. They wanted me to do fifteen minutes, and looking back now, I probably had a solid seven minutes of material with a bunch of drawn-out, crude, poorly-written stories woven in without punchlines. This was a mistake. I wasn't even close to being ready but did it anyway.

I had a choice: Create industry jokes with insider jabs at my colleagues and profession or do my club act. My brother Sean gave me some great advice: If you do industry stuff and it doesn't work, you will regret it and wish they saw your real show. If you do your real show and it bombs, you can at least say you did your way. I did it my way, it bombed, and to this day some of the audience thought they were watching career suicide. Others thought it was the greatest thing they ever saw and couldn't believe I did it.

My fans became bigger fans, and the others, well, they never would have been a part of my community anyway. The coolest thing was performing at the iconic House of Blues venue where some of the greatest musicians and comedians have performed. The highlight was sitting in the green room with my best buddies Lance Gill and Mark Blackburn, surrounded by signatures on the walls from my favorite bands and entertainers. When I hit the stage and looked out at the crowd, it felt like home, with a sold-out show at the two floors of balconies looking down at the stage. Who knew that that picture that I had as my screensaver, was actually the House of Blues in New Orleans? Goosebumps.

Since my show in New Orleans, I have dedicated myself to my comedy. I work on my act like I work on my business, writing every day and performing each week in Pro Am booked shows and the occasional open mic. I record, edit, and rewrite my sets with my comedy mentor. I have performed all around the globe, including Beijing, London, Los Angeles, and New York. Even after all these years of refining and mastering my set, I still can't say I am ready to open for a band at the House of Blues. But am I ever glad I had the guts to try.

If you want to OverDeliver, you need a plan. Break down your plan into checkpoints and build a checklist of tasks you can start today. Each checkmark gets you one step closer to your DreamBIG.

TODAY'S TASK: Start.

CHAPTER SEVENTEEN:

SPEAKING SKILLS

I n this chapter, I share my secrets to becoming a world class public speaker. Whether your public speaking future involves a boardroom presentation each fiscal quarter or you plan on motivating the masses, you can benefit from these tips and tricks of the trade. Your ability to communicate your message effectively could be one of the most important skills you possess when trying to get others to buy into your DreamBIG. It isn't enough to just speak—you need to OverDeliver.

Get Over Yourself

Many people fear public speaking so much they say they would rather die than get in front of a crowd and speak. I get it—it is like the camera or the audience is seeing right through you, through all your bullshit and exposing the real you. At first, you may want to take on a persona that empowers you or makes you feel like a superhero. You can use it to get over the vulnerability of speaking but it will only work for a short while. Pretty soon you will notice what the audience knew all along: You aren't being authentic.

One of the most common techniques to calm the nerves is to visualize the audience naked. This never worked for me. A better approach for me has always been imagining that the audience *needs* this talk. You are helping them by providing education, entertainment, or my favorite, edumatainment. It took the eyes off me and put the focus on them.

Present from the inside looking out and not the outside looking in. Think, *How can I help these people?* I would make eye contact with them and speak to their souls. The feedback from audience members was that I came across as relatable, humble, and funny. They felt a sense of *connection*.

Make it about *them* and not *you*. You're not really that important, so get over yourself.

ABC123

I have always believed that the number one skill that all great speakers have is taking incredibly complex concepts and making them easily digestible. I call it *ABC123*. Make whatever you are speaking about so simple that you could teach it to a five-year-old.

While making my first DVD, my director/producer Joseph Hefera would direct me by saying, "Pretend you are speaking to Jock." My son Jamie (Jock is a Scottish name for Jamie) was five years old at the time. Looking into the back of the camera lens, I pictured my boy sitting and listening to his dad share his exercise philosophy. This technique helped me create a speaking style that mixes simple analogies with highly complex information that feels as comfortable as macaroni and cheese.

Once you have the audience in your grasp, you can drop a few ingredients that add a little depth and pizzazz, like sprinkling truffles on that mac and cheese. Your audience will eat it up.

Practice Makes Polished

Many people think that I have a natural gift of gab and the ability to speak concisely off the top of my head without a script. This is not a gift but instead comes from years of practice, most of it away from an audience.

I practice chunks of material hundreds of times before I bring the material to the stage. I will take a concept, build an analogy around the topic, and share it with as many people as I can in casual conversation. I pay close attention to their body language, what they focus on, questions they ask, and how they respond to the conversation. Every session in my gym, I would share the concept and tweak it different ways until I saw that their attention was captured.

I practiced my craft of communication six to eight hours a day, five days a week, client after client. As the years went on, I started to notice patterns and techniques that sped up the process, over time learning a rhythm and style of speaking that could turn a casual talk about core training into a TED Talk in under five minutes. My podcast became a practice ground for long-form concepts and add-

159

ed the pressure of getting it right the first time. I made a promise to myself and my listeners that I would never edit my show, which raised the stakes.

When you practice your pitch or the core concepts in your presentation, you will be able to create more impact when you share it with your audience. Think about the questions you are asked regularly at a dinner party or in an interview. Your answers should be on lock. Once you know your content, you can play around with your timing and delivery to make it sound less rehearsed.

I learned this lesson after my first WGFS presentation. This was a huge opportunity for me, and I wasn't going to screw it up. I practiced my speech in my head every night and practiced in front of anyone willing to be an audience for months leading up to the event. Every step, every word, every movement was choreographed in my mind. The event was a huge success that launched my speaking career, but looking back at it, I was like a robot on stage with no authentic personality and no humility. I practiced each sentence like I was memorizing a script, which was a mistake.

Now I practice my speeches in chunks with nothing but bullet points in my mind guiding me from thought to thought. This allows me to play between the bullet points and fill in the gaps with casual, conversational moments that make the audience feel like it's just the two of us talking over coffee.

Push and Believe

Every time I take the stage, I push my speaking skills to the limit. Before each show, I create a speaking goal and then try to execute it in the middle of my presentation without anyone knowing that it was pre-planned. I may try to walk through the audience and touch someone in the middle row on the shoulder while delivering a heartfelt statement, make eye contact with everyone in the back row, or physically act out a story. I challenge myself to see how long I can pause between statements to build tension in the room.

The little speaking games I play are experiments that expand my speaking toolbox. If I see that touching an attendee's shoulder gave the audience a sense of oneness or my long pause gave them time to absorb the point I was trying to make and provided more impact, I put it in the back of my mind and save it for future use.

If you experimented every time you got on stage over ten years of lecturing and doing stand-up, you might just improve your speaking skills too.

If It Works, Keep It

My colleagues who travel and present with me stand in the back of the room and roll their eyes when I tell the same joke over and over or act out the same story each and every show. "Here he goes again." If something works, it stays in the act. Over time the story gets refined and edited down to its true essence. Once it is mastered, it becomes a button that I can push at any time to deliver a perfectly-formed bit that is guaranteed to get my desired reaction. My fellow speakers may be bored of hearing it, but for the audience, it is their first time.

It's all about your audience. If you have something in your back pocket that is guaranteed to inspire, create conflict, or make them laugh, it is your duty to use it. If you see the crowd looking down at the floor or fidgeting with their phones, you need a bit that will punch them in the newts and get their attention back.

We have learned that changing speakers every 30 minutes to an hour maximum will keep the audience engaged. The change in tone, delivery, and cadence keeps the energy fresh for the crowd. If you are speaking solo for more than one hour, you will need to change your cadence and style of speech throughout your show.

I will often refresh the crowd by getting them to stand up and perform a physical challenge. I may get them to rub their tummy with one hand while patting their head with the other and then deliver a silly joke that makes the awkward coordination challenge feel lighthearted and fun. It will reset their attention and keep them attentive for the next 20 minutes or so. I am constantly scanning the faces in the crowd to see if I am going too fast, they need a break, or I have them in the palm of my hand.

If you find a fun way to break up your show and it works, keep it.

They Want You to Succeed

Many of you who struggle with public speaking, view the audience as this gathering of towns folk with pitch forks and torches ready to burn you at the stake. This puts enormous pressure on you to perform and deliver your best. The added stress usually brings out the nerves and causes you to stumble on stage. If you make the audience the focus when you are speaking, it takes away the fear of speaking.

It is all about the audience and their experience. No one wants to sit in an auditorium for eight hours listening to someone suck. They want you to succeed. When you picture the audience rooting for you, it makes you more comfortable. It also sharpens your mind and forces you to be present in the moment. Take in the energy of the crowd and turn it back on them. As someone who constantly wants to grow and develop as a speaker, once I felt comfortable in front of an audience, I started seeking more hostile environments.

At a conference, the audience wants you to succeed, but in stand-up they want to watch you burn. When you step on stage, the audience gives you the *Who is this guy? He better be good.* You have 15 seconds to make the unwilling crowd get on your side. The first joke is a make or break. Lose them at the start and you are done.

If you have an hour lecture, the attendees will be a little more patient. You can make up for a slow start by putting the pedal down later in the show.

You Better Ask Somebody

One of the best tips I received from one of my mentors, Greg Rose, was to never open your talk with a who you are. You don't need to validate why you are you are speaking to them. The fact that you are on the stage validates you have the credentials to present at the event. I've seen many make this mistake. They want to convince everyone in the room that they are worthy of this stage time. "My name is Steve. I have worked with Tom Dick and Harry. I won the first race I ever entered. I beat out 100 million swimmers to the ultimate prize. Nine months later, I was born. In first grade I...." Yawn.

Greg said, "Walk on stage like everyone in the room knows who you are. Those who don't know you will look you up after the show if you execute." You don't know me? You better ask somebody.

Nobody wants to hear you talk about your personal accomplishments. It's awkward. It's more natural to weave your accomplishment into your presentation by dropping some subtle flexes. "When I was working with the Masters champ, I realized that there was a special quality that all the greats possess." This sentence is a humble brag that you worked with some of the best players in the world, and you might just know a thing or two about the topic you are presenting on.

Never make it about what you did for them but what they taught you. "The first time I worked with an NFL quarterback, I learned that the body is such a small contributor to the success or failure of the athlete. He taught me that you can have a broken leg and lead a team to the win, but even Usain Bolt can't outrun a bad strategy." The audience hears that you worked with NFL quarterbacks, and you are humble enough to recognize that your contribution as a coach is a drop in the bucket compared to the intangibles that the athlete brings to the table.

You Are the Show, Not the Slide Show

Novice speakers spend more time building their slide shows than crafting their message. Don't get me wrong: I spend an inordinate amount of time on my slides, but they are just there to support my message, not *be* the message.

Nancy Duarte's book *Resonate* was a huge influence on me when it comes to crafting a slide show. She teaches you the art of storytelling and how to weave your presentation from creating a problem to solving it in the clearest and most compelling way. Build slides that set a tone or emotion that supports what you are saying with your spoken word. Wherever possible, have no text on your slides. Otherwise, the audience will read your slides instead of listening to you. Try reading a book while watching the news. One will be your focus, while the other becomes a distraction.

In my Mentorship, I spend a whole section on the art of building slides. The process of slide building mirrors the process of building your marketing plan. Create a problem in the mind of the audience and then be the solution.

This Is It

This could be the most important presentation of your life. This is it. You need to craft your speaking skills and your style of presentation like it is life or death. You need to get your message out to the world. It is your top priority.

Then you need to make your message *their* top priority. Have you ever watched a documentary about something that had never crossed your mind, and suddenly you would give up your firstborn for the cause? "Cocaine addicted turtles are washing up on the beach with straws in their nasal cavities. Well, that's it. We must come out of our shells and stand up for these helpless, little nose ninjas."

It is easy to get wrapped up in a compelling story, but now it is time for *you* to be the story. You need to master the art of storytelling and get your story to your audience in a memorable way. The best way to do this is to become a better speaker. You don't have to start dragging your ass out to open mic night or join your local Toastmasters to work on your craft. You just have to have the intent to improve your ability to craft messages and have purpose behind your communication when speaking to others.

Hold staff education meetings or client appreciation info nights for stage time. This way you will be practicing in front of an audience who is familiar and speaking about things that you are passionate about. Every opportunity to speak is an opportunity to get better. At least that's what I tell myself some nights at 2 am in the comedy club after performing to three drunk, open-mic audience members who forgot their names. Every opportunity must be treated like *This is it*.

Be the Greatest Salesperson

Whether you are a coach, actor, teacher, preacher, lawyer, or parent, you are a salesperson. You are selling your ideals and trying to convince others that what you are proposing is something they need to get behind. A mom trying to get her son to brush his teeth or a lawyer trying to get their client to take the plea bargain — it is all the same game. As soon as I say, "salesperson," you may conjure up visions of the cheesy, cologne-drenched car dealer or the pushy commission salesclerk at the cell phone store. "Good morning. What can we get you to purchase today that you had no intention of buying when you walked in the door?"

But this is not what I am talking about. I want you to picture a woman who just found the cure for cancer, but unfortunately it requires putting dill pickles in your nostrils while you do the Hokey Pokey. She emphatically tries to convince the world that this is the cure. What if it really was the cure for cancer, but she sucked at communicating her ideas and getting people to buy into her treatment?

Coffee Is for Closers

One of my favourite movies is *Glengarry Glen Ross*. A group of salesmen in a New York City office find out that the two lowest salesmen will be fired. As one of the salesmen goes to grab a coffee, he is blasted by Blake, played by Alec Baldwin: "Put that coffee down. Coffee is for closers only."

The need to close the deal was all that mattered. Getting leads is an important part of sales, but all the leads in the world mean nothing if you can't close. Instead, ABC (**A**lways **B**e **C**losing). In an attempt to excuse his inferior ability to sell, the lowest salesman on the list states, "The leads are weak." Blake responds with, "The leads are weak? Fucking leads are weak? *You're* weak."

You may not be trying to sell New York real estate, but you are trying to sell your message, whether it is training techniques, better nutrition, the importance of sleep, why you should get the promotion, or who should be in the starting line-up. You are selling your ideals, concepts, or beliefs constantly. You need to become a better salesperson, and the best way to do this is to sell something you truly believe in.

Animals have a built-in bullshit detector. If you hate cats due to an allergy, they will sneak up and brush against your leg until you start sneezing. If you are afraid of dogs, they sense it and will avoid you. The only way you are going to get a dog to be comfortable around you is if you convince yourself that you are not afraid of dogs—in fact, you love dogs.

You give them one glimpse of the truth inside, and they will see right through you. Luckily for salespeople like us, humans don't have the same sophisticated bullshit detector. I will wait for you to finish telling yourself that you are different and that I am referring to others in this example, not you.

Done yet? Okay, let's move on to the skills portion of this chapter.

Believe in What You Are Selling

To avoid becoming a sleazy salesperson, you need to truly believe in what you are selling. Your sales technique must match your intentions. As discussed in the previous chapter, you must set your intention for why you are selling what you are selling. Your intention should follow your passion. People follow passion. If you are passionate about what you are selling, the buyer will want to get behind your mission and OverDeliver for you. If you are successful in conveying your purpose with passion, not only will they take your mission on themselves, but they also will be motivated to help you spread the word to others.

Malcolm Gladwell termed these people "connectors" in his book, *The Tipping Point*. When an essential oils salesperson convinces you that lavender on your temples will help you sleep, you want to be the first person to save the lives of your family members who are slowly dying from a lavender deficiency. Once they fall off to their blissful sleep, the connector starts to think of whom they can share this wonder drug with next.

Arm Yourself with the Facts

The more you know about the concepts you are selling, the better you will be at convincing others that you know what you are talking about. I know some professional golfers who could easily transition into becoming prosecution lawyers if their clubhead speed dropped below 112 mph. They question everything I prescribe, and for good reason. One percent change in their performance can be the difference between winning the tournament or losing their PGA Tour card. If you are going to introduce a new technique or alter a training protocol, you better come armed with all the facts and present it like you are O.J. Simpson representing yourself in a murder trial.

PGA Tour winner, Adam Hadwin, has helped me formulate and clarify my training philosophy over the years. He has a very analytical mind that questions everything, but not in a bad way. He wants to know the *Why?* so that he can get 100% behind what he is committing his mind and body to.

He is not an athlete you want to just try something out on. Whenever I gave him an exercise that didn't fit with what he was trying to accomplish in his swing, he would confront me with it. If I didn't know why it was in the program, I would always reply, "To be honest, I just put it in there to see how it fits. I see how it is negatively affecting performance by tiring you out for the elements that do help. I'll take it out." I would then go back to my laptop, bandage up my fresh wounds and wipe the tear from my eye while I rebuilt his program. His focus has helped me become a better trainer.

Be Open to the Idea That You May Be Wrong

If you want to be trusted, you need to be open to being wrong. If I tell someone that the Ferrari I am selling is the fastest road car in the world, but they show me stats on a Bugatti, I have to be open to the idea that I am wrong while still closing the deal. "Wow, that Bugatti sure looks fast, not that you would ever be able to get it up to top speed. Plus, it costs three times as much. Dollar for dollar, you are getting a better value with the Ferrari." Has anyone ever bought a Ferrari because it's a better value? That customer just did.

When I am wrong, I not only admit I was wrong but also find a solution. Many times when I was on stage lecturing, someone would ask a question that was more of a statement telling me that I was wrong. If I didn't know the answer, I would say, "I'm not sure, but I will look that up." The first chance I got, I looked up the information and determined whether I was wrong or not and whether I should change the way I think.

"I'm not sure, but I will look it up" shows you are open to being wrong and are willing to learn. A lot of people are afraid to admit they are wrong, especially in public, as they feel it is a sign of weakness. I completely disagree. It takes strength to admit you are wrong and intelligence to then find out why.

The Undersell

Nobody trusts the pushy salesperson. If it sounds too good to be true, it probably is. I prefer to undersell myself and my message. Underselling a habit, for example, that you incorporated into your life will make the audience feel like they might want to get on board as well.

Here is an example of me trying to convince my athlete to take cold showers in the morning: "Well, I like to take a cold shower because it cuts a toughness groove in my soul. It's not for everyone. I don't recommend it, but it sure makes a difference in my life." When you tell someone it's not for everyone, they instantly think, *If it's not for everyone, then who is it for? Am I one of the people who it's for? I want to be the type of person who that is for. I'll show him.*

I may undersell a package I am selling. "Some people buy the yearly package, but it's really only for those who are 100% committed to their practice. I think you should start with a month and see if this type of training is the right fit for you first." The key is to be honest. Do you really want to sell a yearly package to someone who isn't committed? Do you want to see them no-show you every third session, and when they do come, they are taking up a spot of someone who actually wants to be there?

I want my athletes to under-commit and OverDeliver. This goes back to intent. Do you really want to help them or do you want to just make money? If it is money, you want to take the approach of the big-block membership gym. Sell 500 memberships and hope no one shows up while you collect their monthly payment of $9.99. I would rather have people come to my gym five days a week on a reasonably-priced, unlimited monthly package and get results. When they get results, they will spread the word. They become your sales force.

Be Humble

You don't have all the answers, and you are not the only solution. You are, however, the best solution for the person standing in front of you at this time. Know that what you are selling is not the cure for lupus, and, no, lavender is not the magical sleep solution the world has been waiting for. It is just something that you believe in and want to share with your customer.

If you are selling from the right place and your product matches the customer's needs, the sale will come naturally. A humble and honest approach is better received than the oversell "This product will increase your driving distance and improve your sex drive."

Offer Less and Deliver More

By now you know I love to OverDeliver. At the end of the day, I am offering my customers an experience, and I want them to leave feeling that I Overdelivered for them. One of the best ways to do so is to save a little extra and put it off to the side to be given at an unexpected time.

Never give the customer the whole package in writing. If you put in your marketing that everyone who signs up for the monthly package gets an exclusive Coach Glass t-shirt, you will have people walking in the door asking, "Where's my shirt? I was promised a shirt. Where is it? It says right here I get a shirt. I came all the way down here not wearing a shirt because you said you were providing the shirt. Now my nipples are cold, and people are starring at me."

Make the giveaway a bonus that they were never expecting—that is what makes it special. When people are expecting something, it becomes something they feel they are entitled to and therefore it loses its value.

Every year I do a speaking event in Newark, New Jersey, AKA the armpit of New York and home of the Sopranos. One evening, after speaking all day, I went out for dinner with my co-speakers and Lance Gill and Mark Blackburn. We found a little mom and pop Italian place in a rough part of town. Long story short, we had a wonderful meal that was hand-picked by the multi-talented son of the owners who acted as the maître d', waiter, bus boy, and bartender. As the meal concluded, he brought out a cheesecake that his mother had made that day and offered it to us on the house. Without asking, he then brought us some limoncello liqueur, also on the house. The limoncello was served in unique, handcrafted shot glasses. I told him how cool I thought the glasses were and, on my way out the door, he handed me a kitchen rag with two glasses folded inside.

You may think, *This is too good to be true,* and *What's this place called?* The bill that night was higher than a normal meal of this standard, but they made up for it with the little bonuses. Or were the bonuses already "included" in the cost of the meal? The next year, we went back to the same place and this time brought all the vendors and our colleagues to make up a table of 12. When I walked in the door, our server from last year remembered me and said, "It's a good to see you again, my friend." Once again, we had a hand-picked, family-style meal, nice wine, limoncello and dessert on the house. He now had nine new customers who will rave and recommend his restaurant from that day forward. I thanked him for the shot glasses he gave me a year before and shared how special it was for him to OverDeliver for us once again. All he could say was, "Fahgettaboudit." We now look forward to going to Newark each year—which is a statement that has never been made before by anyone—all from a little Italian shot of OverDeliver.

Do you think we would have had the same experience if there was an item on the menu that read like this: "Family Style Dinner. Includes chef's choice entree, appetizer, cheesecake, liqueur, and a souvenir shot glass." I would look at that and think, *There has to be some kind of scam here. The entree will be whatever they have too much of, the cheesecake will be store-bought, and the shot glass is probably plastic. I think I will fahgettaboudit.*

Regardless of the technique you choose to use, you need to ensure that the motivation or intent behind the technique is authentic. You need to use these powers for good, not evil. In my eyes, it is evil to sell people things that you know they don't need for the sake of you making a buck.

The key is to help people accomplish their goals and dreams, be it losing weight, improving performance, improving their overall health, or improving some other aspects of their lives. You are providing them with a service that they cannot perform themselves.

CHAPTER EIGHTEEN:

POLISH THE TURD

Overdelivering requires preparation. Eliminate the unforeseen obstacles that are destined to appear by preparing for their arrival in advance. But what do you do when the unforeseen blindsides you while you are attempting to OverDeliver?

There will be times on your journey to your personal greatness where you will have to polish a turd. Not everything is in your control. Sometimes you will be put in a position where all your preparation and planning get thrown out the window. It may not be your fault; it could be due to others dropping the ball.

Imagine preparing for months to do your big event. You rehearsed it in your head and used your imagery sessions to create the ultimate demonstration of your skills. You arrive and the host who hired you dropped the ball. Not just dropped it—your host deflated it. Audio was cutting out, lighting was off, they didn't have a projector, the equipment was broken, the participants weren't told to bring a change of clothes, they neglected to bring water, there wasn't enough space, or a combination of all the above. That is exactly what happened to me.

My desire to OverDeliver pressures me to over-prepare for events. I try to think of every possible element that

177

could go wrong and then come up with an alternate plan of action in the unfortunate event that everything goes sideways. I play a game called Worse Case Scenario, which we will cover later. One of my mentors and speaking coach, Thomas Plummer, said you should always duplicate your equipment. Bring two projectors, two clickers, and a backup hard drive with your presentation on it in the event your computer blows. Carry a backup outfit in case you spill coffee on the one you are wearing and an extra pair of underwear for when the shit really hits the fan or the cotton, in this case. *A little overkill*, I thought, as I went on the road with only one of everything.

The Plummer system was put in my toolbox the day after I experienced one of the worst speaking gigs of my career. I had just started speaking for TPI and was teaching seminars across Canada with my righthand man at the time, Gord Workum. We traveled to a chiropractic college that was hosting our TPI Level 1 course for one hundred fitness, medical and golf professionals. We arrived at 7 am Saturday morning, which was two hours before the event—plenty of time to get set up and acclimatize to the environment before we welcomed our guests. The frigid Toronto winter wind was howling on our backs as we shook the locked entrance doors to the college. I slammed the side of my fist against the sign that read, "Closed Saturdays, Sundays and Holidays," hoping that our host was inside and would hear our now obnoxious door banging, but no luck. Maybe a janitor? Nope.

All we could do was wait in the cold while our attendees started to show up asking the same question and getting the same answer. "Is the door locked? Is anyone inside?" Fifteen minutes before showtime, the intern showed up. We had 80-plus people standing in the cold, and this second-year student, who was put in charge of a $100,000 event, walked up and said, "Is the door locked?"

We finally went inside, where we were led to a gymnasium that had hockey nets and sticks lying on the floor, which was covered in three inches of dust. No seats, no projector, no nothing. But the show must go on, so it's time to *polish a turd*.

I gave that audience every ounce of me that day. Energy poured out of every orifice as I put on a show that would have had Sammy Davis Jr. wishing he had two eyes so he could take notes better. My preparation as a speaker taught me that the best thing you can do when stuff fails is to continue like it was meant to be. I couldn't stop the nagging feeling in my gut that was telling me to stop the show, apologize and to give everyone their money back. How would this reflect on my personal brand? I decided to motor on and told myself that, if at the end of the day the product was not up to standard, I would look at getting them some form of compensation.

We rocked the house party at the drop of a hat and delivered the goods as promised. The audience appreciated the efforts we put forth on Day 1, and the show was saved. I demanded that for Day 2 the organizers had to put us in an appropriate space and meet our minimum requirements. I learned to never leave your name, brand, and reputation to chance. I now demand an itemized list of requirements before booking gigs and check out the facilities the night before the show in the event of any last-minute changes need to be made.

Every time you fail at Overdelivering, you need to learn from it and adjust your systems. You add new lines to your preparation checklist. What do you think the OverDeliver Prep Checklist looks like at Disneyland, a Tony Robbins event, an episode of Oprah or a Bill Belichick pregame plan? They all take the time to put in systems to consistently put out a perfect product. Why should you be any different?

CHAPTER NINETEEN:

THE SET-UP PUNCH METHOD

Taking the *polish a turd* mindset to everything you do can be incredibly beneficial. After I finish a newsletter, podcast, training video or chapter for this book, I look for ways to polish it up and make it better. With your audience's ever decreasing attention span, you can't afford to waste time. I learned the art of condensing my message from one of my comedy mentors, Sam Tonning. Sam takes my comedy sets or written premises that I come up with and trims the fat.

He is constantly challenging me to find the funny and deliver it in a simple *set-up punch* format. He would ask me, "What is the premise?" The premise is a one-sentence description of the entire joke or story. "Okay, now give me the set-up." The set-up is the part of the joke that takes the audience on a ride in one direction and sets up the punchline. "Now give me the punch." The punchline is the joke, misdirection or play on words that delivers the laughter. "Write five tags to go with it, and then get it to the stage." Tags are little side jabs that keep the laughter going and provide more depth to the punchline.

Here is an idea I tried a few times on stage before I trimmed the fat and applied the set-up punch method.

Before I met my wife, I used to date a blind girl. Her name was Iris, which was kind of ironic. She was a schoolteacher at a school in my neighbourhood. Her students called her Mrs. Iris.

When I was a young boy, my grandma used to always say, "You can't miss something you never had." And Grandma was always right.

Well, I sure miss Iris. Out of nowhere after three months, she said we shouldn't see each other anymore.

She said she wanted a man with a clear vision of what he wants in the relationship. She said we should start seeing other people. I said I've been seeing other people the whole time. It is you that had the problem with that.

Here is an example of me taking this simple premise and turning it into a set-up punch with tags:

I used to date a blind girl. (Premise)

She was a schoolteacher; her students called her Mrs. Iris. (Set-Up)

My Grandma use to say, "You can't miss something you never had." (Punch)

After three months, she broke up with me. (Set-Up)

182

She said we shouldn't see each other anymore. (Punch)

She said we should start seeing other people. (Set-Up)

I said I've been seeing other people the whole time…. (Tag)

But if she would start to see people that would really be something. (Punch)

I don't think she will ever truly find the love she is looking for. (Set-Up)

Unless it can be located by a red and white stick with a ball on it. (Punch)

"Oh, a puppy." (Tag)

One night I shared that joke with a visually impaired man in the audience.

Luckily, he didn't get upset with me. (Set-Up)

He did, however, yell profanities at the at the speaker he was facing on the back wall. (Punch)

As you can see, it packs a bigger punch when you cut out the fluff. This approach took a long-drawn-out bit that would get some groans in its original form and transformed it into a bit that kills.

I take this approach in all my writing. Whether it is a presentation description or promo for a new online product I am selling, I am always trying to maximize the impact of my message. I try to pack as much punch in every sentence and cut away anything that doesn't deliver a direct blow. Here is an example of a lecture description I wrote for my 2020 Perform Better Summit presentation.

Combining rotational plyometric training with High Triplexity neuromuscular training will help you produce the most explosive rotational athletes on the planet. In this session, you will learn Coach Glass's training philosophy, techniques, and exercises that you can use to turn any athlete into a rotational Tasmanian Devil doused in rocket fuel. You will learn how to effectively load and explode rotational slings and ignite the nervous system. Leave this session with specific cues to help train rotational sequencing, understand how to utilize ground reaction force, and create unmatched athleticism. You will learn a ton and have way too much fun. Load and go....

You need to stand out. Every word and every sentence must be carefully structured to make an impact. Now that I have the audience's attention, it is time to OverDeliver on the presentation. I lay out the presentation slides using a Set-Up Punch format as well.

Here is how it would look like as a process:

1. Set the stage in the opening slides by creating a problem in the mind of the audience. (Set-Up)

2. Spend the rest of the presentation solving the problem we created. Once I have the presentation mapped out, I fill it in with high quality content in the form of dynamic videos or impactful images. (Punch)

3. I rehearse in my head each night before I go to sleep the order and flow of the presentation. I add little jabs of gold to the presentation in the form of misdirection, insight, or jokes. (Tag)

   When I wake up in the morning, I hope I can remember the great ideas I came up with last night as I drifted off to sleep.

You can apply the Set-Up Punch process to anything and everything you do. Next time you are at a family dinner or out with friends for drinks, try cutting the fluff out of your stories and see the impact they deliver. It helps if you also cut out the double martinis before dinner.

TODAY'S TASK: I want you to apply the Set-Up Punch process to your bio (the one you use when people ask for a headshot and bio). I want you to trim the fat and add some tags and extra punch to your descriptors. Turn your bio into someone *you* would be excited to meet. Do people really care that you played varsity volleyball and have been a personal trainer for ten years?

Punch it up. You are now a field-tested fitness assassin who leaps over his competitors to spike inspiration into his clients. BOOM.

CHAPTER TWENTY:

STAY FRESH

You need to continually reinvent yourself. Your products, website, presentations, and content need constant tweaking to keep them fresh. Each major presentation I do evolves over a two to three year period. After the two years is up, I throw it out and reinvent myself. I learnt this from listening to interviews with David Bowie and Madonna. They stayed relevant by reinventing themselves every five years. They were always pop stars, but they would change their hair, clothes, and style of music each album.

I will always be a strength coach who specializes in rotational power, but I will change my topic, slide design and style of delivery every two years. Not only does doing so keep it fresh for the audience, but changing keeps it fresh for me too.

The two-year process starts with the creation of the new topic. I usually will present it first on my podcast and use the platform to spit-ball new ways of describing my thoughts through story and analogies. I then write out the key points in a blog-style post. I may never release it publicly, but writing it out formally helps refine the message. Once I have developed the slideshow, I will present it to a small group of professionals either on its own or worked into my LoadXplode Live workshops. I then go back to the office and cut, trim, and throw out the stuff that didn't grab the audience and expand on the elements that got them on the edge of their seat.

This editing process may involve anywhere from one to three workshops before I start to really polish up a finished product. The next step is presenting it in lecture form and hands on at a Perform Better Summit. This is the Lollapalooza of fitness summits with the greatest names in the game invited to present. I usually retire the show after a World Golf Fitness Summit or if I presented it at a keynote event. The finished product is filmed professionally and turned into a promo piece or pay-per-view on my website. Then it starts all over again.

If you could reinvent yourself and your brand, what would it look like? I know you just started your DreamBIG, but now is a great time to stylize it so you can OverDeliver on it. Take some influence from other professions or other things in your life that inspire or entertain you.

I buy skateboard magazines when looking for brand inspiration. I watch comedy specials for presentation-style inspiration. I also listen to old-school and underground hip hop to get a feel for delivery of messaging. You can draw from anything that excites you. Find a website that you love to visit and copy its template for your new business. Take the logo from your favourite t-shirt and adapt it into your logo design. Copy the photo style of your favorite Instagram account. You don't have to create everything from scratch. Instead of stealing your ideas from your competitors, find your inspiration from other genres.

TODAYS TASK: Make a list of your favourite bands, sports stars, music, movies or pop culture references that get you excited. Go online and either using screen grabs or Google images, take pictures of what gets you wet and wild. Put them in a folder on your desktop, or if you are really crafty, you can create a vision board (how 90s of you!). When you are designing something for your brand or creating marketing pieces, go to your inspiration folder and get some juice.

What is the next frontier for the Coach? Depending on when you read this book, you may already know the answer. My last four years was a rabbit hole of neuromuscular training ("neuromuscular" refers to the interaction between the nervous system and the muscular system). I put my stake in the ground on Neuromuscular Training for Rotational Athletes. For coaches I developed a neuromuscular training certification called LoadXplode. For the athlete I created a 16-week training program version of LoadXplode, an 8-week consumer spinoff called High TripleXity, four Perform Better presentations, a keynote for the WGFS, and countless blog posts and podcast episodes on the subject. I squeezed every last drop of goodness out of this topic.

I am now going further up the chain and researching and studying the brain. Neurology is the study of how the brain interacts with the body via the nervous system. This has forced me to become a student once again and go back to school for the first time in 20 years. It is exciting to be back in the position of the pupil and not the teacher. I truly believe this is the new frontier of performance coaching, and I want to be on the tip of that spear.

This is more than a change in hairstyles and wardrobe—sorry, Bowie, but Ziggy Stardust can sit back down. This is a journey that could take the next ten years. Why would I go down this rabbit hole at 47? If you have been following along in this book, I can't do anything but this. I am following my gut.

Think about your brand. Is there part of it that is getting a little stale? Is it time to reinvent yourself? Does your website need a rebuild or new images? Does your social media need some new angles or a change in perspective? If your community has made Janet Jackson's "What have you done for me lately?" their new anthem, it may be time.

CHAPTER TWENTY-ONE:

PROBLEMS AND SOLUTIONS

Three of my biggest DreamBIG opportunities came from my creating a problem for which I was the solution. I am sharing these stories in the hope that you can copy and apply this technique to your DreamBIG.

Remember when you were in college or high school and the teacher gave you an assignment? "This book report is worth 40% of your final grade." How much did you get paid for that book report? *Nothing.* Did the grade you received for putting the clear report folder on it with the plastic spine change your life? *Not a bit.* But you gave it everything you had for that short spell of time that it took to complete it. Once you were finished and handed it in, you forgot about it. Were you forever scarred from the hours of sweat you put into writing your masterpiece? *Nope*—it was like it never happened. But it did: You created something from scratch that previously didn't exist.

I want you to marinate on this for a minute. I came to the realization that my entire collegiate career was contained in a piece of paper on my wall. I thought, *What if instead of doing all that work for a grade or a degree, I used it to get my dream job?*

By now you have invested an enormous amount of time and emotional energy into creating a DreamBIG that will

191

change your life once you OverDeliver on it. What if your DreamBIG was a homework assignment? You would have a deadline dictated by someone else, and you would cram all night to get it done in time to avoid losing two percent each day that it's late. The analogy initially may seem a bit silly, but when I had this revelation, I decided to apply this assignment-based mindset to my first DreamBIG.

U of DreamBIG

I was a personal trainer with a young family and a dream to work with the best athletes on earth. I was tired of working with middle-aged clients who had lofty goals and no work ethic to back it up. As I dreamt of working in the pros, I quickly put the reality brakes on: *Whoa there, little buddy. If you want to work with the best in the world, you probably need to start with some amateurs and work your way up.*

At the time, I was having success with tennis and golfers and thought the next natural progression would be to take my skills to the collegiate level. My alma matter, The University of British Columbia, at the time was the USC of Canadian collegiate sports. If I could get a job there as the head strength coach, I could work with some real athletes.

How do you get your foot in the door at a university? I thought. They probably already had a superstar stud of a trainer with loads of experience. I wasn't sure what they had in place for fitness, but I did know one thing for sure: They didn't have me.

What would I do if I got this job? What would I do differently? Maybe I could write out the program guidelines and periodization plan and see what it would look like. I had free time in the evening, and watching *The Golden Girls* wasn't going help me move forward professionally. I remembered writing programs for my human kinetics projects for various sports and athletes and came up with the idea to write one for golf. I needed to treat this as though I was writing a final paper that my professor had assigned, but for a job rather than a grade.

I worked every night for a month writing my paper on how I would design a College Golf Strength and Conditioning Program. When I finished, I placed it into a clear report binder (for bonus marks) and sent an email to the UBC golf program's head coach Chris MacDonald asking for a meeting. Chris accepted my meeting, and I shared my report with him. He said they had worked with a trainer in the past but never really got buy-in from the players. I asked him to read through my paper and let me know if he was interested in having me help his team.

He called me back an hour later: "This is very impressive and looks very golf specific. I'll give you six months. If the players like it, you got the job. If they don't, we will chalk it up as an experiment that went wrong and part ways. Cool?"

I worked with the golf program for six seasons. We won multiple National Championships, North America Championships, and countless tournaments during my time with the team. As much as we enjoyed the trophies and accolades that went with them, the thing I was most proud of was the culture that we created at UBC. We became a program that attracted athletes during a time when golf was considered a mere pastime. One of our proudest moments as a program was when Cory Renfrew was named Varsity Athlete of the Year. A golfer? Athlete of the year? This is a school that had Olympic athletes and players being drafted to the pros. I ended up coaching Cory through his amateur and professional career, which highlighted him qualifying and playing in the PGA Tour's Waste Management Phoenix Open.

I created a job that no one thought was needed. My paper put a problem into the mind of the head coach: What if adding fitness actually helped take the team to the next level? Other teams were doing so, and maybe we needed to as well if we wanted to compete. But who should be hired to provide the fitness element?

I was the solution.

The Create a Problem Institute

In 2008, I was watching a program on the Golf Channel, the *Golf Fitness Academy*. It was a half-hour show where a chiropractor, Dr. Greg Rose, and a golf pro, Dave Phillips, shared golf specific exercises and how they affected the golf swing. It was the first time I had seen my profession represented on TV. I was hooked. I taped and watched and re-watched every episode like I was breaking down game tape for the big game.

I critiqued the form and cuing they used and found it strange to hear a chiropractor teaching the elements of fitness, who saw fitness through a medical lens. I thought, *Why would you do that? Just use a contralateral single leg deadlift.* I imagined myself hosting the show, sharing my techniques and my exercises. I couldn't stop fantasizing how cool it would be to have a performance show about training athletes on primetime TV and focused on what I would do differently.

After training the golf team one morning, Coach Mac-Donald called me into his office. "Hey, Jay, have you seen the Golf Fitness Academy?"

I'd been studying and utilizing their techniques with our players for the past six months. I coolly said, "I think I've seen an episode or two. It's that Golf Channel show with that doctor guy and golf professional, right?"

"Yeah, it reminds me of the stuff you do with our players. They are coming to Vancouver in a few months to teach their Titleist Performance Institute certification. You should go."

Fast forward to the night before the seminar. My wife Julie asked, "Are you looking forward to the seminar tomorrow?" I then said one of the stupidest things I've ever said to my wife: "Yeah, but I'm not sure if I'm going to get anything out of it." Hello, ego.

The seminar was hosted by Dr. Rose, Dave Phillips and assisted by a young Lance Gill. I saw them on stage and instantly thought, *I want to do that*. But not screen people and train them—I was already a successful strength coach in college golf. I wanted to be the one on stage.

I wanted to teach TPI seminars, and I wanted it bad. I went to bed each night fantasizing about standing on stage and teaching my training techniques to the attendees. I decided to apply the same technique I used to get the job in college golf and see if it would work for getting a speaking gig. But there is no way Dr. Rose and Dave Phillips would allow someone else to teach their classes no matter how good they were at training golfers. I knew my training knowledge wouldn't get me in the door as they had an advisory board with superstars such as Al Vermeil, Mike Boyle, Gray Cook, Dr. Voight, and Tom House. I decided to approach this one differently.

I wrote a business plan for how I would run TPI Canada. I broke down the number of golf pros, fitness professionals, and medical pros across Canada and in each major city. I put a plan together for how I would teach five seminars a year and went as far as breaking out the revenue, projected profit and loss sheet, and a marketing plan. I thought the process would be a valuable lesson on how to write a business plan, and if they didn't want to use it, I would.

Each evening during the time that I would normally be watching Seinfeld, I again focused on a project that I wasn't getting paid for or graded on. Researching and writing out my business plan was a pro bono job, and the client on trial was me.

I mailed the report to Dr. Rose. Lance Gill shared with me the story of the day that Greg received my TPI Canada business plan. Greg walked into Lance's office and threw the 20-page document on his desk and said, "Read this and let me know what you think." Lance read my report and went into Greg's office. "If this guy can do what he says he can do, you would be crazy not to hire him." I created a problem in Greg's mind that he didn't know he had. What if someone *else* was able to teach his courses in a different country and could make TPI money while he focused on growing the business. But who could teach the classes?

Greg asked me to come down to TPI, and we started the process of becoming a lead speaker for TPI. That's an entirely different story. I had no idea that the next day was going to be the start of a journey that would span a decade of teaching TPI seminars, travelling the globe, and being featured on two episodes of the Golf Fitness Academy. Just as I dreamed it.

Be the Solution

The secret to creating opportunities is building a problem in someone's mind that changes the way they think from that day forward. The next step is to make yourself the solution. What do you want? Who holds the key to the door that would allow access to what you want? What are some challenges that they may encounter in trying to acquire what they want? What could help them achieve their goal that they are unable to perform on their own? How can you fill that need?

In the UBC opportunity, Chris wanted to win. For TPI, their driver was growth and revenue. How could I help these people achieve their goals using my skillset? I am an innovative strength coach with the gift of gab and an entrepreneurial mindset. The more niche you make your skillset, the easier it is to fill a void that only you could be the solution for. This is where your Golden Nugget comes into play.

What is that special thing that separates you from the rest of the pack? Go back to the Golden Nugget chapter if you need a refresher or ask your closest colleagues and confidants what they see as your superpower. Now you need to Polish the Turd, Set-Up Punch, and deliver it to your unsuspecting gatekeeper in the form of a problem that your superpower will solve.

Picture a comic book hero who is obsessed with basketball after his father died in a dunk-off against a radioactive supervillain. He wants to avenge his father's death but can't compete in the game he loves due to the fact he was born with a bad case of gout. His superpower is statistical analysis. Can you come up with a scenario where he could apply his superpower to the game he loves? Who would hold the key to his future of using his statistical analysis to revelutionize the NBA? Could he frame his ability to analyze data and make the Seattle Supersonics GM hire him? Could he put together a report on how statistically the team is underachieving in shooting percentages from outside the arc? Could he share that better shot choices could mean the difference between missing the playoff and winning the Championship?

It is easy to see the connection when you put it in the land of fairy tales. The thought of my being on the Golf Channel or teaching seminars in China with a translator is the stuff fairy tales are made of. You got to DreamBIG and be the solution. Picture the craziest thing that you would want to achieve. How can you create a problem that you would be the solution for to get you in the door?

Once you're in the door, OverDeliver.

CHAPTER TWENTY-TWO:

TIME TO OVERDELIVER

My wife and I were in Vegas at a NSCA conference and walking through the Forum Shops in Caesars Palace. I pulled her into the Rolex shop and went straight to the Submariner—I always had wanted one. It's a classic, sporty, yet elegant stainless-steel watch with a black face and bezel. I had owned numerous knockoff versions of this classic throughout my life that would tarnish or just straight up stop working.

I asked the salesman if I could try it on. He didn't even need to adjust it. It fit perfectly, and a chill went up my spine. I looked at Julie: "I will have one of these one day." She said, "It looks good on you—you should get it. How much is it?" As she glanced down and saw the price tag, she quickly changed her tune from *you should* to *yeah, right.* We had just gotten married, put a down payment on our first home, and were paying off my student loans, so this wasn't the time to buy an expensive timepiece, but I never waivered: "When I accomplish my dream, you won't even flinch at the price."

It started that day. I said if I could earn $100,000 a year for three years in a row, I would buy the watch. I must have been earning around $40,000 at the time, so the idea of doubling or tripling my income seemed like a goal that would deserve a reward at the end worth $10,000. If I set aside three percent of my earnings each of those three years, I could justify the purchase.

Two years later, I was earning over $100,000 annually, and kept increasing from there, so it was time to pay the man. The problem was that I was enjoying reaching my goal each year so much that I didn't want it to stop. My wife reminded me that I had a made deal with myself and that I should see it through. I told her I wanted to recalibrate the deal and OverDeliver on it by making $200,000 per year.

The previous goal was too easy—I needed to dream bigger. That year I surpassed my new goal and set another even bigger one for the coming year, and I nailed that one too. Finally, my wife said, "Enough is enough. Buy the watch. I know you are enjoying the challenge, but the person you were when you set the goal so many years ago deserves the reward." I want to highlight that statement: *The person you were when you set the goal so many years ago deserves the reward.* By raising the bar higher and higher, I was disrespecting the man who made the dream.

I bought the Rolex Submariner No Date with black face and black, ceramic bezel, which was the exact one I always had wanted. Everyone says the one with the date bubble is worth more at resale, but I'm never selling my watch. It is my dream, and I wear it every day. Every time I clasp the safety clip on my wrist, I feel a sense of pride. I'm not a materialistic person and certainly not flashy. This has nothing to do with anyone else but me.

Lesson to Be Learned.

The motivator for your goal accomplishment can never come from materialistic things. That might seem crazy to me say after the story I just shared, but if you look deeper, you will see that the motivator wasn't a Rolex. The watch was a symbol of the bigger goal, which was for me to provide for my family and build a business that could afford me a future to explore my creativity. If it was all about the watch, I would have bought it the day I broke the three-year $100,000 mark.

I shared my Rolex story with a colleague who was admiring my watch. He was quite inspired by the romantic notion that a beautiful timepiece could represent my success as an entrepreneur. Three months later, he showed me his matching Rolex. He looked at me like we were somehow connected because my story inspired him to reward himself since he had made over $100,000 for the year.

But he had missed the point of the story. It's not a Boy Scout badge you get for helping an elderly woman cross the road when you were 12. The *journey* is the reward, not the watch. The watch means nothing without the struggle it took to get it. When I strap it on each morning, I am reminded of the dreamer who tried it on in Vegas. It reminds me that anything is possible, and I can OverDeliver on dreams I previously thought improbable.

I earned that reward over ten years ago. I have reached so many loftier goals and could afford to buy more expensive watches today, but I would never spend that kind of money on a materialistic item again. Yet I couldn't disrespect the young, hungry entrepreneur who walked into the Rolex shop on that fateful day with a dream.

You don't need to have a separate reward at the end of your DreamBIG. The DreamBIG final destination is the reward. If you make the DreamBIG something that will fulfill your soul, at the end you will be fulfilled. A watch can't fulfill your soul. It can only remind you what time it is — and it's time to get to work.

The next chapter will help you acquire the skills needed to be Undeniable in the face of adversity. If you dream big enough, adversity will find you. I want to make sure you are ready to not just overcome it but OverDeliver on it.

PART III: BE UNDENIABLE

Think about the word *Undeniable*. You will not be denied. You will not deny yourself from expressing your greatness to the world. This term is less about others denying you and everything to do with you not denying yourself.

If you are Undeniable, you don't have to worry about what others do or don't do. It is all about you and the Undeniable mindset. You make a deal with yourself to never deny that gut feeling that wants to break through walls to get what you want like the Kool-Aid Man. *Ohhhh Yeahhhh!*

CHAPTER TWENTY-THREE:

NO HOLDS BARRED

Holding back is a form of denial. When you deny what is in you, it creates a state of uneasiness or *dis-ease*. I know this is a bit of a stretch, but I also feel that certain cancers can be the growth of suppressed or denied dreams. I know that when I feel unable to execute my creativity or I am held back from an opportunity to truly express myself freely, I feel dis-ease in my chest. Before I go on stage or if I am about to seal a deal that will greatly affect my life, I feel like my bowels are about to fall out and my armpits begin to sweat.

It's trying to get out. What if I suppress it and try to hold it all in for days, month, or years? Don't you think it's possible that we may develop some detrimental physiological response by our bodies? "I can feel it in my bones," "It's a gut instinct," "She broke my heart," "My mind was racing," or "Don't sweat it." The mind, body, and your dreams are connected. If you won't listen to your mind, listen to your body—and don't deny it.

If you want to be Undeniable, you need to not only decide in your mind, but you need to convince your body that you cannot be denied. If you want to be mentally strong, you need to challenge yourself physically. If you want to be physically strong, you need to overcome discomfort with mental determination and will power.

I push my comfort zones both mentally and physically on a daily basis for this exact reason. I am constantly finding ways to make myself uncomfortable. I feel the more you can challenge yourself and push the limits of your abilities in controlled environments, the more you will be resilient during the unexpected catastrophic events in your business, personal life, or inner self.

Comedian Brody Stevens was someone who was near and dear to my heart. He used to always proclaim, "Push and believe." He committed suicide, which angers me. He pushed, but he didn't believe. Now he is bereaved. I want to save you from this fate of living a life of dreaming big and underdelivering because deep down you don't truly believe in the most important thing in the world: you.

How can you believe in yourself and your abilities? Challenge yourself with small, measurable goals and start tracking your progress. If you can run 5 kilometers in 23 minutes, push yourself to finish it in 22. If you can endure 30 seconds of a cold shower, work your way up to a minute, then two, then three, and so on.

Once you have some momentum, you can make the goals bigger and riskier. Take them to the streets and put your money and talents on the line. I am constantly looking for new challenges in my career, in stand-up comedy, and in my interpersonal relationships. Put yourself in uncomfortable situations when you get a chance. Have the uncomfortable conversations when conflict arises in your relationships. Take a job or a project that you may not know if you have the abilities to complete. Get uncomfortable.

Navy SEALS are the baddest mofos on the planet. They weren't born Navy SEALS. They were created. How do you create the ultimate Undeniable weapon? You create a safe environment to challenge your ability to handle discomfort.

This training ground is called BUD/S training. I visited BUD/S in San Diego when I was consulting and training their medical and strength staff on how to assess function and connect it to performance. To complete BUD/S, you need to survive 24 weeks of hell. If for any reason you feel the need to join the 75% of soldiers who quit during this training, you ring a bell. The sound of the bell ringing is the sound of you losing your undeniability. I would never judge anyone for ringing the bell as I don't have the balls to even attempt BUD/S, but I feel for them. I feel empathetic toward anyone who sets out to accomplish a goal and fails.

You can create your own BUD/S training program for the real world, and I encourage you to do just that. Find your threshold of physical and mental comfort and design a training program to push those boundaries. I go to Hot Yoga five days a week and lift weights in the heat, hold poses for excruciating long periods of time, and sweat to

209

the point where I can't decide whether to pass out or puke first.

Why the hell would a man in his late 40s who doesn't compete in any sport or isn't training for a movie or magazine cover put himself through this? Discomfort fortifies my ability to be Undeniable in all aspects of my life.

The Undeniable Game Plan

This chapter provides a follow-along game plan for you to develop yourself into an Undeniable machine. For some of you, this part of the book will change your life, and for others, it will reinforce what you already know. Regardless, it will challenge you to find the chinks in the armor and expose your weaknesses in your daily habits and routine.

I have always said that the strongest people have the ability to expose their weaknesses and take action to make them strengths. The Undeniable Game Plan breaks down all aspects of your life, which I call the Foundations for Overdelivering. You need to be proficient in all these foundations to truly be Undeniable. You may crush one area and feel vulnerable in another. Don't shy away from the weakness. Look it in the eyes and take action.

The Foundations for Being Undeniable

The following foundations for performance are solid fundamental elements that everything you do is based on.

These fundamentals are consistent and unyielding. You can add a ton of fluff to your programming and nutritional plan, but if the foundations aren't solid, it will all be a waste of time.

My foundations are simple:

1. *Hydrate*: Drink one half your body weight in ounces of water each day.

2. *Eat Clean*: Eat whole, natural, unprocessed foods from a good source whenever possible.

3. *Move Beautifully*: Move with purpose for a minimum of 20 minutes every day.

4. *Sleep Like It's Your Job*: Provide recovery for the mind and body.

5. *Be Mindful*: Have intention.

You can do CrossFit classes five days a week and eat grass-fed beef and organic broccoli for breakfast lunch and dinner, but if you aren't sleeping and drinking plenty of water, you will fail. You can also drink three liters of water a day and sleep from 10 pm until noon, not workout, and drink protein shakes till your stool samples look like a Wendy's Frosty Soft Serve Ice Cream, and you too will fail.

All five foundational elements need to be present in your performance plan. You may be thinking, *This is too simple. Not what I signed up for. I bought this book to get the secrets that you use with the world's top athletes, not this namby-pamby drink more water bullshit*. Patience, young grasshopper. This is the foundation that all the high-performance variables will be layered upon.

1. Hydrate.

Do I need to share with you how your body is made up of 120% water? That's right. And the rest, you ask? Well, if you are good at math, you would see that there is 10% left for all the other stuff.

Seriously, though, water is essential to life. The order is oxygen, water, food, and, finally, coffee. You can live for three minutes without oxygen before brain damage and death occurs, three days without water, three weeks without food and life without coffee is not worth living. I don't have to remind you to breathe and eat. One you do without thinking and the other is all you think about.

Water, on the other hand, seems to be a hang-up for many people. If you are like me and consume three liters (a little over three quarts) or more per day, skip forward to the next section. If you are one of those people who proudly holds up a 12-ounce water bottle and boast to your friends that you drank it all today, you need to read this.

My good friend and nutritional guru, Robert Yang, recommends you drink one half your body weight in ounces per day. If you weigh 200 pounds, you need to drink 100 ounces of water a day. A glass of water is 8 ounces, and a normal water bottle is 16.9 ounces or equal to 2 glasses of water. That means a 200-pound athlete will need 12 glasses or 6 water bottles a day. If it is a hot day and you are out in the sun sweating like teenager waiting to see if there is one line or two on the pee test, add another 2 glasses of water. Exercising? Add another 2 glasses for moderate and 3 for intense training sessions.

Water is water. Anything else is not considered water in this situation. Beer, coffee, tea, booze, and soda are all diuretics. That means that not only are they not hydrating you, but they are causing you to urinate, which is a negative unit of water. For each dietetic beverage, you need to add one glass of water.

Not all water is created equally, by the way. You want water that is rich in minerals. That is why some water costs $3 per bottle and others are two for $1. Tap water has a ton of treatments added to make it safe to drink. Water treatments such as fluoride and bleach remove the mineralization from your water. Cheap water is tap water. It may say, "Poland Springs" on the label, but I assure you the closest thing to living up to its name is that it was poured from the tap into the bottle by a guy named Yurgey.

Want to turn your crappy water into the good stuff? Add a pinch of Grey Celtic Sea Salt or Pink Himalayan Salt to your water. It will also improve your electrolyte balance and help keep you hydrated while exercising. Throw out that Gator Sugar Water and grab some sea salt. The bottom line is you need to drink more water. Period.

2. Eat Clean.

I am not a nutritionist. I am, however, a student of nutrition and have many colleagues and team members who advise me and help my athletes with their nutrition. I will keep this really short and sweet for you so you can get back to your coffee and donut: Eat good shit, know where it came from, and eat it in moderation. Eat real food that is unprocessed and as close to the natural version of the food as possible.

I love to cook for my family every night. It is one of the ways I like to show love. "I made this for you. Eat it. I made it with love." I start each dish with fresh produce, chop it up, heat it up, mix it with spices, and serve it. I used to take fresh produce and chop it up, sauté it in oil, and add a store-bought sauce to make my creations. With a little practice, I was able to make my own tomato sauce, bone broth, and curry pastes.

The more I cook, the more I want to make it the way it was made in the old country. When I make it myself, I don't have to add any fillers, preservatives, stabilizing agents, or sugars like the store-bought variety. Just veggies and protein. I am not saying you need to take up cooking as a hobby, but I am encouraging you to be aware of what you are putting in your body for the sake of convenience.

Here is my daily food plan that you are welcome to copy and adjust according to your lifestyle and taste. I am a creature of habit, and I don't like to have to think about what I am going to eat first thing, so my morning routine is the same each day. I read somewhere that you need to *chew* your calories and not *drink* your calories. I start with a smoothie poured over a sliced banana, nuts, seeds, and coconut shavings. My smoothie has a handful of spinach, pea protein powder, organic collagen, blueberries, almond butter, and almond milk in it. My goal is to meet my essential vitamins and mineral requirements early in my day, so I try to get nutrient-dense food into my breakfast.

Lunch is almost always the same: salad with protein. The salad consists of tomatoes, cucumber, red onion, green onion, red cabbage, lettuce, spinach, and some form of protein (usually fish). How much nutrition have I had before 1 pm each day? Enough to allow me to add variety to my dinner. Dinner varies from night to night, but as mentioned earlier, I like to be creative and enjoy cooking for my family. Real food from a real source cooked by a real dad.

3. Move Beautifully.

What does moving beautifully mean? In the Undeniable Body chapter, I share a ton of ways for you to move your body for performance. Below, I share a great way to start your day with movement. The key is to do it with purpose. What are you trying to accomplish? Stressing the body to create adaptation? Rest and recovery?

I have a set schedule that I follow, which is a mixture of running, yoga, lifting, recovery stretching, and soft tissue work. Each day sets up the next. The day after a heavy lifting session, I will schedule some recovery work. I space out my cardio days with yoga. The key is getting 20 minutes of dedicated body work in each and every day. Listen to your body and *move*.

4. Sleep Like It's Your Job.

I go deep into this topic in your Evening Ritual, but for now just know that you can do better. Most of you would be fired from your job if your job was to sleep. Sleep like you are getting paid for every minute your head is on the pillow.

5. Be Mindful.

If you need more rest and recovery in your life, you will need to decide whether you need physical or mental recovery. Physical recovery does not mean sitting on the couch. It means doing physical activities for at least 20 minutes each day that leave the body feeling more rested and recovered from the stresses of the day. This could be a walk, yoga, stretching, massage, or a relaxing bike ride.

If you need mental relief, I recommend mindfulness. Meditation is just one form of mindfulness. You can be mindful while you walk, ride your bike, cook, sit in the bath, or enjoy a hobby. The key is that you are present and not stressing about the past or fretting about the future. To revisit the concept of liminal thinking, you can influence the conscious mind by repeating affirmations that promote positivity in your life.

One of my favorite affirmations is one that I repeat to myself while I am on a walking meditation: "I am good and always getting better." I will repeat this to myself in my head and sometimes quietly out loud. I like this one because it is humble ("I am good") while also optimistic ("and always getting better"). I can apply it to my work, comedy, relationships, or personal development. Make up your own. Just make sure the words elicit joy and happiness in your soul.

Each of the five pillars needs to be in place for you to truly be Undeniable. Take one away and the rest will fall. *Focus.* If you miss a day, start the success of tomorrow right now. These pillars will provide the foundation for the greatness you will create in your career and life. Add to that foundation, but never subtract.

Below, I have put together a game plan that I have tweaked and implemented over the past decade. It is a follow-along guide that provides structure to your habits and daily routine. I researched the world's top performers from the sports, arts, and business world and applied these principles to my clients and my own life. The principles I am about to share with you are things that all top performers have in common. The order, duration, and intensity may vary, but the ingredients are all the same.

I have found that adding structure to my morning and evening routine allows me to maximize my potential. What happens in the middle of the day is anyone's guess, but how I wake and how I end my day is in my control.

217

The Undeniable Game Plan: Morning Ritual

Your morning ritual could be the most impactful thing you do in your day. I want your morning routine to be automatic. Wake, move, shower, fuel, get on with your day, and end your day with a evening routine. Then repeat.

The unknown variable is what happens once you "get on with your day." The start and the end should be on autopilot.

Hydration

Your day starts with hydration. Have a glass of water by your bedside or grab some when you rise. I would like you to drink 25% of your daily intake within the first hour of waking. "But I want coffee." Think about it. You haven't had any water for 6–9 hours. "But I haven't been doing anything but sleeping." Respiration and sweat throughout the night can place you in a dehydrated state when you wake.

Start the day with two glasses of water to replace fluids lost in the night and start the hydration for the day ahead. Set a water table for the day. If you are ever thirsty, you are already dehydrated.

"But Coach, if I drink all that water in the morning, I will be running to the toilet every five minutes." You have a water threshold that you can shift over a week or two of steady water intake. If you gradually increase your water intake over two weeks, you will shift your ability to hold and utilize water more effectively. I can drink four liters (16 glasses) of water in a day and only drain the main vein three or four times.

Spirit

I start each morning with meditation. It sets an intention for my day. Just sitting in silence for 10 to 20 minutes allows me to get in touch with my mind and body. It is time for myself before the world demands my attention and dictates my schedule. If you wake up and look at your phone first thing, you are opening yourself up to others' needs. Starting your day with meditation is putting you first.

Movement

Start every workday with movement. I don't care if it's 10 minutes of dynamic stretching, a 20-minute run, or 30 minutes of kettlebells. Just *move*. Its not what you do that counts—it's the fact you had an intention to be active in the morning that creates the mindset of a kickass athlete. Attack the day like an athlete preparing for a major event.

Getting muscles, organs, and connective tissue moving also elicits a hormonal response. When you wake, you have a rush of the stress hormone cortisol flowing through the body. This hormone helps you wake up, but it also breaks down body tissue and suppresses the immune system as well as reproductive and growth hormone secretions. Let's think of this relationship through the voice of

Dana Carvey playing George Bush on SNL. "Cortisol: bad. Testosterone and growth hormone: good. Recap."

Exercise can elevate cortisol if the intensity of the exercise elicits a stress response from the body. It can also trigger cortisol when the duration of the exercise is over an hour and the athlete's glycogen stores are depleted. Starvation triggers cortisol to break down tissues for energy.

Why do I care about cortisol so much in this section of my daily routine? This hormone dictates the following routine for me each day:

1. Move early in the morning to help reduce morning cortisol stress.

2. Slow and low intensity for 10-30 minutes is ideal.

3. Stretching, yoga, body prep activations, Kinoga, calisthenics, a light run, or moderate cardio are ideal ways to get moving in the AM.

4. Save the super-intense workouts for later in the day.

5. Exercise on an empty stomach, but eat immediately afterwards.

3. Wake and train at the same time Monday to Friday to help regulate your sleep cycle and endocrine system (hormones).

The more often you expose yourself to exercise, the better your body becomes at reducing cortisol levels and handling the effects of it.

Fuel

Start your day with good fuel. Food is fuel. Good food is good fuel. Great food is—I think you get the idea. I start each day with high density nutrition. I try to reach a high percentage of my vitamin and mineral requirements in the AM, which leads to healthier habits in the PM. At night, your body will crave what it didn't get in the day.

I want you to think of food as the fuel that drives your body and mind. Clean fuel will lead to clean bodies and clean minds. What you eat and when you eat it will affect your energy levels, overall health, body composition, and brain function.

There is no perfect diet for everyone, but in this section, I want to share my views on nutrition in a simple format that is easy to adopt. Let's divide our fueling needs into fuel for the mind and fuel for the body.

The brain at rest consumes about 20% of the body's energy. The brain functions best on a low-carb, high-fat, protein diet. Want to stay awake and focused? Eat protein and healthy fats. Want to sleep? Eat simple carbohydrates. So how is that donut and a coffee with milk and two sugars before your big meeting or athletic event serving you?

Your body, on the other hand, requires fats, protein, and carbs to maintain the energy levels needed to produce work, keep your vital organs running, and accomplish daily physical tasks. My goal is to get as much nutrient density per calorie in my food. I want less food but more nutrition. This is a challenge because the more nutrient-dense a food is, the more calories it often contains.

Finding the right balance and combination is the key. I eat bright-colored veggies, berries, nuts, and seeds in the morning to fuel my body with vitamins, minerals and all the micronutrients I need for my day.

Whether you are Paleo, Weight Watchers, Vegan, Keto, or a person who just eats what they see, this thought process will fit your needs:

Brain: Fats, Protein.

Body: Nutrient dense foods from natural sources.

Simple.

Evening Ritual

Sleep

Sleep like it's your job. If you were getting paid to sleep, we would all go to bed at 9 pm and wake at 8 am. There have been countless studies done on the effects of sleep on your overall health. For those of you who think you are different ("I don't need sleep, I work best on 3–4 hours of sleep a night"), think again. Ideally, you would get a solid 7–9 hours of sleep a night. The only way that happens is if you decide when you are planning on getting up and then reverse the math to determine the time you need to go to bed.

If you need to be up at 6 am, you better go to bed at 10 pm. Ideally, we would go to bed when the sun goes down and rise when the sun comes up. Left to our own devices, we probably would. Our natural sleep cycle is dictated by our circadian rhythm controlled by the hypothalamus, which responds to light. The invention of fire, electricity, televisions, and now smart phones allowed us to stay stimulated past sunset and get us up before sunrise, which throws off this natural, rejuvenating cycle of sleep. My rule? No TVs, computers, or smart phones in the bedroom or at least while you are in your bed.

Make your bed a place of sleep. Have a ritual where you get in bed, the lights go out, and you trigger your sleep cycle. Many of you will use your bed as a TV watching apparatus, late night snacking station, and home office for last minute emails while sneaking in a YouTube video before you sleep. You are confusing your brain into thinking the bed is a multipurpose space that is occasionally used also for sleep. Clean your room and go to bed.

I could write a whole book on sleep, but that is not the purpose of this section. Just follow these guidelines and you will find yourself more rested, along with increased energy and a decrease in stress. Enjoy overall better health, improved body composition through a better functioning endocrine system, a better sex life, and improved alertness during the day.

All that from making sleep your job? Yup. Sleep like it's your job and do everything in your power to not get fired.

Night Nutrition

Ever since I was a child, I had to have a bowl of cereal before bed. As I got older, my cereal was replaced with chocolate bars, desert, or a night cap. As you can imagine, this affected my sleep in a negative manner. My good friend and colleague Dr. Ernst Zwick challenged me to replace my evening indulgences with dark chocolate and herbal tea. He informed me that my cravings at night were based on what I was lacking in my day.

Changing my palate would require me to stop eating after dinner and adding a square of dark chocolate to level my blood sugar and a caffeine-free herbal tea to calm the system. I know what you are thinking. Dark chocolate? Healthy? This is the type of dark chocolate that makes you look at the wrapper twice to see if someone replaced the ingredient chocolate with chalk. *"Does that say 70% Chalklate?"* He said I could start with 70% and gradually work my way to 90% chocolate over a few months. One small square each night was all it took. Sure enough, my cravings subsided, and I started to crave dark chocolate and red wine instead of beer and cake.

TODAY'S TASK: You control how you start your day and how you end it. Start by writing out your current routine. Be honest with yourself. If you can't identify any routine, you now have one.

Write out a personalized game plan that works for you. Include things that make you Undeniable during your day. If meditation seems too New Age, then try walking first thing in the morning. If you can't fall asleep at night without watching Sport Center in bed, try watching it on the couch for a week. Then drag yourself to your crisp, cold bedroom and make your bed a place for rest and recovery, not entertainment.

CHAPTER TWENTY-FOUR:

UNDENIABLE BODY

I don't need to convince you that fitness is important and that you need to make exercise a part of your daily routine, do I? Because if I do, this probably isn't a book you would pick up off the shelf at the bookstore (if they still have those by the time, I finish this). We all agree that fitness is an important aspect of a healthy daily regime. The healthier we are, the better we can perform both mentally and physically to accomplish our DreamBIG.

With that out of the way, we can now dive deep into your unconscious and drop some liminal nuggets that will change the way you see your body and guide the way you train it to accomplish your goals.

Liminal learning is an approach that involves setting unconscious thoughts in the mind that will guide your conscious actions. The information I share with you in this chapter will break through the threshold of the conscious (supraliminal) and leave nuggets of truth in the subconscious and unconscious (subliminal) mind. These seeds will sit in the background and guide your actions.

Scientific studies have shown that your brain starts the process of taking action a third of a second before you consciously take action. Let's fill that subconscious computer with data that drives positive actions when they reach the conscious mind and, even more importantly, when the conscious mind is completely unaware.

How Did You Get Here?

The body you currently reside in is a combination of your genetics and the actions or lack of action you have taken throughout your life up to this point. Nutrition, training, environmental factors, and internal and external stressors sculpt your body into what you see in the mirror. Apply a stress to the body and the body will adapt. You choose the type of stress that will elicit the type of adaptation you desire. Some of you consciously took matters into your own hands and sculpted a body by design that you envisioned in your mind. Others have a body that seemed to just happen.

Let's focus our attention on those of us who purposely applied training regimes to our body to create specific adaptations. If we look at the two ends of the spectrum, we have the body builder and the ultra marathon runner. Both of these dedicated athletes put in hours and hours of training, adhered to nutritional guidelines, and made huge sacrifices in their lives to achieve their desired bodies. The bodybuilder decided at some point that they wanted to develop the biggest and most proportionately balanced body they could build. The massive muscles he or she developed amazed onlookers but also restricted their ability to perform certain activities and functions like scratching their nose. "My bicep, delt and forearm are conspiring to keep my finger away from my nose. That's why I use this adapted selfie stick to pick."

The ultra marathon runner wanted a body that could run at high speeds for an excruciating long duration. Consequently, they created a body consisting of long, lean muscles and a face that looks 20 years older than they really are. Their bodies adapted right down to the subcellular level. My point is that with each modification we make to our bodies through training and nutrition, we gain on one side and lose on the other.

What motivated each of these athletes to start the process of transforming their bodies to these extremes? What would make our body builder want to train for hours every day and live on a diet of protein shakes and endless Tupperware containers full of chicken and broccoli? The classic 1940s Charles Atlas cartoon of a man named Mac who got sand kicked in his face for being skinny comes to mind. In the 1940s, this ad ran in magazines and comic books around the world and pushed the idea that the bigger your muscles were, the tougher, more confident, and manly you would be. And the more of a man you were, the more women you would attract.

You think this messaging might have set a subliminal message in the minds of a young reader that might manifest itself in actions taken years later? Even if you scoffed at the cartoon of the weakling being bullied by the strong man, there is a part of you that absorbed the not-so-subtle messaging. You are influenced by your experiences, observations, and the constant bombardment of images and information around you. Those images and experiences create a belief about yourself and how you fit in the world around you, which in turn guides your actions.

What if the beliefs you have are based on misinformation? Does building a body that allows you to pick up a compact car optimize your function in the world we live in today? Do we need the ability to run from one city to another today in under four hours? You drive an electric car to the next city and sit outside a café, flipping through Instagram. Luckily, your maladapted thumb tendonitis won't interfere with you sipping a frappé mocha grande no-foam latte.

The two examples I just used are extremes. Your fitness goals will likely live somewhere between these two bookends. The regime you currently use to achieve your goals is based on your environment, experiences, and observations. Are you even aware of why you train, the way you exercise, and what led you to this type of training in the first place? How is it working for you?

My Body, My Story

I love running. I was a sprinter in high school and college, but as I got older, I started to enjoy going for longer runs. There was something about being outside in the fresh air, music in my ears, and the trance-like rhythm of the run that put me into a meditative state. During my working hours, I was a strength and fitness coach. When I had an hour off, I lifted weights. I continued with this regime of running and lifting for 20 years.

What I didn't know was that this regime was building some tight hips, an immobile t-spine, and sciatica. If you said to me 20 years ago, "I've got this fantastic exercise program of only 20 years of hard work. At the end, you will be left with back pain, a hip replacement, and a shitty golf swing. Are you ready to get started?" The sad thing is that I am one of the most respected functional strength and conditioning coaches in the world. If I can screw this up, I can't imagine how bad you could botch your personal program. Do you think the body builder would have signed up for 20 years of training to obtain a body that makes his penis look microscopic in proportion to the girth of his legs?

Where has your program gotten you? What is your end goal with all this huffing and puffing?

The Perfect DreamBIG Body

What is a perfect body for the demands of today's world? If you could start from scratch without any of your unconscious conditioning telling you that bigger is better, what would the perfect body look like and how would it function? If I had it to do all over again, I would build a body that was lean and strong and could perform a variety of skills and endure long bouts of sustained work.

The basic building block for human performance is a functional body that has ample mobility and inherit stability; is athletic and efficient; and has a high capacity to perform work. How would we go about designing a program or training regime to optimize this body? The following is my attempt to do just that. I am framing this section in this manner so that you can drop preconceived ideas about your own strengths and shortcomings while implanting quality performance strategies in your subconscious. These subconscious, golden nuggets of performance goodness will guide your future actions. Am I fucking with your mind? You bet I am. But it's for your own good.

We are programmed to think that training or going to the gym is for the purpose of building muscles, sculpting our bodies, and getting "swole." I want you to change that mindset and think of training as the daily practice of moving beautifully. You choose what activity gives you joy while acquiring your physical goals, but it has to be something that at the end of the activity you feel better for doing it.

If going for a run in the woods on a cold rainy morning makes you feel alive, do it. If being in a group CrossFit class and pushing yourself to the limits fills you with incredible energy and vitality, then do that. My rule is do an activity that you can practice for 20 plus minutes every day. After practicing your activity, you should feel better, not worse.

Now you may be thinking, *Coach, you can't get gains doing 20 minutes a day*. This is true. I said nothing about making your body adapt to the stresses you apply to it for the sake of changing performance. If you want to get bigger, smaller, faster, or more athletic, you will need more, but not at the expense of not doing something every day for at least 20 minutes.

Let's use a CrossFit warrior as an example. Training for CrossFit is like playing a tackle football game on the body. How many football games does a running back play each week? One. The rest of the week, they practice the elements they will use in the game at slow motion. If you want to be a recreational CrossFit competitor, I recommend you practice the technical elements associated with your competitive WOD (Workout of the Day) for a minimum of 20 minutes each and every day. Then perform them at speed once or twice a week. You can now enjoy CrossFit for life.

Back in the day, every morning I ran in the mountainous forest in my backyard in beautiful Vancouver, Canada. I had two routes: The first one took me 17 minutes and involved cutting through hilly paths covered in stumps, logs, and squirrels. The second one was on a 4.5 kilometer, rolling, groomed path that took me 23 minutes to complete, which I would run once or twice a week. I would add to this regime kettlebell training and gym work for 20 minutes 3 times per week.

I was extremely consistent with this program for close to 10 years. I would wear my heartrate monitor and track all my run times and workouts. I was obsessed by a number my app would spit out that would provide me with the recovery time needed before I could train again. The harder I ran or lifted, the longer the recovery needed. Most workouts had a recovery time of around 8 to 14 hours. I had low-back issues, sciatica, and neck pain, and for all the work I did, I didn't look like I was training as hard as I was. To be fair, I was also counteracting all my hard work by drinking a few beers or half a bottle of wine a night. But I thought I deserved those drinks.

My wife, on the other hand, was going to spin class and hot yoga every day she could. She kept telling me I should go to hot yoga. I had tried Bikram Yoga for a short stint years before and it wasn't for me. I was about as flexible as a dining room table.

Years later, Julie finally got me to commit to coming to a class at her new studio. They had an offer of unlimited classes for one week for $10, and I am one cheap son of a bitch, so I agreed. I attended my first class, which was called Total Body Conditioning. This wasn't yoga—this was CrossFit in heat. The next class was Yoga Flow, and after the beating I took in TBC class, I enjoyed the more mellow transitions from pose to pose. But I was grunting and groaning while attempting what should have been relaxing stretches and soothing holds. My competitive spirit kicked in, and I was determined to learn all the poses and perform them with an Ujjayi breathing technique of four count inhale, hold, four count exhale, hold. My breathing technique at the time was one second inhale, hold for five seconds, and then hard exhale with a loud groaning sound that sounded like Grandpa getting off the couch.

I stuck with my yoga practice five days a week and added a long run on the weekend. After six months of committed practice, I was able to get my breathing under control and found freedom of movement and ranges of motion I never dreamed possible. More importantly, my back pain, sciatica and other nagging joint discomfort was gone. I went from seeing my soft tissue chiro twice a week to now going once every three months just to catch up and visit.

At the start of each yoga class, the instructor has us sit in child pose and dedicate the class to someone you love or reaffirm what brought you to your mat that day. Each class I say these words to myself: "I am here because this is what I do." I have made it part of my day: Like breakfast, brushing my teeth, and taking a shower. It's just what I do.

I added weight training to my yoga and running routine and found a balance that I could commit to long term. I cut out drinking during the week, get tons of sleep, and started to see my body transforming into something that looks athletic and shirt-off-worthy at the pool. I am pain free. What else could I ask for?

The moral of the story is that you need to find your version of hot yoga. If you need some tension in your life, start strength training. If you need more mobility, take up a stretching routine. It doesn't matter what it is, but it does need to match your body's needs at this point in your life.

It should provide you with the all the physical, mental, and emotional joy you desire. You will know it is right when you can see yourself continuing this practice for years to come.

TODAY'S TASK: I want you to write down three to five activities that you like to do. Ideally, they are all very different and require varied intensities and recovery times. This week I want you to perform each activity and write down the following:

1. How did you feel about the activity before performing it? Did you look forward to it, did you dread it, or were you indifferent?

2. How did you feel while performing the activity? Challenged, energized, in pain?

4. How did you feel afterwards?

It should be obvious to you which activities you need to add to your weekly routine and which ones you need to remove or use as a litmus test from time to time. You may need to tweak your routine from season to season.

Changing the stimulus forces adaptation. At the end, you should have a plan that leaves you feeling energized, moving freely, and maintaining a physique that you are proud of.

Function First

I have screened countless athletes over my career. The art of screening involves getting the athlete to demonstrate a functional range of motion and control while performing various movement patterns and holding postures. I have had the opportunity to work with some of the best athletes in the world from the NFL, MLB, the PGA Tour, and Extreme Sports. Everyone has disfunction and compensatory movement patterns. The better the athlete, the better they are at disguising their compensations.

One athlete in particular stands out in my memory. I was down at the Titleist Performance Institute consulting for a PGA Tour player who brought with him a friend. He asked if I would screen his buddy so they could resolve a long-standing bet about who was the most functional. His friend was *Dancing with the Stars* champ and professional dancer, Tony Dovolani. Tony moved beautifully. He was tall, lean, and graceful. Tony was also a mess. Tony shared with me that dancers are always injured and that the greats find ways of masking their injuries by using compensatory movements. What made them great was their ability to create an illusion of freedom when in reality they are in constant pain.

The body has an incredible ability to adapt. Dissect a hamstring and the body will use an adductor as a hamstring and keep on trucking. Sometimes the adaptation is good, and other times it can cause compensation, disturb function, and cause pain. The key is to always strive for function first above all else. Its better to move good than to look good.

Not sure if you are functional? Find a TPI or Functional Movement Screen (FMS) practitioner in your area. If you are in pain, look for a Select Functional Movement Assessment (SFMA) doctor. Before you start adding performance variables, clean up your disfunction.

What Drives Your Actions?

If we are a culmination of our actions over time, then this raises the question of what drives our actions. It can't just be our personal experiences and social influences. At the end of the day, we are simply organisms. The human organism has a few basic inner drives that underly our actions. The first driver wants to grow, acquire, and procreate, while at the same time, an opposing second driver wants you to rest and conserve your resources.

The first driver, which we will call the Growth Driver, wants you to hunt and forage for your food to give you the resources needed for survival. The second driver, the Rest Driver, wants you to use as little energy as possible after acquiring your newfound resources so you can last as long as possible. The resources you required when you were a cave person were calories, water, and shelter. As resources such as food and shelter became easier to acquire, we could use our excess energy to pursue other commodities like money, material items, and things to make our rest time more restful.

We became so efficient at acquiring the basic resources needed for survival and improved our ability to rest that we created a surplus. We can now acquire an abundance of resources (calories) and need to create false work environments where we can simulate hunting and gathering to burn off the excess. This is called going to the gym.

Your need to grow is still the underlying driver that gets you up in the morning. You are driven to grow physically, spiritually, intellectually, economically, and emotionally. To create physical growth, you need to apply a stress to the body, forcing it to adapt to that stress. To grow intellectually, spiritually, and emotionally, you need to add stress or tension to your belief structure, studying ideas created by others and opening yourself up to new ideas creates adaptation. To grow economically, you need to create a resource that is desired by others that they are willing to pay you money for. The better you are at performing that resource, the more money you will make. You improve the quality of your performance and the efficiency of delivery by adding stress or tension to your systems and technique.

Your Undeniable self is driven by the first driver. To be Undeniable, you need to add tension to your life. When you add tension to your life, your life will adapt to that tension and become stronger and more Undeniable. Your intension each day should be to be in tension: Focused and sustained bouts of tension followed by intervals of intense rest will create a body and mind that are truly Undeniable.

239

The key is applying the right type of tension and balance it with the appropriate amount of rest. We all know people who have either too much tension or others with too much rest in their lives. The Yin-Yang balance between these two drivers is what you seek.

Let us look at a few different ways that you can efficiently and effectively add tension to your life that will yield maximum adaptation with minimal toxic side effects.

Interval training HIIT

Physically speaking, there is no better example of a work-to-rest ratio under tension than High Intensity Interval Training (HIIT). HIIT training involves maximal all-out effort for 15 seconds to 1 minute followed by a rest interval allowing you to fully recover before doing it again. A higher intensity of the activity will deplete the energy stores faster and require a longer recovery time.

During recovery, your body is still working, burning calories, flushing waste, and replenishing your energy stores. When you train in this fashion, you realize that the discomfort of high intensity work is short-lived. Once you recover, you are ready to perform another round.

Your ability to work and recover and the knowledge that you *will* recover allows you to work harder. This will pour into other areas of your life. You may find yourself during your workday trying to accomplish as much as possible in a set time frame while knowing that immediately afterward you will enjoy a well-deserved break. I find some of my best work comes from work sessions where I set a countdown timer and challenge myself to get a small project completed in 90 minutes. I block out the rest of the world and put my head down and get it done.

Just like running the stairs at the stadium, you know the goal, how long it will take and how much stress it will put on the body. *Go.*

Strength Training

It doesn't matter what the implement is. Just pick up heavy shit and put it down. Repeat.

Strength training is simple. Apply the right recipe of sets and reps, and you will get the results you are looking for. Need size (hypertrophy)? Lift 10-12 reps for 3-4 sets. Strength without size? Use 1-4 reps for 5-6 sets. The recipe has been perfected over centuries of training trial and error. I won't waste your time sharing a recipe for chocolate chip cookies when you came here for my Undeniable Pie. If you feel you have a strength deficit, find the recipe that works for you. Like a good cookie recipe, your strength training plan should be made up of simple ingredients. Once you have the strength base you desire, it's time to move it.

High TripleXity Training

My goal for you is to move beautifully and efficiently. This requires you to train like an athlete. I like multijointed, multi-plane exercises that challenge your nervous system. I spent the past 25 years developing my own brand of this style of training that I call High TripleXity Training. It puts an emphasis on complexity of movement over adding more pure strength. Instead of using weight to add resistance to the muscle-skeletal system, we are adding complexity to stress the nervous system. Once my athletes have established a baseline of strength, I add High TripleXity.

Kettlebells

If you want to get strong and powerful with minimal equipment, get some kettlebells. Kettlebell training is ancient and has endured the test of time. To master the kettlebell, you need functional movement of all your joints, core stability, balance, coordination, and agility. I incorporate kettlebell training in my workouts as it allows me to express my athleticism and power in the shortest amount of time.

Olympic Lifts

Olympic lifts and barbell training are standard in athletics. If you want to express true power, you need to be able to move weight efficiently. Most Olympic lifting involves maxing out your one rep max by systematically increasing your weights over time. In my program, we do things a little differently.

For me it's all about speed. Use a weight you can lift with perfect form and move it as fast as possible. No throwing the weights from the top of your snatch in my gym. We lower the weights back to the ground under control. I always say that, if you can't control it, you can't lift it. I use this technique to work the body eccentrically. Eccentric loads require the body to act as a braking system. You can only accelerate as fast as you can decelerate.

There are thousands of different styles of training out there for you to explore. These are just a few of my favorites. The key is finding the one that works for you. Find a qualified trainer to teach you the proper lifting techniques and listen to your body. Remember that every stress you add to the body will cause adaptation. Make sure the training style you choose adds the right stress to illicit the right adaptation.

Recovery

Every four to six months, my wife and I go to the Scandinave Spa in Whistler, B.C. If I have been putting too much tension on my life for a sustained duration while working on a big project or traveling around the globe lecturing, my wife will say," It's time to go to the Spa." I know that sounds so bourgeoise, but this spa isn't about facials and pedicures. In fact, it is the opposite. This spa is a mini-cycle of tension and rest, which resets the imbalances of life. It is designed around the Scandinavian tradition of sauna, steam, and ice water plunges.

The recipe is 10 to 20 minutes in the heat followed by 30 seconds to 2 minutes in the cold followed by 30-60 minutes of relaxation. Stressing the body with intense heat from a sauna or steam room forces the body to dissipate heat via dilation of the blood vessels, moving blood flow to the extremities, increasing perspiration, and decreasing blood pressure. The cold plunge releases endorphins and increases your heart rate. Blood vessels constrict to move blood flow from the extremities to the vital organs. The rest periods are performed in atriums with incredible views of the mountains and forest. This rest interval allows your body to regulate your body temperature and stabilize your heart rate.

The cycle creates a physiological response that is energizing while at the same time relaxing and soothing. The rest intervals create deep sessions of intense introspection and DreamBIG time. And the spa has rules such as no talking and zero noise, as well as a strictly enforced ban on electronics. Now you know why my wife says, "It's time to go to the spa"—not for my health but for some peace and quiet and a break from my nonstop banter.

Now you may be saying to yourself, "That's great, Jay. You live a life where you can take time off work, drive to Whistler, and spa with your wife while I am here working my ass off to make ends meet." The point of my story is to share the relationship between rest and tension and how, when they are in balance, you can improve your life.

Pete Rock has a line in his classic hip hop album *Center of Attention*: "Damn right I like the life I live." I love that line because there are no apologies. I created this life through dreaming big, OverDelivering on those dreams, and being Undeniable. It is a self-curated life that is built through hard work, determination, sacrifice, and living within my means.

Want to go to the spa? Curate a life where it is not only possible but it is an integral part of your routine.

CHALLENGE: Don't have the cash to go to the spa? You can do it hobo style. You can create your own Scandanave Spa in your very home. Next time you have a shower, turn on the cold for 15 seconds followed by hot for 1 minute. Repeat. I challenge you to do this 5 times each morning for a week. I was introduced to this technique by an old Navy Seal who started each day with a cold shower. He said it cut a toughness groove in his skull. Anything he did after that was easy.

The second driver wants us to rest and recover to reserve any resources and energy we acquired from the Growth Driver. Most of you know how to relax, but let me share with you the following: With my pro athletes who travel and train constantly, I have to put active rest in their programs. These are intervals of rest that could be anywhere from an hour to 24 hours. The key is the word *active*: Active rest is a conscious act where the intent of the activity is to maximize recovery. This could be for relief of mental, physical, or emotional stress. Each type of stress will require a different strategy. Physical stress may require an active rest using a casual bike ride, leisurely hike, or some pool work. Mental stress may require meditating, going to a movie, or watching the sun set. Emotional rest may need some dedicated time journaling, having coffee with a friend, or hitting the heavy bag at the gym.

The key is that you go into the activity with intension to recover from the stress that is taxing you. Going out for coffee without intent is just a coffee. Meeting a friend who knows how to make you laugh and is empathetic when you are having a bad day is intentional.

Massage is a fantastic modality to help you recover physically, mentally, and emotionally. There are so many different forms of massage, each with their own focus. Need a physical flush after intense exercise? You can seek out a fascia release specialist, athletic masseuse, or trigger-point specialist. Need to relax? Swedish massage or the touch from a loved one can melt all your troubles away. It is helpful to find a therapist who can get in tune with your body and deliver what you need that day.

Self Evaluation

Periodically, it is a good practice to perform a self-evaluation and ask yourself the following question. Do you need more tension or more rest in your life? What would yield better daily performance, more fulfillment, and bring you closer to achieving your personal greatness?

If you need more tension, you will need to decide what form or tension would yield the best results with the least amount of collateral damage. Do you need yoga or HIIT training, muscle hypertrophy or weight loss, speed, or endurance? I recommend you balance your forms of tension in the following manner: 4 days a week you should focus on your tension of choice, then 2 days of the opposing tension, and 1 day of active rest. If you wanted to add muscle, I would strength train Monday, Wednesday, Friday, and Saturday, with yoga on Tuesday and Thursday, and finally a walk on Sunday.

The Dali Lama once said, "Exercise because you love your body not because you hate it." So many of us fat-shame ourselves and train out of spite. Get your mind right. Exercise and care for your mind, body, and spirit because you love yourself. It should not be a punishment. Have a sense of humor about yourself and love yourself enough to move and progress toward the ultimate version of you. Where you are right now is not where you will be tomorrow. Remember you are already good—and always getting better.

This chapter is called the Undeniable Body. You should know by now that you cannot separate the mind and the body. Be patient: There is a chapter just around the corner where we go deep into the Undeniable Mind. But for now, we need to create a strategy for when your Undeniable Body hits an inevitable obstacle.

CHAPTER TWENTY-FIVE:

THE INJURY OBSTACLE

Y ou are doing everything right: building that Unde-niable Body, training each day, eating clean, sleeping like it's your job, and drinking so much water you need a catheter. Then out of nowhere, *Pow!* You blow your back out lifting a 4 kilogram container of pea protein out of the back seat of your car. All that hard work gone to waste. All your momentum halted, and you feel like you have to start from scratch. What do you do next?

First you need to figure out what the real problem is and then put together a game plan to get yourself back on your feet as fast as possible. The following is a triage and treatment guide for you when the shit hits the fan.

Let me be extremely clear here: This is meant to help you understand the mechanics of injury and should not be used as a guide to self diagnose and treat. You should always defer to a medical practitioner in the event of an injury. This guide will, however, provide some insight into the problem-solving process your health care professional will go through to find the problem and rectify it. I will also demystify the various treatment techniques so you can make an educated decision when picking a treatment option.

Injury can be either acute or chronic. Acute injuries occur suddenly, like blowing out your knee after a defender slide checked your patella from the front of your knee to the back. Chronic injuries are injuries that occur after smoking the chronic with Dr. Dre and Snoop. *Not.* Chronic or overuse injuries are caused by faulty movement patterns being performed over and over, causing wear and tear on the tissue. Overuse injuries occur when repetitive movements are performed with increased intensity, duration, or faulty patterning. Injuries such as tennis elbow or carpal tunnel syndrome (which for some reason all my male junior athletes seem to develop in one arm) are avoidable. Whether it's an acute or chronic injury, there is some form of damage to the body, causing pain and dysfunction.

The first step is figuring out what tissue is damaged or compromised. You have muscle, tendon, ligament, and nerve as potential suspects. Ligaments don't have a lot of nerve endings or blood supply, so ligamentous injuries rarely cause pain at the site of the injury. To injure these structures, there is usually collateral damage in the tissues around the ligament. Dysfunction and lack of joint integrity will definitely be present. Tendons are prone to overuse injuries or catastrophic ruptures. When you hear the word *sprain*, think *tendon* and when you hear the word *strain*, think *muscle*.

Muscles are quite resilient and usually will become injured due to imbalances in the antagonist (muscle on the opposite side of the joint) or from a blunt force causing bruising or contusions. Nerve issues usually radiate pain from the source of the injury either up or down the limb or spine. So what did you injure?

If it is a mechanical problem, you need to let the damaged tissues repair themselves. Tears, strains, and sprains will cause inflammation in the injured area. Inflammation is your body's natural response to injury. Your body increases blood flow to the area to flush out any waste and help repair the tissue. Most first aiders, coaches and moms will use ICE (Ice, Compression, and Elevation) to reduce the swelling and relieve pain. There is, however, new research and evidence that says inflammation is your body trying to heal itself and reducing it will slow down the healing process. Many medical practitioners and athletic trainers now use stim units like the Marc Pro and other soft tissue techniques to speed up the inflammatory flushing process in the area. Keeping the joint moving will also help pump out inflammation and speed up recovery as long as the joint structures are functional and the injury is of a soft tissue nature.

Tony Finau was playing in the 2018 Masters and dislocated his ankle after a hole in one celebration. Running backwards he rolled his ankle, and for some strange reason he knelt down and popped his ankle back in place like he was putting on a shoe that fell off. I was fortunate to be in the medical trailer each morning and watched his medical team try to put him back together so he could compete in this prestigious event. His chiropractor, Dr. Love, acted fast to get the joint moving and flush the inflammation through massage and aggressive soft tissue treatments. They also used some natural medical patches that were charged with turmeric and other minerals and vitamins to accelerate the healing process. From Wednesday to Sunday, you could see the ankle go from red to purple to yellow to full function.

Pick Your Poison

There are thousands of techniques out there that can help you recover from injury. The key is finding the one that works for you. The majority of treatments work the musculoskeletal system. Others work on the nervous system, endocrine system, energy systems, or attempt to balance your chemical and hormonal levels. The treatment should work on the system that is causing the problem. This is why the best therapists have a plethora of techniques at their fingertips. Often the symptom and the problem causing the symptom are two different things. This is why proper assessment and screening is needed to properly treat the injury or discomfort you are experiencing. Below is a bastardized description of some common treatment techniques. I am purposely describing these techniques in this manner because this is how I describe them to my clients. It is important that you describe complex concepts in easy-to-understand deliverables or through your personal stories.

Dry Needling

Dry needling is a treatment that involves the therapist inserting long thin needles into the muscle causing the muscle to contract and relax. I personally think they should rename it *moist stabbing*, but that's neither here nor there. My experience with dry needling is a love-hate relationship. I love the results it gets but personally hate the feeling. While being treated, I break out in a cold sweat. My therapist said it was my fight or flight mechanism kicking in. It was inappropriate to run from the table or punch my therapist in the solar plexus, so my body just said, "Oh well, I guess I'll just lie here and sweat."

Dry needling is a treatment that is available in some states and countries, while others won't allow it. Controversial? Not really—it's more to do with a turf war between the therapists and the acupuncturists. It is like when McDonalds started selling pizza, which ruffled a few feathers.

Acupuncture

Acupuncture is an Eastern medicine made popular by the Chinese. It works on the ancient philosophy and belief that the body is made up of "meridians" which are pathways in the body that energy flows through. An injury is a blockage in the path that restricts the natural flow of energy. The acupuncturist uses needles to re-establish these pathways. At times the therapist may add stim (small electric current) or heat up the needles to enhance their effectiveness.

Soft Tissue

Soft tissue is a broad term for body work. Massage is probably the most common technique in this category. The therapist uses their hands, forearms, and even feet to apply pressure in rhythmical flowing patterns that relax the muscles and connective tissues. ART or Active Release Therapy does the opposite. The therapist places their thumb or elbows in the muscle or tissue and then moves the limb, causing the muscle to glide under the pressure. For me, ART is the most effective at releasing tight muscles and restoring function in my tight body. Some soft tissue techniques use tools like dull blades or scrappers to release fascia or muscles at a deeper level. Instrument Assisted Soft Tissue Mobilization, Gua Sha, and Graston are some of the more commonly used techniques in this category.

Neuro

The brain is a powerful tool when it comes to unlocking the body. There are theories that claim that a lot of back pain, joint pain, and inflammation can be the result of the mind creating pain to distract you from other stresses you are under. Some range of motion restrictions are caused by your body trying to govern or protect itself from potential injury. Neuro therapy uses drills, eye tracking, movement, and other types of stimuli to unlock the mind and in turn unlock the body.

My interest in the brain-body connection led me to researching and experimenting with brain-busting coordination-based exercises. Developing complex neuromuscular training techniques for the purpose of enhancing performance in healthy athletes became the foundation for my popular High TripleXity and LoadXplode programs.

The coolest thing about neuro drills and exercises is the response of the athlete when we unlock their range of motion or enhance function. Performing eye-tracking drills results in newfound balance and stability. Performing some simple breathing exercises unlocks mobility that had been "locked up" for years. The science of neuro is the next frontier in the world of human performance, and I plan on being at the tip of the spear.

There are countless other techniques and schools of thought which get incredible results, but for the sake of brevity, I have kept this list to the techniques I feel are widely used and often misunderstood. Fascial release, stim, PRI, yoga, Pilates, Eldoa, DNS, and many others could be listed here. I use all of them in different forms, but describing them all in detail can be left for a different book by a different author. This author needs to get back to helping you OverDeliver.

CHAPTER TWENTY-SIX:

How to Be a Road Warrior

You have started your Daily Routine for OverDelivering. Great. It is easy to get into a healthy routine when you are at home in your own time zone and you can control your environment. It seems that every time I settle into my routine, I get a call from a player who needs me in Phoenix or about a speaking opportunity in New Jersey. Traveling for work can either kill your momentum, or it can become an opportunity to reinforce your new habits and test your undeniability.

I think it was Will Ferrell who once wrote in a song about Portland, "If I can make it there, I'll make it anywhere"—it's up to you whether you let the road beat you, or whether you come home better than the person you were when you left. It is time to take your Undeniable Body on the road. Here are my tips for travel and how to maintain your brain, body, and self control when on the road.

One of my responsibilities as a performance coach is to create travel strategies for my pro athletes. The pros have tight travel schedules that take them all around the globe, and they need to perform at the highest level once the rubber hits the runway. It's no different than a business executive who lands in a foreign country and needs to ink the deal of the century. Personally, I often squeeze a four-day round trip to Asia that includes two eight-hour days of lecturing and performing. By the time I get in my seat in Vancouver, I am already on Beijing's time zone. When I land, I am fresh as a daisy and ready for some dumplings, bed, and full night sleep to prepare my mind and body for the following day.

Want to avoid wasting the first two days of your trip acclimatizing to your new time zone? Of course, your answer is yes. We all try to cram in so much into our travel plans to ensure we optimize every second of the trip and we don't miss a thing. Or even worse, just so you could squeeze in one more day abroad, you convinced yourself that you could be in your office the day you return if you take the red-eye!

The following are some tips on what to do the day you depart, what to take on the plane, strategies for staying awake or sleeping the entire flight, the first thing you do when you arrive, and how to return home without looking like you were just run over by a baggage cart.

Road Warrior Travel Tips

Tips for the Plane

1. Don't eat unless you are in first class. The ingredients in your meal were designed to sit in the plastic microwaveable tray for months before being heated. It will take you longer to process the foods through

your system than it took them to process the meal in the factory.

2. Set your watch to the destination's time zone as soon as you take off and not a minute before. I once sat in my seat, changed my watch, and fell asleep only to wake 30 minutes later still in Vancouver and then had to depart the plane for maintenance. I almost missed my reboarding time due to my watch being three hours off.

3. If you want to sleep on the plane, eat high carbs to promote sleep plus take a natural sleep enhancer such as ZMA, melatonin, or CBD.

4. Want to stay awake and get some work done? Consume high protein foods with no carbs. This will keep your brain alert and focused.

5. You can't drink enough water. It may not feel like it, but the air is different up there. It is sucking you dry. Drink water, and double it if you plan on having an adult beverage on the flight.

6. If you are flying to a destination that is currently sleeping, get some sleep early in the flight. Carb up and go to sleep for as long as you can. You can wake yourself up with a coffee once you get to the hotel.

Upon Arrival

1. Get on your destination's eating schedule ASAP. I know it's 8 am back home, but you will need to eat dinner if you are in London at 6 pm.

2. If it's morning, eat a breakfast that triggers your mind to think breakfast. The first few days, you will want the same style breakfast you have back home. Once you acclimatize, you can try chicken feet and dumplings for breakfast.

3. After dinner, have a desert before bed to increase carb and help trigger sleep. ZMA or other natural sleeping agents can help you sleep throughout the night. Avoid sleeping pills whenever possible as they are extremely hard on your liver, especially if you are planning on indulging on that business trip. Cheers.

4. As soon as you get to the hotel, try to get to the gym. A quick 10- to 20-minute sweat session will reset your system before you meet up with your colleagues.

5. Sit in the steam room or create one by using the shower on full for 20 minutes. Steam helps hydrate you and helps respiration.

6. Eat clean, low-carb foods early in the day. You don't want to trigger the need for a nap at 10 am on your first day of business.

7. Squint directly into the sun for 10 seconds x 3 when feeling tired or if you are indoors for more than 8 hours. On a trip to the Philippines, I was speaking in a dark arena filled with athletes. Every break I got, I ran to the exit and stared into the sun. I had to remind my body that it was daytime, and I should be awake.

8. A great pick-me-up is a Scottish shower in the am. Start with a warm shower and then turn on the cold water for 10 seconds, followed by warm for 30 seconds, and repeat 3 times.

At the Conference

1. I don't care what time you start in the am. Get moving for 10 to 20 minutes as soon as you wake to energize your system. You will look at the other conference floor patrons and secretly know you have done more before the show than they will do in the entire day.

2. Eat a high-protein breakfast with healthy fats. This will fuel your brain and body for the day. If you add simple carbs or sugar, you will crash by 10 am.

3. Eat clean all day. It's easy to grab crappy, processed carbs, but you will regret it when you are yawning and looking at your watch all day. High protein, low carbs for alertness.

4. Entertaining or being entertained at night? Drink a glass of water for every alcoholic drink you take in. It will slow your roll, keep you hydrated, and guarantee you won't be the talk of the show tomorrow for the wrong reason.

5. Set a rule to get to bed before midnight. Nothing good happens after midnight or in the VIP room.

The most valuable tip I can give you for travel is to set a mindset as soon as you enter the airport. When I walk through the sliding doors at the terminal, I repeat the mantra "I give myself to travel." Long line at check-in? "I give myself to travel." Your flight to from LA to San Diego is rerouted through Chicago? "I give myself to travel." Your flight is so delayed that your departure is now later than your return flight? "I give myself to travel."

You can't control what happens, so don't stress about it. You will get there when you get there, and you will make any adjustments to your plans once you arrive. Give yourself to travel.

Follow these tips when you are on the road and you too will be a hardened road warrior. People often ask me how I can teach a course in San Diego for two days, fly a red-eye overnight to Toronto, perform on stage at 9 am, lecture for six hours straight, go out for dinner and drinks, and be on a flight home the next morning. The answers are all here for you—you just need to follow them.

CHAPTER TWENTY-SEVEN:

THE UNDENIABLE MIND

The human mind is one of the most untapped and under-utilized resources we have in our mission to OverDeliver. We have been brainwashed to think that you are either academically gifted or you inherited your parents' 2 + 2 = 3 gene. The rest of your mental potential is left to the quality of your education and the heap of self-help books that continues to mount on your bedside table.

It may be refreshing for you to know that brain placidity is real. This means that you can improve your brain power and deepen the mind by engaging in brain exercises and fueling the mind with nutrition.

Just like your body, your mind needs regular doses of exercise followed by rest. I like to call this cycle Ramping Up and Ramping Down. Having the ability to ramp up and ramp down at your fingertips gives you an edge on your competition.

When I used to play late-night Beer League Hockey, we would finish our game at 10 pm, sit in the locker room with a few icy-cold "recovery" beers, and get home at 11:30 pm. I would head straight to bed and stare at the ceiling until 1 am, trying to figure out how to get to sleep and why I missed the net on my breakaway. The clock said it was past my bedtime, my brain said it was time for sleep, but my sympathetic nervous system thought there was a 200-pound defenseman still chasing me.

I have also been in situations where I had to ramp up. Presenting in front of large crowds gets the adrenaline going every time. Adrenaline isn't enough, though, when you need to be articulate and present. I remember flying to the Philippines to speak to their Olympic team coaches and athletes. My times zones were flipped upside down. I was to hit the stage at 8 am after an 18-hour journey. My head was foggy, and my body felt like I just completed the Cross Fit Games. Time to ramp up.

There will be times in your life when you need to ramp yourself up for the big moment and other times when you need to ramp down so you can reserve your energy for when you need it. Here is a list of tools you can use to Ramp Up or Ramp Down your mind throughout the day.

Ramp Up

Exercise: Start the day with 20 minutes of movement.
Breathing
Music
Caffeine

Ramp Down

Breathing
Meditation Mindfulness
Yoga or Movement
Rest

Power Nap

Sleep

In the following sections, I have broken down the tools that have not been previously covered in more detail.

Breathing

The act of breathing is something we all take for granted. I'm not sure if you are aware of this, but you have been breathing ever since you came out of your mother's cozy uterine-lined sleeping bag. Every few seconds of every minute of every day, you breathe in oxygen and breathe out carbon dioxide. You can voluntarily speed up your breathing, slow it down, or consciously hold your breath. At some point, you will once again begin to breathe involuntarily. Once your focus is placed on more important things like "Ooooh, a squirrel," your brain's medulla oblongata regains control over this basic life function.

Focused breathing is a powerful tool to help you Ramp Up or Ramp Down. Right before a stressful event like performing stand-up comedy, you may take a few deep, slow breaths to slow down (Ramp Down) your racing heart and calm your mind. When you want to get yourself psyched (Ramp Up) before taking a freezing ice plunge, you may take a few fast and shallow breaths before exclaiming, "This is crazy, this is crazy, this is—" *Splash.*

Comedian Kirk Fox's father, Bamboo Ben, use to trudge through the sands of Mission Beach every morning and stop from time to time to raise his arms high in the sky and release a RIA to the heavens. Kirk once asked his father what "RIA" meant. Bamboo Ben replied, "It's AIR backwards. It's the first thing we take in when we're born, and it's the last thing we let go of when we die."

I go for a run in the woods by my house as part of my weekly exercise regime, not so much as an exercise for my body, but more as an exercise for my mind. There is a gathering of three cedar trees on a trail that I run by each day. As I pass, I give each of them an RIA. These trees represent my wife Julie, my daughter Emily, and my son Jamie. My screensaver on my phone is a picture of these three trees. This image grounds me when I am traveling and I want to feel a piece of my family and my home in the Northwest.

At the end of every training session, I have my athletes lie on their backs and breathe. My favorite one is a 5-second inhale, 7-second exhale, followed by a 3-second hold. Repeat this for 5-10 sets before getting off your mat. While they are breathing, I share my thoughts on the day with them: encouraging words about the work they just completed and how great they will feel when they go into competition.

I call these *Motitations* or motivational meditations. Once the body has relaxed, the mind opens and is ready to receive these positive affirmations. Breath is a powerful gift. Use it.

Power Nap

My good friend, colleague, and sleep expert, Brandon Marcello says that a 20-minute nap can be extremely beneficial. It won't replace the sleep debt you incurred from staying in the lobby bar till 3 am, but it will refresh the brain and improve cognitive function. Brandon recommends a Napachino, which involves drinking espresso or coffee right before you lie down for your nap. It takes approximately 20 minutes for the caffeine to kick in, which will help you wake up at the desired 20-minute mark.

Why 20 minutes? There are different phases of sleep that you cycle though while you nap. If you sleep too long, you may drop into a deeper sleep phase and feel tired and disoriented once you wake. It's a nap, not a hibernation, so keep it short and sweet.

Speaking of sweet, high carbs help you sleep, and protein helps you stay awake, so a tasty treat with your Napachino followed by a hind 1/4 of elk when you wake is ideal, unless, of course, you are vegan, which in that case don't nap. Use that time to call someone and inform them you are a vegan.

Yoga

Most of you will be thinking that yoga should be listed in the Undeniable Body chapter. In reality, yoga is more about the mind. The word *yoga* translates as *join* and signifies the joining of body and mind. The practice of yoga movements and postures is meant to free the body to enhance mindfulness.

Ideally, you want to perform the various stretches and postures using a rhythmical breathing technique called "Ujjayi breath." The Ujjayi breath consists of a 4-second inhale with a 1-second pause, followed by a 4-second exhale with a final pause, and then repeated throughout your yoga practice. Trying to maintain that rhythm while contorting and holding postures under tension takes 100% of your attention—attention you would otherwise be attaching to your daily tasks and personal stressors.

Once you have completed your yoga postures, the real meditation can now take place. In traditional yoga, you lie in the Savasana or Dead Pose at the end of your yoga and meditate. In North America, they use this meditation time to wipe down their equipment and role up their mats so they can run and check their smart phone and catch up on what they missed. What you missed was an incredible opportunity to connect your mind, body, and soul.

In Western yoga, a 20-year old-instructor in Lululemon leggings finishes class with some words of wisdom and a "Namaste." For most of the students in these classes, "namaste" translates as "time for a kale smoothie and an Instagram selfie #livingmybestlife." *Namaste* actually translates as "I bow to the Divinity in you," which is a Buddhist belief that each of us has a Buddha inside.

Like most things that stand the test of time, there is a value in practicing yoga the way it was intended. Embrace the mindfulness aspect and reap the ramp down rewards of a deepened yoga practice.

The Conscious and Subconscious

Understanding how these two parts of the mind work is important to controlling your brain's energy levels. A simple way of understanding the difference between the conscious and subconscious mind is to compare it your smartphone. When you open your smartphone, whatever you are looking at is the conscious mind.

The conscious mind can be described as the *active mind*. If you were to push your home button, you can see all the other apps that are running in the background. These background running apps are similar to the subconscious mind. These apps are running without you being conscious of them. Why is my battery draining so quickly? You can multitask with multiple apps at the same time, but doing so takes an enormous toll on your phone's battery and computing speed. Better add some more juice, or just close the apps you aren't using and run more efficiently.

The conscious mind can be trained to become more efficient and compute at higher speeds, but you need to be careful. More doesn't equal better—more can equal burnout.

You may, like many people, say that you are great at multitasking. The truth is that you aren't—you just don't know what it feels like to be 100% present in your task. Any great performance in sports, business, acting, art, or surgery requires the performer to enter a focused state that blocks out all external information, producing 100% focus on the task at hand. I discuss how to get into this state in a moment, but please understand that no great performance has been executed while running a grocery list app in the background.

The unconscious mind is the mainframe that takes all the information from the conscious mind and makes sense of it. The more you stay in the conscious mind, the more items the subconscious needs to process. The great news is that the subconscious is like a supercomputer that can handle enormous amounts of work. Meditation is like double-tapping the home button and closing all the apps that are running in the background. It turns off the running mind and allows the subconscious to become the primary drive.

I developed a ringing in my ears at age 45. I only hear it when I am in a quiet environment, turn off my inner dialogue, turn off the external world, and go internal. At that point, the ringing is noted. It is always there. When my mind is active, it drowns out the ringing and replaces it with the noise of my conscious mind.

One of the coolest things about the subconscious mind is that it seems to sort out the day's events when you sleep, meditate, or perform repetitive activities. Need a mental break? Go for a quick run: 10 to 20 minutes of low to moderate intensity jogging will allow your mind to take a break from the active mind and allow the subconscious to make sense of your last focused mental session.

Learning a Novel Skill

When you learn a new skill, you lay down neural pathways that connect the various parts of the brain and nervous system to perform the desired task. Increasing the number of attempts to complete the task results in a more efficient routing of these pathways and increases skill level, speed, while decreasing the neural load needed to perform the task. The more times the task is performed, the deeper the connection and "groove" of the pathway.

Let's put all of this in the real world. Have you ever tried snowboarding? If not, please replace snowboarding with a novel skill you tried to learn but initially failed at. I started snowboarding when it was at its infancy, back before we were even allowed on ski hills and were banished to the back country and local toboggan hills. I have taught countless people how to snowboard over the years. The experience for the novice shredder is always the same.

Day 1: Student takes 10 minutes to put on the first binding and for some reason 12 minutes to put on the second. We start on the bunny hill with the tow rope, which starts with the board beneath the student and quickly changes into a snow scraper as our student gets dragged up the hill on their belly. Once standing, they develop a look on their face that can only be described as *Now what?* This is followed by falling on their butt, then falling on their face, then falling on their—you get the idea. Fast forward three hours and we have a cold, wet "snowboarder" who has officially completed a cumulative two runs on their backside and one run sliding on parts of their body that they didn't know could bend like that.

Day 2: Sore and weary from a day of body sledding, they arrive at the lift. Bindings go on in a snap. Chair lift is successfully mounted and dismounted. No more need for the tow/drag rope for this shred dog. Our athlete drops in and makes three or four surprise turns, followed by a "Oh my God, I am doing it! Whoa, whoa, ow, *shit*." Day 2 score: 11 runs with the bottom of the sled on the snow for 80% of the ride.

What was the difference between Day 1 and Day 2? Your first thought may be experience and time. What you may not have taken into consideration is the magic that happened in between Day 1 and 2: sleep. While you sleep, your brain has time to compute the lessons learned on Day 1 and sort these failures and short-lived successes to build a framework for future success.

A scientific study was done using our favourite experimental animal, the rat. "No-one will care if it doesn't work—it's just a rat, right?" The scientists put the rat in a maze. Here comes the cool part: They then hooked up wires to the rat's brain to record the sounds of the brainwaves. What they heard at first was a randomized sequence of bleeps, pings, and blops. Once the rats found the correct path through the maze and discovered the cheese, they would repeat the same sequence over and over again. Bleep, bleep, plop, bleep, ping, pong, ping. Even the lactose intolerant rats reached the end of the maze with the consistent sequence of sounds, followed by them telling everyone around them that they are lactose intolerant and feeling better now that they also recently cut gluten from their diet.

Now here is the really, really cool part. When the rats went to sleep, the scientists heard the same sequence of bleeps and pings from each rat but at an accelerated rate. They were replaying the sequence ten times faster in their sleep than they did when they were running the maze. It was like they were deepening the sequence into memory for better recall tomorrow. This may help us explain the snowboarder phenomenon.

I always say to my kids that a good night's sleep without studying is better than a night of cramming. Ideally, you would work on your studies and combine it with a solid eight hours of sleep. The problem with cramming is you have consciously taken in all the information for the test but haven't allowed the subconscious time to make sense of it. Now take this approach with any of your novel tasks you come across in your daily working life, and you will see how a good night's sleep may just make the biggest, scariest, problem you are facing manageable.

Taking mental breaks in your focused studies or work bouts can allow a data dump to the subconscious. I like to work for a focussed two to three hours max and then take a mindful break by running for 20 minutes, preparing a meal, cleaning the house, or meditating. The repetitiveness of chopping vegetables, running, or sitting in silence allows the subconscious supercomputer to do its magic. Once you return to your work, try a different task or a different way of working with that task to engage different pathways. Build that Undeniable supercomputer.

Meditation

Q: So how can I develop an Undeniable mind?
A: Meditation.

"Oh no, you don't. I'm not going to sit cross-legged and chant, 'Om.'" Although there are some amazing benefits from this type of meditation, there are other forms of meditation that you can practice that you are already good at.

Meditation Through Movement

You don't need to buy granola, wear Teva sandals, smell like BO covered in patchouli oil, or drive a VW van to meditate. Far from it. Some of the world's greatest leaders, entertainers, CEOs, entrepreneurs, and artists make meditation an integral part of their daily routine. Bill Gates, Def Jam's Russell Simmons, LinkedIn's Jeff Weiner, Joe Rogen, Oprah, and Madonna, just to name a few, formally meditate on a daily basis. Oh, and I left out the Coach. I meditate in a couple of different forms. Some are very formal while others are passive in nature. I want to share with you some techniques you may not be aware of so you can dip your toe in the warm water of meditation.

Walking in Nature

Behind my house, I have the most incredible forest full of evergreen trees, rocky boulders, trails, fern gullies and everything else you would expect from the Great Northwest. I try to get out in the woods every day—not for the exercise, but for the sense of calmness and tranquility. Whether I am running, hiking, or walking, I am one with the forest.

Bill Gates uses walking in nature as part of his weekly routine, especially when he is working on a project that requires a clear and uncluttered mind. He will take walking meetings with colleagues or his wife, or go solo. And he is not the only CEO who holds walking meetings. No-names like Steve Jobs would conduct walking meetings and swore that they enhanced the thought process and communication.

The connection between walking and deeper levels of thought have been studied for centuries. Eastern philosophy has investigated the meditative quality of rhythmic movement and its ability to separate the conscious and subconscious mind. Westerners may look for a biological clue to explain this phenomenon, but for the purpose of this book, *get out and walk.*

Walking on its own is great, but the forest adds a whole other layer to this practice. The Japanese have used "forest bathing" to help heal depression and reduce anxiety, which makes sense. Our surroundings have evolved faster than we have as biological beings. The more density you add to a population, the greater the increase in pressure, social stress, and stress-related illnesses. Trees are replaced with concrete, and the urban jungle becomes a buzzing metropolis. Forrest bathing returns the "bather" to their roots, grounding them.

Try it and be open to the energy the forest, mountain, beach, field, or riverbank is giving you. Doing so requires that you unplug the earphones and turn off the rest of the world. If you actively walk with the intention of connecting with nature and disconnecting from the digital world, you are meditating.

Cooking

One of my favorite forms of meditation is cooking. I love every aspect of it: shopping for ingredients, cutting the vegetables, creating the sauces, cooking the various elements, and seasoning to perfection. There is a delicate harmony between the creative vision of what you want to create and controlling the temperature, acid, sweetness, sour, and salt. When the combinations are correct, beautiful things are created for my family.

Sharing my cooking is like sharing my mediation with my loved ones. They see my happiness and know how much I enjoy seeing them enjoy my food. When I cook, my conscious mind shuts off, and my subconscious kicks in, like driving a car and not remembering each time you placed your foot on the brake or gas pedal or whether you indicated before turning. It's all a blur until you reach your destination. Cooking is the same, but the final destination is when it hits the taste buds of the ones you love.

Art

Winston Churchill used painting as a source of meditation throughout his career. It doesn't matter whether you are good at it or not. What matters is that you are performing the art form with an intention of being creative and for the sake of enjoyment, not work. It doesn't matter if your art is physical like dance, audible like music, or visual like painting, sculpting, or doodling. Artists lose track of time and move into a sort of trance when they are deep into their art and not thinking about their checklist, unread emails, deadline, or an upcoming meeting. They are not even thinking about art—just being it.

Exercise

I either run, lift, or do yoga every day. Two out of the three are used for mind and soul, and the other is for my body. I lift with the intent of inducing a stress on my body, which forces adaptation to occur. Yoga and running also put stress on my body, but my intention is more of a meditation or exercise in mental defragmentation. The cadence of running—feeling each heel strike, my heart beating in rhythm with my respiration, and being out in the fresh air—is pure bliss. I don't like treadmills for that very reason. I want to get some sunlight and enjoy a journey through the city, forest, or wherever I happen to be calling home that day.

Hopefully, this part of the chapter has helped you realize that the big, scary world of meditation and being in silence isn't just for the yogi or the bong-rippers of the world. It is part of being a high-functioning human being.

CHAPTER TWENTY-EIGHT:

PRESENT–FORMER–FUTURE SELF

One of the biggest obstacles you will face along the journey toward your DreamBIG is maintaining your momentum. Being consistent and persistent with daily focus on your goal is crucial to completing big projects that create impact. So much has been written about goal-setting, the use of checklists, and breaking down your large goals into smaller, easier-to-digest chunks. If you want more on that topic, you can find all you need by searching "How to get shit done" in your Google browser. Getting shit done is easy. It is called *Get up off your ass and do the work.*

Understanding what makes you do what you do is a trickier animal. This chapter is about dealing with the person inside you who wakes up each day and must decide whether to do or not to do. Then you have to decide what to do and how much energy you are going to put into it. It's about who you are as a person and, more importantly, the person you were and are willing to be.

Present Self

One of the most common exercises performed by the world's top performers is the practice of meditation, which

I discussed in previous sections. You need to develop the ability to live in the present. Being present allows you to act without fear of what's to come or the weight of carrying around what has been. Being present during your daily activities, sport, training, social interactions, relationships, and work is critical.

Presence allows us to execute these activities without the cluttered mind. Imagine trying to have a deep conversation with a colleague while you are writing a tweet that can't seem to stay under the 150 characters without losing the context of the message. How do you think your listening skills would be? How do you think your colleague would rate your engagement? How well do you think you would be able to react to the twists and turns that your conversation is taking?

Your lack of "presence" in your day-today activities is very similar to the example above. Instead of your focus being on writing the perfect tweet, your mind is busied with "What if?" "What happened last time?" "What will happen next time?" "I wonder if they notice the stain on my shirt from lunch? They probably think I'm a slob. Why did I order the meatball sub?" "Oh, I'm sorry—were you saying something?"

Let's assume you are now present, which is a massive assumption seeing that you are probably craving a meatball sub right now. *You are focused.* Are you ready to take on a task that is so critical to your future success that you will commit your next one, three, or five years to it? Are you ready to wear out your pen checking off your to-do list and slam dunk life? Great.

Where was this goal-crushing superhero yesterday? Will you be able to recreate this alter ego again tomorrow? Let's come back to the present after we discuss the former and future self.

Former Self

Does the past affect the future? Of course, it does. If your house burned down yesterday, it will still be affecting you today. On a more psychological level, your ability to accomplish things in the past will give you confidence and fuel you to accomplish things in the present and future. Having in the back of your mind *I got this* makes whatever task you are focused on seem doable.

The opposite is also true. We carry around our past failures, and they are relived via a little voice in our heads warning us, *Remember the last time you tried that? Failure.*

Negative actions from our past selves can develop into habits that repeat themselves over and over. I'll use the example of a person who is trying to overcome a substance abuse issue. If you woke up today with a hangover, your former self has delivered you a gift from yesterday into your present. Many people in this position will look back at the decisions they made last night and say to themselves, "Oh my God, did you have to say yes to one more drink?" The messaging for the rest of the day is that yesterday's self wasn't able to override the urge to drink with willpower, so why would today's self be any different? I will return to this story in a moment when I discuss exercises that create dialogue between the former, present, and future selves.

Future Self

So much of our energy is put into creating the ideal future self. The future self is always somehow better, more refined, free of faults or failure. The future self, at least for the short term, is inevitably the same as the present self with the only difference being that we are one day older. The long-term future self can, however, become vastly different from the present self if we take daily actions in the direction of this "New you."

We create dreams of who we could be and develop life strategies to accomplish these dreams. These strategies are made up of the life skills we have acquired through our life experiences. The skills and confidence needed to execute the strategy laid out before us comes from the experiences we acquired through our former self. This is where your philosophy of life and how you perceive challenges, victories, and defeats comes into play.

Let's go back to the drinker who had too much whiskey the night before. He curses the person he was yesterday, has zero expectation that his present self will be any different, but longs for the future self who has more control. The secret is to start *today*. Today, in the present, you have an opportunity for tomorrow's self to be proud of your present actions. If you wake up tomorrow without a hangover, you need to celebrate it. Pat yesterday's self on the back and thank him for giving you a clear head and energy to make the most of today. This builds confidence in yourself that you can again get through another sober day and create positive momentum moving forward.

Too hard to take on? Start smaller. Yesterday you had eight drinks, today you have six, and tomorrow you will have five. Still too hard? Seek help. There are systems and support groups that will walk you through the steps. If you think I'm just talking about you stopping your addictive habits, you are way off. This former, present, and future self inner dialogue works for anything and everything you want to change in life. Fewer chocolate biscuits today leads to even fewer tomorrow. Finishing your checklist today leads to an eagerness to see what you can accomplish tomorrow.

Awareness of which self is driving the bus will determine whether you can accomplish your true DreamBIG. It can only be created by the present self drawing lessons from the past and creating a plan for the future self. The work is done in the present, and you need to present for it.

Optimist or Pessimist

Are you a pessimist or an optimist? I always thought I was an optimist, and anyone who has spent time with me would probably agree. An optimist walks through life thinking that the future will unfold in a positive manner, and all good things will be bestowed upon them along their journey of life. A pessimist, on the other hand, is someone who always expects the worst in life. The more I reflect on my life, the more I think I am a pessimist.

How is this possible if I wake up every day in a good mood and spend my waking hours laughing, smiling, and trying to make the world a more positive place? I have come to the realization that my happiness has come from preparing for the worst and being pleasantly surprised and joyful that the worst-case scenario didn't come true.

We all know people who go through life with a black cloud over their heads. They are constantly under attack from Life. "Nothing ever works out the way I planned it. Why me?" These people are usually seen as pessimists, but in reality, they are optimists: They want everything to be positive and perfect every day. They wake up expecting the day to go their way, for their project to be a success.

But reality kicks in and life deals them, like all of us, some ups and downs. The optimist takes the downs as a personal attack and the ups as what they expected, so no need to get excited about it. On the contrary, the pessimist takes the downs as what they expected and the ups as an unexpected bonus.

I do an exercise with my staff where we perform a *pre-post-mortem* on any projects we are working on. A post-mortem is performed to figure out what went wrong after a catastrophe. A pre-post-mortem is pretending that the project was a failure before it has even been launched. This exercise allows you to analyze any elements or actions that could have potentially caused the failure, which in turn allows us to act on those potential disaster elements before they happen.

This is a very pessimistic approach, but it allows us to celebrate later when the disasters are averted. It is like projecting into the future your former self while being in the present.

Have the strength to acknowledge your weaknesses and either accept or change them. Don't be blind to what is holding you back from greatness.

CHAPTER TWENTY-NINE:

CREATING CHANGE

In the previous chapters, I presented to you a strategy to create change in your mind and body. Many of you may have scoffed at the ideas of positive change. You tried it before, and it didn't work. Sure, it was great for a few weeks, but then you fell back to your old ways and ended up even more unhappy. You need a system for creating true change.

Liminal thinking is happening while you read each page in this book, reinforcing the need for change. Your DreamBIG is giving you a destination. Your routine is providing a foundation for positive progress. You also have the knowledge needed to make real change. You are no different from anyone else. Even the greatest champions in sports have to deal with the challenges of change at every stage of their careers. What I am about to present to you is a systematic approach to problem solving that can be applied to athletic development, business, or personal growth.

I have had the opportunity to coach Canada's most celebrated, successful male golfer and Masters Champion, Mike Weir. Late in his career, he developed some compensatory movement patterns that threw his game into a negative downturn. This phase of his career was challenging both physically and mentally. Mike was struggling with inefficient "feels" of reversing out of his loading pattern and having to manipulate his elbow and hands through impact to create his desired shot outcome. Whenever we corrected the pattern, he would respond with how different it felt from his compensatory movement. By sharing how different it was, he was reinforcing how good the new move was, but, unfortunately, he was also reliving the bad movements.

What does that have to do with your goals? Well, a hell of a lot if you want to understand how to break down aspects of your life that you struggle to find strength in. I need you to find strength when you look in the mirror and ask yourself if you have what it takes to achieve your goals. I need you to have the ability to step outside yourself and see your weaknesses for what they are and have the strength to change them.

Allowing yourself to see your reflection and not cower— and see your weaknesses and insecurities inside and take action to change them—is the strongest thing you can do.

Chocolate Biscuits

I want to share with you a story I use with my athletes called "Chocolate Biscuits." Come along for the ride because there is some deep-rooted performance psychology in this story. What I have created will have you seeing yourself, your actions, and the outcome of your actions through a different lens.

I want you to start by picturing a chubby, little funster named Chitsy, who loves chocolate biscuits. Who doesn't? The problem is that Chitsy has lofty goals: She wants to be the world's number one female model. Unfortunately, Chitsy's love for biscuits has made her a chubby, little funster. She knew that filling her face with chocolate biscuits wouldn't help her chances of becoming the model she envisioned. She needed a change. To make a real change, we must look at the behavior that led to Chitsy to become overweight

Obviously in this story the chocolate biscuits are the culprit, but what is the real problem? Could it be an inner hunger for something Chitsy desires that is unfulfilled? Regardless of the cause, we need to start by changing the behavior while we dive deep into the cause of the behavior. If you simply take the delicious biscuits away, Chitsy will crave those crispy, golden, mocha-covered mother fuckers like never before.

What we need to do is replace the biscuits with an alternative that is healthier but, in some way, satisfies Chitsy's empty hole. She tries dried figs and almonds and proclaims, "These aren't bad." Brilliant. When we gave Chitsy the new treat, she enjoyed it, but kept coming back to how they didn't have the same crunch and chocolate coating the biscuits had. We had to be very stern with Chitsy and rule out any comparisons, fantasizing, or glamorization of the chocolate biscuits while she ate the new treat. The new treat was a step toward her goal to being a model, and the biscuit was a one-way ticket to band camp. Eat an almond and visualize the runway. Eat a fig and see your new FIG-ure (I almost feel like apologizing for that one).

I shared the story of Chitsy with Mike Weir the week of the Masters while we tried to change his compensatory feels (chocolate biscuits) and ingrain his new, more efficient pattern (figs and almonds). Offering an analogy that is easy to recall allows me to say nothing more than "Chocolate biscuits," and I get a response of "I know, I know—you are right. You won't hear any more talk about my negative 'feels.' It's all figs and almonds from this point forward."

What are the chocolate biscuits you devour in your life?

TODAY'S TASK: Write down three "chocolate biscuits" in your life. These are the actions you take that you know sabotage your goals but you do them anyway. You can't resist—they may be a weakness you know exists but can't resolve or a craving that leads you away from your ideal self.

Now that you have your list, I want you to write down beside each biscuit an alternative action or pattern to replace your chocolate treat. It may not be as tasty, but when you add on top of it a heaping serving of your desired goal, it resembles something quite edible and satiating. When you feel a desire to indulge in a biscuit, you will replace it with your newly-approved treat and celebrate how it brought you closer to your goal.

Do not compare or romanticize about the biscuit of days gone by. Instead, celebrate the new road to your personal greatness.

If change was easy, we would have no addictions, everyone would be able to hit perfect 300-yard fades, and your significant other should have nothing to nag you about. Focusing on what you used to do, how much better glutenous bread tastes, or how great it was to just sit on the couch all day Sunday watching football will not help you move forward.

Get excited about the new you, how much less bloat you have on your new diet, and how great it feels to complete the Sunday 10K race. Don't compare—just leave the chocolate biscuits behind you and enjoy accomplishing your goal.

CHAPTER THIRTY:

SETTING THE UNDENIABLE STAGE

All the world is indeed a stage and we are merely players.

—Rush.

To truly be Undeniable, you need to first set the stage: Create an ideal environment for you to excel in. I can picture it in my mind: Getty Lee, wailing out his lyrics into the sold-out arena, full of fans with their lighters in the air, like he is the only one in the building. To free yourself and express your true greatness, you need to feel like no one is watching—no judgment, no critiques, without the fear of failure. Just you, executing your greatness to the world.

Sound cool? Well, that moment isn't possible unless you set the stage for greatness first. The greatest moments of my career started with me making my bed. Let us reverse-engineer this.

The closest thing I ever had to feeling this freedom in my career was when I performed the keynote speech at the 2018 World Golf Fitness Summit. No, that is a lie—I also felt it on stage at the 2010 Summit and on stage doing comedy at the House of Blues in 2016. The thing that all three of these events have in common is not what occurred

293

on stage, but instead it has everything to do with what happened the months that preceded the event. I knew that each show had the potential for greatness as I planned on riding the razor's edge of risk and reward. Shooting t-shirts into the crowd using a three-man slingshot, running up on stage in a lab coat during my entry song, having planted "fans" throwing panties on the stage, and taking Skype calls from Mathew McConaughey are just a few of the elements I added to the shows. I knew that each risk I took would either be a huge win or career suicide. If executed properly, I had the opportunity to deliver a performance that people would never forget.

Every night, months before each event, I would lie in bed and run through the show. During each run-through, I would get a new idea or a new analogy that would help me get my point across better while my wife slept quietly beside me. I would lie there thinking, *I should get up and write this down*. Then I would spend the next five minutes telling myself that the idea wasn't that good and not worth getting out of bed for, then another ten minutes trying to convince myself that if it was such a good idea, I would remember it in the morning.

After many sleepless nights, I decided to put a pen and notepad next to the bed, like the ones in hotels (which no-one uses) in the event that another gem of an idea came to mind. I would write one-word or one-sentence notes in the dark that would spark a memory in the morning of what I wanted to remember.

To prepare my mind each night for my presentation run-through, I needed to create an environment conducive for creativity. I need a clean, clutter-free room, with black-out blinds, crisp, clean sheets, and the room temperature as cold as possible. To ensure I have a clean bed and clutter-free room, I know I need to ensure that all my clothes are put away each day, and I start the day by making the bed. Starting your day with making your bed is not a new concept, but for many of you, this could be a catalyst that starts a snowball affect of productivity in your day, especially if you are single. "Why make my bed if I am just going to get back in it and mess it up again tonight?" Making your bed creates a mindset of order in your life. You start the day with a win—you have completed your first task of the day.

When you finish your day, you will come home to a crisp, clean bed for you to climb into. This is your opportunity to thank the former self for setting the stage for a great night of slumber. You will remember that positive feeling upon waking and want to repeat the routine again.

The same can be said about your place of work or the environment in which you express your creativity. If you set the stage properly, you will create a setting that will allow 100% focus and dedication to the task at hand. If you walk into your office and your desk is covered in clutter, your mind will be distracted and cluttered all day.

Picture walking in your office with your desk clear of anything other than your laptop and mouse. Maybe a ficus in the corner and a picture of your favourite kid, but that's it. How productive could you be? What if you turn on your computer and the desktop is clear other than the screen-saver you put on it of your entire family, your pet, second favorite kid or your DreamBIG? You check your email inbox and see that you have five new emails in your otherwise empty inbox. No flags, notifications, or unopened junk mail. No tabs on your web browser of unfinished searches from the day before. Just a fresh computer, clutter free, and a blank slate to start your day. Now I know it is a pipe dream to have this on a daily basis, but if the thought of it gave you some joy, I believe this is the direction we should be moving toward to free ourselves from the shackles of an over-cluttered life.

Marie Kondon became an overnight sensation when she wrote a book, *The Life-Changing Magic of Tidying Up*, about the Japanese art of decluttering your life, which turned in to a Netflix series. My wife read the book, which was a little redundant, seeing that she could write an encyclopedia on decluttering your life. Julie believes that if you haven't used something for six months, you need to get rid of it. She asks, "When's the last time you wore these bowling shoes? Bin it."

Bin it is a Scottish term for *throw it out*. My entrepreneurial mind keeps itching to open a decluttering company called Bin It, but I digress. The decluttering of the house creates an environment that has order and minimalism that allows you to focus on what is truly important. You only have so many decisions you can make in a day and so many computations. If you remember from the previous section on automating your first two meals of the day, you will appreciate how effective you will be in a home that doesn't distract you from your work toward your DreamBIG.

Set the stage. Make your bed, declutter your office, minimize your living space, and write your next great accomplishment. In the next chapter, I share how to go even deeper into this philosophy.

We are going to declutter your desktop and mind. All the world is indeed a stage. So clean up the stage, Getty.

CHAPTER THIRTY-ONE:

FACTORY RESET YOUR HARD DRIVE

To declutter your life and set your Undeniable stage, you should start with your mental hard drive. Every New Year, I perform an action that sets my year up for success. I erase the entire hard drive on my computer and phone. I know, I know it sounds crazy. Take a breath and release your puckered balloon knot for a minute and let me explain. What I am about to present to you isn't just for your computer. Taking time to reset your hard drive in all aspects of your life can free up valuable space that you can use for accomplishing your DreamBIG. The computer is like the catalyst to help you defragment and rebuild your life each year.

I don't believe in New Year's resolutions. If change was that important to you, you would have done it already. This is not a New Year's resolution; it is yearly maintenance. Clearing out last year's metaphorical and physical hard drive and starting the year with a clean slate is a strategy I highly recommend.

Not to get too technical, but your computer and brain are similar in the way that they have open files that are running programs in the background that you are unaware of, as I have explained in previous sections. These background processes take up active memory and tax the hard drive. Think about all the emails, texts, documents, GIFs, and memes that you can access with one click. They are open and running in the background in the event you want to view them. All you see is what is on the screen at the present moment, but there is more behind the screen that you can't see. It is what you can't see that is holding you back.

I will break down the process I use for resetting my year using the computer analogy and paralleling it with my work life as the two processes are identical.

Step 1: Back up to move forward.

Computer: Perform a backup of your hard drive. For your computer, drag onto an external drive all the files you need to save for future use. Take the time to go through each one and delete any files or documents you haven't used in the past year, movies you watched, duplicate pictures or items that were saved for short-term use but somehow got lost in the shuffle. Challenge yourself to see how many gigabytes you can free from your drive. It feels great to remove the clutter.

Work: Look back at the past 12 months and dive deep into the various elements that led to the success or failure of your year. Create a spreadsheet with all the different responsibilities you had, and list of all your clients you service and the jobs you did to fulfill your obligations. Create three columns on the right with the headings Revenue, Fulfillment, and Future. We will be using these columns in a moment to prioritize of each of our obligations for the coming year.

The Pareto Principle states that 80% of our work produces 20% of our desired outcome, while 20% of our daily actions create 80% of our net result. Simply put, 20% of the work you do results in 80% of your income, success, or fulfillment in your job. Everyone has that client or account that brings in the big checks but requires very little effort on your end. On the flip side, there are those clients who are constantly demanding your time and energy for little return.

Step 2: Reset and reinstall.

Computer: Once you feel comfortable with the files you saved, it's time to erase the hard drive. There is no going back, so make sure you've got everything either in your time machine, external drive, or cloud. Once the computer is wiped clean, it is time to reinstall the operating system. You can decide at this point if you want your old system put back in place or want to install the newest updated system. Newer isn't always better. I still run an operating system on my MacBook Pro that is two generations old. It works great while I wait for the bugs to be worked out of the newest OS. If it works, don't mess with it.

Work: This is a perfect time to rank your list of jobs, clients, or responsibilities in order of how they contributed to your year. For myself, I have eight key pillars to my business: My pro athletes, lecturing for TPI and Perform Better, my own LoadXplode workshops and certifications, consulting for teams and corporations, the Coach Glass podcast, online LoadXplode business, yearly Mentorship, and finally running my local gym/junior golf academy. I rank each of these items on the spreadsheet from 1-8 under the columns Revenue, Fulfillment, and Future. Revenue is an obvious one: How much money did each of these entities generate? Fulfillment represents the joy each of these items provides me in my working life. If you love helping your athletes but hate dealing with administration, you will rank them accordingly. Future represents how you feel these various jobs will lead to future success. For instance, my LoadXplode Certification I started this year in China took an enormous amount of my time to create while generating very little in compensation. However, this venture will reap huge dividends in the future once it builds momentum, and therefore it ranks high in this column.

Step 3: Fill your plate and repopulate.

Computer: This final step takes some discipline. Keep the external drive with all your files handy. Only drag over files or documents to your fresh hard drive as you need them. You will be amazed at how fast your computer will run with the bulk of your stored documents left on the external drive. While you are actively using a file or app, drag it over to the hard drive to avoid any interference or lag. You are only as fast as the cable that connects the external drive to the hard drive.

Work: If you successfully completed Step 2, it will become blatantly clear what you need to focus on for the year ahead. If a task ranked high in the Fulfillment and Future columns but low in Revenue, keep it in the plans for the year ahead. If a client ranks high in Revenue but low in Fulfillment and Future, you will need to decide whether you can sacrifice the revenue for the sake of job satisfaction and making time for future opportunities that will replace the lost revenue.

I create a fresh, new spreadsheet but only copy and paste the items I am going to focus on for the year ahead. I then create a weekly time sheet that breaks down the amount of time and the ideal day of the week I will execute the various tasks. This allows me to compartmentalize the various elements in my business to ensure that when I am working on them that they have 100% of my attention.

Try this yearly reset and let me know what you think. I guarantee it will be well worth your time and energy and will quickly become a yearly habit in your life as well.

In the next chapter, we discuss the neuro element when it comes to overcoming injury or enhancing performance. The brain controls the body, and the body performs the task. To optimize the efficiency and effectiveness of the body, you need to care for your brain. Just like the body needs recovery after bouts of exercise or work, so does your brain. That is why I like to regularly schedule a data brain dump.

CHAPTER THIRTY-THREE

CLOSER TO THE DANGER ZONE

In Chapter Seventeen, I shared my love for the movie *Glen Gary Glen Ross*. "ABC: A (Always), B (Be), C (Closing). Always Be Closing." "Coffee is for Closers only." So you want to be a Closer? Closers are closers because they won't be denied. They are Undeniable.

In this chapter, I am going to take you into the Danger Zone. I call it the Danger Zone because many who have gone in never come out. When you enter the Danger Zone, you will either run from it without looking over your shoulder, or you will love it so much you never leave. Once you feel what it is like to live like a Closer, you may not be able to be anything but close—it feels amazing. It will energize your body and mind when you go to sleep each night in anticipation of having the opportunity to be a Closer again when you rise.

When you throw away your return ticket from the Danger Zone, you are a Closer. Not everyone can drain a 3-pointer at the buzzer in game 7, sink a 12-footer for a green jacket, or seal the deal on a million-dollar merger. But anyone can be a Closer.

Closers all have similar characteristics and habits. If you were to apply these attributes and skills to car sales, marketing, law, or entrepreneurship, you are guaranteed a success story. When asked what their secret to success is, I have never met a world class athlete who says, "I don't know. I just kind of do it when I feel like it and try my best." The same applies to anyone successful in coaching or business.

At first, successful people may think of their daily routine and habits as just something they just do:

I wake up and prepare my body for the day with strength training, running, or yoga. I eat the same breakfast every morning and get to work. I block out the world by turning off any access to me while I focus on my craft. I take a break from my focused work from time to time to check in with my team and recalibrate the plan of attack. We meet to ensure we are moving in the right direction and quickly adjust where needed. I get back to work at polishing the product or finishing my current task. I have a hard end to my day, which can be checking off the last box on my checklist or based on a specific time on the clock that I have put in place to prevent me working myself to the bone. I then pack up and compartmentalize that part of my life so I can rest and recover to do it all again tomorrow.

A Closer Checklist

- ✓ You treat whatever it is you do like you are a pro. If you are a carpenter, hammer that nail like it is the world championship. Read about your craft and research better techniques for doing what you do—like a pro.

✓ You have discipline. Your discipline is forged in you, knowing that it is a culmination of your daily action that creates who you are. Wake up and make your bed. You will accomplish your first win for the day in the first 10 minutes of waking. Discipline ensures that the actions needed to be successful are getting done. Successful people return to a made bed each night. Want to be successful? Make your bed.

✓ Nothing you do is by accident. You have a plan, and you execute that plan. You even have a plan for reacting to unforeseen accidents.

✓ You are a perfectionist. You have a way of doing what you do which is constantly being tweaked and fine-tuned until it's a polished work of art for all to behold. You then look at it again, analyze it, and start over to make it even better.

✓ You put your work, practice, or craft first. It needs to be fed daily. Spending quality time with loved ones cannot be fulfilled if in the back of your mind you are focused on what you need to get done in your work. You complete your work, compartmentalize, and then get back to life.

✓ You take care of your body, mind, and spirit because you know that one cannot flourish without all aspects of life functioning at the highest level.

✓ You get results or you die trying.

The Closer Routine

Step 1

Write out your daily routine in detail. If each day of the week has a different schedule, then write out your week. You will see trends, dead zones, and holes that you can tweak to optimize your potential. Here are some questions for you to consider when filling out your routine.

What is your morning routine? What time do you wake? What do you eat?

What is your work routine? Do you answer emails first, or write out your goals to start your day? Do you set the tone for your day, or let others dictate your priorities?

Do you let the clock dictate your lunch, breaks, and end of day, or are your breaks task-driven?

How do you end your day? Is there a clear and distinct separation between work and play?

Step 2

At the end of your day, reflect on how productive your daily routine is. Did you just tread water, or did you swim closer to your destination? Did you feel fulfilled at the end of the day, or did you leave something on the table? Did you feel in control of your day, or did your day control you?

Routine

My daily routine is a culmination of techniques and systems I have learned from my clients, mentors, and personal experience. As a coach, I have been hacking my routine over the past 25 years, and curated this life through the DreamBIG method.

I wrote in my notebook in 2017 that I wanted to work from home and create an environment that would fulfill me monetarily, allow time to optimize my physical being, and free my mind to pursue my creative aspirations. I had to create a business that would generate big payouts for condensed work to free up my time at home to take care of my mind, body, and soul. I designed a life that would allow me to express my creativity.

This routine may sound like a pipe dream to some, heaven to others, and early retirement to those who don't know how hard I grind. I assure you that I have never been more successful in all aspects of life than I am right now, and it is due to the life I have created.

Daily

6:00 am: Wake.

6:15: Coffee, sourdough bread with organic peanut butter, banana, and hemp seeds.

6:45: Turn off my Wi-Fi and write (could be my book, journal, comedy, or anything on my mind).

8:00: Take my kids to school.

8:30: Write my checklist for the day.

9:15: Hot yoga/weight train/run. Basically, try to move beautifully for a minimum of 20 minutes every day.

10:30: Shower and put on my work clothes.

11:00: Two poached eggs on toast, with spinach and peppers, or a smoothie.

11:30: Work on my checklist, record the podcast, meet with my athletes, or prepare for upcoming travel.

2:45 pm: Pick up my kids from school.

3:15: Finish up any loose ends in my day. This is a focused power hour to get it all done. Often requires headphones, hip hop, and a coffee.

4:30: Finish my day, turn off the computer, and change out of my work clothes.

4:45: Start to make dinner for my family and be a father, husband, and human being for the rest of the night.

Weekly

Monday: Set the stage for the week.

Tuesday: Record the podcast and publish.

Wednesday: Get into the deep work on my DreamBIG checklist. Create quality content for my Coach Glass community.

Thursday: Check in with my team to prepare for long-term projects and work on checklist items. Stand-up comedy in the PM.

Friday: Complete any loose ends and try to do something creative (be a silly goose).

Saturday: Family time.

Sunday: Family time and set mind for next week.

Your weekly schedule and daily routine should focus on what feeds your personal fulfillment and future aspirations (DreamBIG), and compensates you financially. If you need to get up at 6 am and open your gym or work with your online community till 9 pm, your schedule will look dramatically different.

The important thing is that it accomplishes your goal and fulfills you in a balanced way. An unbalanced routine leads to burnout and you underdelivering. Now is that what you have learned throughout this book? Or are you different somehow from the truly successful people in this world?

The Starting Point

Being a Closer requires you to go above and beyond what is asked. Being Undeniable and always OverDelivering requires a mindset that drives all your actions—not just when you want it, but *always*. The Closer mindset is built not born.

Life lessons, often guided by a mentor or hearing stories about the greats, reinforces and deepens your ability to OverDeliver. Jerry Rice was the first to practice and last to leave. The same could be said about Jordan, Tiger, and Lewis Hamilton. If you want to be like Mike, you've got to do the extra work no one else is willing to do. It is my job as a junior coach to instill this mindset in my athletes. If you apply the lessons I share below in your own life, I guarantee you will never finish a workout again without going back and giving it one more rep.

Years ago, I had an incredibly talented junior golfer—I will call him, "Roy"—join my academy. He had zero experience in the gym. He was a champion on the course, while off the course he crushed junk food and Lazy Boy recliners like a boss. But the gym was a requirement to be in our golf academy. We believed that golfers were athletes, and athletes needed to train.

His movements were sloppy, he lacked stability, and his hyper-mobility only added to his slug-like appearance. He was put in a group with equally skilled golfers, but his shortcomings in the gym were exaggerated when training alongside the others. What the hell was I going to do with him?

I was watching the TV series *The Wire*. There is a scene where Fat Faced Joe was chatting with Cutty. Both men were boxing coaches and were chatting about their students and life. Fat Faced Joe was more experienced and successful as a gym owner and was helping Cutty understand the business. Joe pointed at a young, beginner boxer punching the heavy bag like an NBA player in a bitch-slap fight. "What do you think of him?"

Cutty replies confidently, "Pretty weak."

"Pretty weak? That's just the starting point," philosophized Fat Face Joe.

The starting point. I rewound the video back repeatedly and played it even more times in my mind when I went to bed that night. *That's just the starting point.* I thought back to the starting point of some of my favorite athletes. The first day, they walked into my gym, then lunged and squatted like newborn giraffes. Years later, they developed into thoroughbreds who were able to compete at the highest level and take on any challenges that crossed their paths.

You don't notice the improvements while you are training them. The process is slow and deliberate, and each milestone is dulled by time. The finished product occurs so far down the road that you often forget where they were when they started their journeys.

Back to Roy, who was starting further back than anyone I had trained up to that point in my career. I honestly thought he would quit before we could see any progress, so I just encouraged him to show up and do his best. He showed up, alright, and certainly did his best. A few years went by, and Roy was starting to lose the chub and gaining some control over his ever-changing body. He was continuing his winning ways on the course and was getting a lot of attention from college scouts. I'll never forget the fateful day when our home course hosted that week's tournament and all the juniors cancelled their training session in fear that they would be too tired after 18 holes of championship golf. Roy asked if it was okay if he still came to training. I would never deny any kid who wants train and agreed to give him a one-on-one session on the house.

The session started like any other. He worked his butt off to successfully complete each exercise I threw his way. He was performing a TRX suspension pull-up and was eight reps in when he gritted his teeth and asked, "How many more, Coach?" I knew he couldn't have had more than two reps left in the tank and told him that he had three more. I saw his eyes focus and his teeth clench even tighter as he trembled through the next two reps. He kept pulling and shaking and pulling some more until he fell to the floor. "Fifteen? Roy. Are you kidding me? Fifteen? I didn't think you could do 10. I challenged you to do 11 because I wanted to see you fail on the last rep and watch how you responded. What got into you? How did you manage fifteen?"

He sat up and looked me right in the eye. "It's this gym, Coach. It's changed my life. I have taken the lessons I learned with you here into all aspects of my life. At school, if the teacher wants us to read one chapter, I do two, if 20 math equations, I do 30. When my mom wants me to do the dishwasher, I finish it up, scrub the pots, and sweep the floor after. Everything I do, I do more. It's becoming a way of life, and I'm seeing the positive results." I know you are probably thinking that this sounds like a Hallmark Sunday Movie, but it's real, which is why it has had such a big impact on me.

I realize that we are all in one way or another at the starting point. Any challenge you take on puts you right back at the start. Knowing the outcome will be what you expect it to be, with some surprises along the way, is motivating, to say the least. Anything worth doing requires small steps fueled with intention in the right direction over time to accomplish it.

The process is the most important part—it is where the lessons and the ah-ha moments live. The fact that Roy got in the best shape of his life, went on to play Division 1 golf, and won championships was secondary to the lessons he learned about hard work, overdelivering, dedication, and overcoming obstacles.

I think of Roy every time I meet a new mentee. When they face personal challenges and ambitions, I am confident that we can help them create a successful path to their desired destination. You just need to acknowledge and accept that this is the starting point and then take your first step toward your DreamBIG.

Moving forward, you need to make a decision: *Am I the type of person who does one rep more than is asked? When no one is looking, do I do that little bit extra?* If you decide this is what you are all about, every thing you do from today on will be enhanced. Just like Roy, you will be a stone-cold badass and someone who can come and train with me any day.

CHAPTER THIRTY-FOUR:

SURFING FAILURE

Applying an extra rep, being the last to leave the office, or getting up an hour earlier to fit in your training doesn't guarantee success. You must be smart to be successful. Many of you are so pumped up at this point in the book you are itching to start your new venture, try out for the rep team, or ask your boss for a promotion.

But you need to learn how to sit on the outside and wait for the optimal time to execute your DreamBIG. My lack of patience on some of my early DreamBIGs almost cost me everything.

My failures in business remind me of the lessons I learned in the impact zone. Surfing has a way of pounding sense into you if you don't respect timing and put yourself in the wrong place at the wrong time.

I will never forget the first time I got pinned and rolled along the bottom of the ocean floor. I was late catching a wave, and this "wave of the day" picked me up, suplexed me to the bottom, and sat on my chest waiting for the ref to give me the three-count.

I've had this experience both in surfing and in life. You get yourself into an opportunity that is way over your abilities and say, "Fuck it, let's go" and jump in with both feet.

317

Don't get me wrong, I have taken this approach in the past and had the ride of my life as well. As I mature and refine my systems, I am having a much higher success rate at identifying the perfect wave or right opportunity.

I am a huge fan of legendary surfer Kelly Slater. (Side note: He actually made me feel comfortable with being bald. I thought that if he could proudly display the chrome dome, then so could I.) When Kelly Slater or any experienced surfer arrives on the beach, they don't just strap on their leash and jump in the water. They sit on the beach and look out at the waves. No two waves are the same, but they do follow a predictable and repeatable sequence. Waves come in sets that gradually build in intensity, followed by lulls of calm waters between sets. Each set of waves will have a similar characteristic. Some will have five waves with the fourth wave being the biggest. Others may come in packs of six, start strong, and then taper off. The best surfers will sit and get an idea of what to expect before entering the water so they can best predict the right wave for what they want to accomplish.

Business is the same. The best businesspeople don't just jump into opening a store or a restaurant. They sit and watch the swell and decide when would be the best time to jump into the market. Knowing that the best month for retail is November followed by a huge lull in January would help you decide whether you want to have your grand opening on New Year's Day or Halloween.

The timing of when you choose to paddle out into the surf will determine how much energy you will expend on getting out past the break. Setting out in the lulls will make for an easier paddle and leave you fresh and rested for your ride back to shore. Time it wrong and you will be battling headfirst into the oncoming waves.

Beginners try to paddle over the white water, with each wave throwing them back farther than they had initially paddled. Getting stuck in the impact zone will have you gasping for air and rolled around like you are in a wash-and-rinse cycle. As you become more experienced, you learn techniques for getting out of these situations or avoiding them all together. The Duck Dive, for example, is a technique where you go under the wave with your board and pop up on the other side. A good duck dive will get you past the white water and efficiently get you out to the line-up with ease.

It is critical that you develop these same techniques in your life and business. You need a strategy to help you avoid the inevitable onslaught of bad breaks and obstacles that will come your way.

Having the ability to dodge incoming waves is great, but veteran surfers do something even smarter before entering the water. The experienced surfer looks for the rip, the spot in the surf where the water returns back to the ocean. The surf looks like a never-ending pounding of water onto the shore, but if you really think about it, the water must go somewhere. Well, it does: It returns back to the ocean depths in nearly invisible rivers called *rips*. If you paddle out on a rip, it is like getting a tail wind or driving in the HOV lane.

The secret is sitting on the beach long enough to evaluate and find the right timing based on the sets, wave count, and rip. Savvy entrepreneurs can also identify these rips in their industry and take the easy street to success. Before you jump headfirst into your DreamBIG, you need to take the time to evaluate the conditions in which you plan to start your journey. Can you forecast and predict the lulls in your industry? Do you feel capable of finding the right time to start your DreamBIG? If not, you may need to seek out a mentor who has been pinned at the bottom a few times and can teach you how to duck dive and locate the rip.

Many entrepreneurs get so excited about starting their DreamBIG that they forget to consider what it will be like once the doors of their new venture open, like a young couple who decide one night to have children and nine months later are chin deep in diapers, wondering how they got there. They know they want to get their product out in the world, but then what?

I learned this lesson on that faithful day that I almost lost it all. I had paddled out into some waves that were way bigger than I was accustomed to. I was so eager that I didn't watch the sets but just jumped in the water and tried to smash and crash my way through the white water. I knew how to duck dive, but my paddling was so weak it made little difference. With each wave, I was giving back all the forward momentum from my ineffective paddling. I was exhausted and gasping for air while I flailed my Jell-O arms in the water.

A slick local encouraged me by letting me know that another set was coming, and I needed to get a move on or I would get pounded again. He directed me to paddle sideways toward the rip. I paddled my ass off sideways, which seemed counter intuitive as I wanted to get past the waves not sideways to the beach. I found the shoulder of the waves that started to barrel in and looked back to where I was only a few minutes before. I saw the impact zone throwing violence and mayhem. I kept paddling and ducking, paddling and ducking, until I finally reached the line-up.

The line-up is where all the surfers sit past the break, resting and waiting for the perfect wave to take them back to the beach. I was so tired I that laid my head on the board and tried to catch my breath. I was too tired to even sit on the board and enjoy the tranquility of the line-up. I saw another wave coming in as an opportunity to get the ride of my life. I conjured up enough energy to turn my board around and point it toward the beach. Too tired to look back, I paddled with all my might and hoped I was in a good position to catch the wave.

There is this moment when the wave is building behind you where everything gets quiet. I could hear the guys in the line-up gasp as one of them yelled out, "You are late.

Oh shit—" I was late. Not looking back to see where I was in the wave was a big mistake. I was so focused on moving forward I thought I could leave the rest up to the wave.

It picked me up and pitched me over the falls headfirst. The wave pile drove me to the bottom of the ocean. Every ounce of oxygen was punched out of my lungs as I was pinned against the sandy floor. I didn't know what way was up and what way was down. I just kicked and crawled for my life. I felt my head break through, and I took a salty gasp of air just in time to be thrown back to the bottom again and again by the ensuing waves.

If you think this story was about surfing, you are mistaken. This is the story of a business venture gone sideways. Avoid this fate by taking the following steps before you jump in the entrepreneurial waters.

1. Take your time on the beach to analyze the venture you are about to embark on and prepare yourself for what's to come. Ask yourself if today is the right day to start. Do you have the skills needed to take on the current market conditions?

2. Take the time to explore the rip or any strategies that may make your transition into your venture more efficient. This may involve bringing in a mentor to help you identify ways to expedite the process and avoid any wipeouts.

3. Before entering your new venture, make sure you know how to duck dive any potential obstacles that are inevitably coming your way.

4. Once you get past the white water, take a moment to rest and recover before you open your doors. Don't open shop while you are out of breath with Jell-O arms. A soft open while you work out the kinks can be helpful but requires you to budget for this transition period. Can you afford to open for the first month with zero sales while you train staff and put your systems in place?

5. Once you catch your wave, remember that you don't have to ride it all the way to the beach. You can peel off on the shoulder for an easier paddle back to the line-up. Regroup and attack again and again.

Surfing is fun, exhilarating at times, and potentially dangerous if you get in over your head. I always say that I could go surfing for four hours, never catch a wave, and have the best day. Starting an entrepreneurial venture can be described the same way. It is the duck diving, paddling out, and reflecting while waiting in the line-up that make it worth the effort.

If you catch that ultimate ride, it's a bonus.

PART IV: BALANCE YOUR LIFE

CHAPTER THIRTY-FIVE:

COMPARTMENTALIZATION

I am often asked, "How do you accomplish so many different things, with diverse formats and genres on different platforms, each week?" Training and programming professional athletes, podcasting, working on graphic design, filming videos, editing, writing, running a junior golf academy, coaching, keeping up with social media, travelling the world, lecturing, creating certifications, consulting for pro sport teams, and mentoring coaches are just a few of my weekly tasks. As I write out what I do for a living, I can see how people might see it as exhausting and impossible, but I see it as an energizing list of activities that I am blessed to be able to engage in each day.

The secret to accomplishing so many diverse activities and tasks each day is to compartmentalize each item and attack it like it is the only thing in the world that needs to be accomplished at that moment. Stay in the present.

A great way to stay present and compartmentalize each task is to create an environment that is conducive to accomplishing the task effectively, as I have suggested in a previous chapter. I will change my desk, lighting, music, clothes and even go as far as changing the smell of the room using essential oils. I find writing is best performed first thing in the morning in a low-light office while wearing a cardigan with leather patches on the elbows while smoking a pipe. I'm just joking about the cardigan and pipe, but I do feel that your output will differ based on how you feel. If your clothes and work environment change the way you feel, then you need to be conscious of what you wear and where you do your work.

Wear the clothes that fit the job. An example of this is when I play golf, I like to wear pants. This is coming from a guy who wears shorts 365 days a year and wrote in his high school yearbook that my life goal was to "Wear shorts to work every day." I find that, when I golf in shorts, my swing is too fast and too explosive, and I feel like I am jumping out of my shoes. When I wear slacks, I feel like I'm at a business meeting or formal event. I walk slower, talk slower, and swing in rhythm.

If I want to be creative, I listen to loud hip hop in my headphones and wear skater clothes. When business planning, I like to be in a Starbucks with background noise or some jazz. For DreamBIGs, I seek out opulence. I will go to the lobby of a fancy hotel, a classy, old lounge bar, or an upscale coffee house. When I'm looking for life balance and serenity, I go for a hike in the forest or relax in the hot–cold plunge pools at the Scandanav Spa in Whistler. Your environment matters.

Changing your clothes or your environment is one thing, but you also must be able to compartmentalize your life mentally. I picture my home and work life as rooms.

When I transition from my work life to my home life, I walk through the imaginary door and close it behind me. I change out of my work clothes and put on my home clothes even if I never leave the house. My wife reminds me at times when work is on my mind by asking, "Are you going to get out of your work clothes and relax, or are you planning on working all night?" The work clothes she is referring to may be the golf shirt and shorts I am wearing or just a metaphorical description of my mindset.

Visualizing a room with a door you can close behind you will keep you from having work on your mind while you eat with your family or worrying about your kid's messy room while you are doing your month end.

I used to struggle with the work–life balance. I wore my entrepreneur spirit as a badge of honor. I would think of work the moment my eyes opened in the AM and keep the preverbal hamster wheel running until my eyelids slammed shut in the PM. "I'm a grinder; this is what it takes to be successful. These other weak-minded 9–5 workers will never get ahead punching the clock. *Grind*."

That attitude led to burnout and a feeling of disconnect from my family, and left me wandering around in an irritable haze, focused on a checklist that would never be completed. Once again, it took my wife to point out that this way of life was not healthy for me or anyone who kept me from checking off another box. Something had to change.

I decided to keep strict working hours. Once the clock struck 5 pm, I was done. Evenings and weekends were for family. You have a big project to complete or want to write a book? Not on family time. Set your alarm for 5:30 am and start earlier. I realized that I was more productive when I focused for short bursts of work followed by mental breaks of exercise, meditation, cooking, or listening to comedy. When I spent less time in the office, my stress decreased, my energy increased, and the quality of my work improved.

I now open and close my "work door" multiple times a day. Sure, my wife gets tired of me changing my clothes three times a day, but at least I'm mentally available to listen to her complain about it.

TODAY'S TASK: This week I want you to set a work schedule and stick to it. I want you to change your clothes each time you enter or leave your workspace. Try to match your clothes to your task. Change your environment or at least be aware of how your environment affects your productivity and inspiration. Lastly, I want you to visualize each task as a room that you can walk into and close the door behind you when you leave. Let me know how it goes.

In Chapter Twenty-Six, "How to Be a Road Warrior," I shared my secret to travel. The mantra "I give myself to travel" is a form of compartmentalization. Each compartment has different rules, a different energy, and expectations. Some athletes are shocked when they see me doing stand-up comedy. My demeanour and tone are different in the gym from the stage—same guy, just a different vibe.

I learned that there is a difference between family Jay, Coach Glass, business Jason, and my onstage persona. When I was a kid, I remember vividly visiting my dad at his sales office and seeing him in his suit with his colleagues. Work Dad had a swagger that was all business, but somehow it vanished once he left the office.

It is okay to have a variety of shades of who you are. Just make sure each one of them is authentically *you*.

CHAPTER THIRTY-SIX:

THE MIDDLE-AGED ATHLETE

If you are in your twenties and reading this book, you can skip this chapter. If you are 20 and work with middle-aged adults, listen up and listen good.

An overweight, middle-aged man walks into a bar. Bartender says, "What can I get you?"

"Just a soda water. Does that have sugar or dairy in it? Cuz I'm Keto."

Middle-aged woman at the bar leans over and says, "Nice to meet you, Keto, I'm Vegan. Want a french fry?"

"Megan?"

"No, Vegan."

"Sorry, this is my bad ear. Nice to meet you, Vegan."

"Do I look fat in this dress?"

"Unfortunately, I can't tell without my reading glasses."

Bartender says, "I should have followed my gut and finished my degree in psychology."

Forty, fifty, and even sixty? The milestone birthdays force us to stop and truly look at ourselves in the mirror. I am a true believer that your age is just a number, but if you take a snapshot each decade of your life, you will have to agree that you are getting older. Each threshold shines a light on our habits, the choices we make, and provides us

333

with an opportunity to analyze our daily routines. The person you see in the mirror is a culmination of the choices you make over time.

I remember that 39 was a big one for me. For some strange reason, my 39th birthday threw me for a loop. This was the last year of my 30s! At this point, I was happily married and a father of two, with some positive momentum in my career. My brain quickly did the math, and the equation came out to "You are one-half done with your active life and rolling downhill from here. You only have 26 years left in your career to accomplish what you need to accomplish, so you better put the pedal to the medal. You are running out of time."

I was only 15 years into my career at this point and naive to think that life was over past 80. Looking back, I laugh at myself for freaking out, but at the time, *it was real*. The person I saw in the mirror back then was a fitness coach who needed a fitness coach, a leader in the industry who needed mentorship, a healthy-lifestyle consultant who needed to drink less, sleep more, and cut back on the "I deserve this" mindset. I was unhappy with myself inside. I focused so much energy on making sure that my wife and kids were happy and that I was progressing in my career that I forgot about me.

I'm not special—I think this is a phase everyone goes through at some point in their lives. For me, it all came to a screeching halt on my 39th birthday.

Next year, I will hit my next big milestone: 50. I am happy to say that I am in better shape physically, mentally, and spiritually than I was when I was freaking out over turning 40. I am almost ten years older but somehow feel ten years younger. Today, the mirror shows me a bald head, man boobs, and armpits that perpetually think they are at hot yoga, but, somehow, I am in the best place of my life.

What changed should be your next question. I share my pillars to maximizing life and performance in the chapter DreamBIG Body. Want change? Change how you eat, drink, sleep, and move. Simple. What isn't so simple is what is coming next. The *Why?*

I have seen it a thousand times: a middle-aged man in elastic waistband khaki shorts; double XL, horizontal-striped golf shirt stretched over what he calls, "The gas tank for the love machine." Drinks too much, works too much, and is too busy to sleep. He is late, so he grabs some fast food and eats in his car on his way to another pointless meeting. Anything to distract his thoughts away from the life he didn't live. "If only I trained harder when I played high school football, I would have gone to college on a scholarship, gotten a hotter wife, would have been a better role model for my kids, and made a shit ton of money."

His doctor says he needs to lose weight and cut back on the booze but knows that he can't change this man's life in a 10-minute doctor's appointment, so he does the next best thing: prescribes him cholesterol medication to minimize his lifestyle choices and sleeping pills to help him get some critical rest and recovery. A year later, the man is diagnosed with type 2 diabetes and finally is shocked into making a change. He jumps on the next fad diet and swears that this time it's going to be different. I would like to introduce you to Keto Ken. Recently divorced Keto Ken meets recently divorced Vegan Megan.

The old Megan used "It's wine o'clock somewhere" as her life motto. She pivoted her focus away from her husband and kids and obsessed over the lives of people she barely knew on social media. Every image of people living their "best life" deepened her lack of self-worth that would gnaw at her soul until it was dampened by pinot gris. Gravity took what she thought were her best assets and made them things she felt needed covering up. She thought a bold outfit, funky hairdo, and a little glitter on the nails would draw others' attention away from her insecurities and the emptiness she felt inside. She claimed she survived the Big C after her best friend was diagnosed and beat breast cancer. She was there for her every step of the way, while the cancer in her marriage grew and started to metastasize to her relationship with her children. "That's it. I am switching to a plant-based diet. I'm not going to let cancer get me." She is three books and two bad habits away from being her best self — *not*.

The problem in both of these stories wasn't the lifestyle choices or the actions they took on a daily basis. It was the thing that was driving them to make those decisions and take those actions. We all have it inside us. You can't see it in a mirror unless you get your face six inches away from it and look yourself in the eye. Look right through your eye into your soul.

Many of you will try this and have to look away. You look away because you can't believe how you have neglected this precious part of you for so many years. Some people see it as their inner child because the last time they were truly in touch with that part of themselves was when they were a child. It's like their true self has been suspended in time.

All the things that surround you mean nothing if you are not in touch with the inner you. Your job title, your personal belongings, your physical appearance, your health issues, your relationships—they are all in the periphery. They are very important but still the periphery. You can try to change them, tweak them, or polish them until they shine, but it will all be for naught if the inner self isn't cared for. The emptiness won't go away with a new car, imported wine, or a younger lover.

I have always felt a dark void in me. I have tried to fill it many times with many different distractions and never succeeded. But awareness of what the void is has started the process of turning the darkness into light. Meditation, enlightenment through the study of other's journeys, and having a sense of humor and acceptance of my shortcomings are all part of a great start. Making decisions from my true self, trusting that feeling in my gut that's never wrong, and fighting through the fear of failure is my path to connecting to the part of me that is clawing its way out of the abyss inside.

Do you have to wait until you are 40, 50, or 60 to get in touch with the real you? I have provided for you the framework to create change: the knowledge to build a DreamBIG life and pursue a career that will truly fulfill you.

Go back and review the chapter that covers the topic you are so desperate to change. Go. Now.

I will wait for you when you are ready for the next chapter of this book.

CHAPTER THIRTY-EIGHT:
SELF CONFIDENCE AND SELF BELIEF

Recently I installed a motion sensor in my backyard. It lights up the entire yard if anything moves. Living in a forest, we have many visitors in our backyard throughout the night: skunks, racoons, cats, coyotes, and, I soon came to realize, rats.

"Hun. Look, the family of raccoons is back."

"Aww, they are so cute."

Or "Huuuun? Was that a rat?"

"A rat? No. Oh no. You need to deal with that. We can't have rats living under our deck. Gross."

I put out some rat poison and placed a rat trap that could snap a Slim Jim in half, beside the deck. I put it out before bed and went off to sleep. At 11:36 pm, I was awakened by a loud snap. I was stoked. We got him. Or did we?

For the next three hours, I lay there listening to the flipping, flopping, and squealing as the rat fought for its life. Being a vegan, I felt like a hypocrite. I was conflicted whether or not I had made the right decision. When I bought the supplies, the young kid at checkout asked me if I understood the ramifications of my actions, and I told him I did and was going through with it anyway.

But now I questioned my choice. Was it wrong for me to use regular cheddar when a vegan cheddar substitute

339

was available? Saving a few bucks meant that this rat had to die knowing its last meal caused distress and suffering to the cow that produced the dairy that was used to make the cheese that tempted the rat to his demise. All of this could have been avoided if I followed my vegan gut feeling and used vegan cheese. How would I face the pimple checkout clerk at Whole Foods now?

I had a similar morally-conflicted experience when I went quail hunting with some friends. After four unsuccessful hours in the bush, we were starving. Steve was in charge of bringing lunch. When he opened the pack, to my vegan heart's dismay, he only packed egg salad sandwiches. I lost my shit. "How am I supposed to eat those? You know I am a vegan. Now I have to endure another four hours of grueling quail hunting on an empty stomach?"

Okay, I am not a vegan and never was, but this little anecdote that I just shared with you is a reflection on how some of you treat many aspects of your life. You set strict belief barriers on what you can and cannot do. But then your actions are so contradictory to your belief structure that you can't even see the hypocrisy.

Being Undeniable requires you to match your belief in yourself with the actions you take. You are strong and confident when you design your DreamBIG and see yourself as a superhero. Then at the first sign of trouble or hardship, you pack up any confidence and self respect you have and flush them down the toilet. To prevent this con-

340

tradiction of self, it is so important that you set out your belief structure in writing, which I will return to later.

Self-confidence is fleeting. For many of us, self-confidence comes from positive things happening in our lives. When things are going great, we feel great, and our confidence is high. When things take a turn for the worse, we feel stressed, we become unsure of ourselves, and our confidence is low.

How is it possible that you can be on top of the world one day and feel like throwing in the towel the next? Some days the golf hole looks like a hula hoop and the next moment it seems to have clingfilm on it. You hit three pointers like they are free throws, and the next day you are tossing up bricks. Self-confidence is a fickle thing. Your self-belief, however, is something completely different: It is cast in concrete.

I remember an interview with the legendary golfer Colin "Monty" Montgomery. Colin had fallen from being the number 1 golfer on the European Tour and in the top 10 in the World Rankings for 400 weeks due to poor play and a lack of self-confidence. For several years, Colin was known as the best golfer never to win a Major, and the pressure got to him. His public divorce and countless bowls of custard weren't helping, either. In 2005, out of the blue, he returned to his old form and won the European Order of Merit and catapulted back to number 10 in the World Rankings. Colin started contending for the win each week, and was asked, "It seems you have your game and your confidence back. Which one came first?" Colin replied, "They go hand in hand. You play well, and your confidence goes up. When your confidence is up, the game feels easier, and you play better. You can't fake confidence."

It is human nature to have ebbs and flows of self-confidence. But self-belief at its core should be etched in stone. The problem with Monty wasn't that he lost confidence in his putter—he lost his inner belief structure. Missing a few putts and a few cuts will cause a temporary dip in your playing confidence, but life altering events, like a failed marriage, can shake the foundation of your self-belief. Therefore, it is imperative that you take the time to write out an account of who you are and how you truly feel about yourself.

This is the "Look into yourself in the mirror" exercise on paper. You may find this very challenging, but that is a good thing. We shy away from the truth about ourselves because we live our lives playing a character, acting out scene after scene, hoping to convince the world that this is our true self. The list you are about to write out isn't being written by the character you play; it is being written by the actor and writer of the script. You can't hide behind a fake moustache and glasses. Unlike your friends and family, you can see right through the disguise.

TODAY'S TASK: Take out a piece of paper or open a word document on your computer. I prefer paper and pen here so you won't get distracted by notifications and pop-ups on your computer screen, but the choice is yours. Take your time with the following exercises.

1. Rank your self-confidence right now from 1-10, with 1 being Piglet and 10 being Rick Flare.

2. Rank your self-belief from 1-10. This is your deep-down foundation of self-belief. From your worst day to your best, this number should be consistent.

3. Finish the following sentence: "My self-belief is built upon my ability to _____." This should be a unique trait or skill set you possess that makes you who you are—that is, your Golden Nugget.

4. "My confidence is often broken when _____."

5. "My confidence is at its highest when ____."

Review your answers and look for patterns. Is your confidence and self-belief built on ego, fear, others' opinions of you, past success or failures, or is it based on the lies you tell yourself? Was it challenging to be honest with your self evaluation?

This task is designed to look below the surface layer of your self-belief. I remember a craze that swept the nation back in the late 80s. Everyone was buying posters called Magic Eye Pictures. At first glance, the poster was just a collage of thousands of tiny, colorful blobs smushed to-gether. But if you looked at the picture with a blurred, cross-eyed gaze, a 3-D image would appear, kind of like the black-and-white optical illusion that at first looks like an old woman's face but through a different angle looks like a sexy woman's side profile. Once you see the picture in the picture, you can never not see it.

Self discovery is the same. Once you see who you truly are and reveal the true person within the person, you can't un-see it.

Your true self-image and self-belief structure will be the drivers behind your actions when you are faced with obstacles. Wouldn't it be a good idea to know how you would react in the face of danger before you go hunting for the dragon that stole the princess? Whenever I start the process of designing a DreamBIG, I look at what would happen if it didn't come true. It is easy to DreamBIG when you are focusing on the triumphs, but it is equally important to prepare yourself for the worst-case scenario (WCS), which is the one that will challenge your self-belief and the foundation of your confidence.

Unfortunately, too many young entrepreneurs neglect this stage of the DreamBIG. They figure out that they were not prepared for the stresses of potential failure right at the moment that the fire from the dragon's mouth rains down upon them. Planning for success is the easy part. Creating an action plan for failure and accepting the risk of failure is challenging.

Here is a great exercise for you to try when you are creating your DreamBIG: Write out your goal, the worst-case scenario (WCS), and what your action would be if the worst-case scenario came true. Here is an example:

DreamBIG: Open up a skateboard shop.

WCS: We don't sell enough skateboards to pay the distributor in the 90 days they give us to pay the bill for the initial inventory we bought.

WCS Action: Develop contingency float fund to buffer any slow months or unexpected costs. The float fund will need to be a part of the initial business plan budget, and we will not open our doors until the financing and float fund is in place.

TODAY'S TASK: Perform this same exercise with one aspect of your DreamBIG. It doesn't have to be your final DreamBIG end goal but maybe a subset or actionable mini-goal that you need to accomplish to get you closer to the end goal.

I believe this will be an easier task than tackling the big one and will breed confidence in the exercise of preparing for the worst.

As mentioned in previous chapters, I am a pessimist. My lack of optimism is a huge contributor to my happiness. A true optimist wakes up each morning expecting to see the sun shining and to hear their birds chirping. Anything less than that and somehow, they are disappointed.

Living in the Northwest, you wake up expecting rain, sleet, and an overcast sky. If it rains, I am happy, but if the clouds break and that glowing orb in the sky shines through, I am ecstatic, but not so impressed by the sun revealing itself to me that my emotion for the day would be altered.

I am not one to get in an elevator and happily comment to the stranger standing next to me about how great it was to see the sun this morning. Those people should be placed in isolation until they learn how to interact with the world without making everyone around them want to shoot themselves.

I have always been someone who looked for the worst-case scenario in life and decided whether or not I could cope with it. Could I find happiness in a world without sunshine? Could I be happy recording my podcast if no one was listening? The fact that the sun does come out from time to time and that we were fortunate to build an audience and a community of Glisteners is a bonus. (By the way, they named themselves the Glisteners, not me. The Glass Listeners somehow found a portmanteau by blending these two words that sound more like the oiled-up pony boys on the back of a float than podcast fans.)

Everything that comes to me or is created by my team is a blessing. It is all gravy because I have explored the reality that I could live in a world with nothing and still be okay. No house, no business, no fame, no fortune, and I could still truly be happy. When you find a way to find joy in your work without the benefits that go along with it, you are free from the pressures that surround you while you try to protect it.

This doesn't mean that I take what I do in my career lightly. The exact opposite: I value and respect my goals and my DreamBIG so much that I am willing to risk it all in the quest of acquiring it. That freedom breeds confidence and that confidence is embedded in the foundation of my positive belief in myself.

What do you do if your self-belief is low or negatively skewed? If you gave yourself a 5 or less on the task of scoring your confidence and self-belief, we need to dig down and get to the root of this false belief. I say it is a false belief because I know that if we tap into the right areas and dive deep into the underlying source of your lack of self-belief, we can turn it around. The Golden Nugget that we explored in the earlier chapters and an account of how your loved ones perceive you truly reflect who you really are.

We must separate self-esteem (what you think of yourself) from pride (what you think others think of you). When someone puts you down or gives their opinion of you, what they are really doing is holding up a mirror to how you see yourself. If someone came up to me and said, "Jay, you're not funny," that wouldn't bother me one bit. I know I am funny. I have been funny since I was first able to talk. But if they said, "Jay, did you put on weight?" that would probably put me on a course of a negative self-image for two or three days, a gnawing undercurrent that would cause me to make side glances in mirrors and ask my wife, "Do I look fat in this dress?"

The difference between "You're not funny" and "You're fat" is that one of them taps into an insecurity rooted in a half truth. As someone who has been an athlete and coach my whole life, there is a public expectation to be fit. I work my ass off in the gym, perform hot yoga, run each week, and eat healthily to keep fit and feel great. When you have that much invested in one aspect of your life and it's not reflected in how others see you, it is deflating. I know it shouldn't, but it does. "Jay, you are bald." I'm fine with that because there is nothing I can do about it, and I did nothing wrong to cause it. I am just like my grandfather and his grandfather: bald. But my weight, good or bad, is 100% in my power. That makes it personal.

The great comedian and philosopher, Russel Brand, said, "What others think of you is none of your business." It truly is only their interpretation of who you are. It's not real. What is real, however, is how we perceive their opinions. Why don't they like me? Instantly you reflect on all the reasons they may not like you. Be aware of those reasons that you conjure up. Those reflect how you see yourself. I don't care what others think of me, but I do care about how their opinions make me feel about myself. The real sadness is that many of you will morph into a hybrid of what you think others think of you.

If you dive deep into your own self-belief and heal your ego from within, you will see your weaknesses the way I see my humor. I am funny, I know I am funny, and if you don't like it, that's your problem. I learned this lesson from my wife who grew up in Scotland. Scottish people are born with this inherent ability to not give a fuck about what others think of them. She meets people and thinks, *If they don't like me, that's their problem.* And that's a big reason why most people who meet her do like her. How Undeniable is your self-image?

TODAY'S TASK: Let's take an inventory of things that we react to in our personal self-belief. Write down everything that would trigger a downward spiral if a peer was to negatively paint you with a brush of self reflection. I want you to put an "I" beside the items that are "In" your control and an "O" beside those items that are "Outside" your control.

Now cross off the ones with the "O" beside it, and let's focus on the ones labelled "I." How many of them are real and how many of them are you willing to take responsibility for? If you are going to take full responsibility for them, add them to an actionable list that you can build into your daily routine to start the process of removing them.

"Too deep, Jay. Come on, man, I thought this journey was going to give me all the answers, not force me to mine for the answers in the depths of my soul." I won't apologize.

This is the process needed to make you Undeniable. A foundation of self-belief built from balsa wood will not be Undeniable in the face of hardship or obstacles. Concrete requires the right ratio of ingredients to maximize its integrity. Your Undeniability requires a deep analysis of what makes up the recipe that your self-belief is built upon.

CHAPTER THIRTY-NINE:

THE YIN–YANG OF LIFE

The yin–yang symbol that you see on every martial arts studio logo, tattoos from the 1980's, and on surf and skateboards made by T&C is a perfect metaphor for life: the ebb and flow of the positive and negative, feminine and masculine, order and chaos, the light and the dark. It represents balance. The Yang is the white side of the image, and the Yin is the black side. The white Yang side represents positivity, masculinity, and light. The black Yin side represents the negative, feminine, and darkness. Before you get your knickers in a knot, I didn't come up with this. The Yin–Yang is an ancient Chinese Taoist symbol from thousands of years ago.

When I practice yoga, I perform a one-hour yang-yin routine. I start with 30 minutes of masculine, strenuous holds for a set number of breaths, then transition into 30 minutes of passive feminine stretches. Once you complete the Yang portion, you are dying to lie down in the pool of sweat you have created beneath you and release all the tension you built up. If you did the passive stretches without the strenuous holds, they would have no meaning. The masculine holds followed by weightlifting and wind sprints would leave me unbalanced for the rest of the day. You need the Yang with the Yin.

If the Yin-Yang is a true representation of the balanced cycle of life, it would imply that for every positive thing that happens in life, there is an equal but opposite negative. You might think, *Well, that sucks. You are saying that when something good happens in my life, something bad is right around the corner?* Yes. Maybe not tomorrow, but at some point.

If we look deeper, we can see how both Yang and Yin always live in harmony and in balance in all things. If you look deeply at the symbol, you will see that there is a black dot on the Yang side and a white dot on the Yin. This means that each side lives in harmony with the other but also has a piece of the other within. Women are predominantly estrogen and progesterone driven, but at the same time, to a lesser degree, have the male hormone testosterone coursing through their bodies as well, while men have the feminine estrogen hormone in them.

If there is a positive, somewhere within that positive is a negative. When bad things happen in life, there is always some good that comes from it. Your job is to see the light inside the darkness and the darkness in the light in everything that you experience. If you live in a world of black and white, you will be disappointed.

Just because your day starts with a negative doesn't mean you need to throw the rest of the day out the window. "I am only going to have positive things happen in my day today. What is that smell? Burnt toast? Oh shit. I am either having a stroke or I left my toast in too long.

Ugh. There goes my perfect day. It is ruined. I guess I'll just walk down to the SPCA and pound some pound puppies. Punt a few bunnies over Mr. Abernathy's fence and trip old ladies while they cross the street. I might as well — the universe is against me today."

Everything is in balance at all times. If you can accept this statement and truly live by it, you will always be in balance too. You lost your house due to rising mortgage interest rates? Wasn't the journey toward owning your own home the true gift? You now have the tools to do it again minus all the mistakes that you made the first time. You won the lottery? Understand that there are going to be some complications, hardships, and challenges coming your way in the form of money management, relatives looking for handouts, and the loss of your ability to daydream about things that are beyond your reach. Your goal is to make the positives as big as possible and endure the hardships with a mindset that this too shall pass.

There is a mathematical concept known as *regression to the mean*. The best representation of this is in the game of golf. In golf, most courses are a par 72. That means it should take you 72 strokes to make it around the course. On an exceptional day, a professional can shoot 10 under par 62. If he or she averages over multiple rounds of golf a mean score of 72, you would expect that, for every 62, there will be an 82 around the corner.

Over time, you always regress toward your mean. You may shoot 62 followed by a 72, 78, and 76. The mean is still

72. The problem is that if you shot a 62, you would think that you have broken the barrier of greatness, and you expect to shoot 62 or close to it every time you go out. The goal is not to shoot 62 every round but to slowly move the mean from 72 to 70. Over time with consistent quality play based on sound fundamentals, you will lower your mean.

You need to base your life on the mean, not the highlight reel.

The same can be said about the Yang-Yin of life. Your Yang-Yin could be negatively skewed. Being a homeless addict would be a horrible way of life, but within their personal darkness, they have good days and bad days. The handsome, country club, trust fund, Ivy league college student lives a far more positive and stress-free life in comparison but also has bad days—like when he runs out of hair product, or the soft-serve yogurt shop is closed and he is now left to deal with the emptiness inside from a life without meaning.

Both the homeless and handsome live the Yin and Yang of life. The key is where you place the Yin and Yang. Make your bad days grey and your good days fluorescent, or choose to move your mean down toward the darkness where the good days are light grey and the bad days are an abyss.

Your goal is to get uncomfortable. The bigger the Yin, the bigger the Yang. The bigger the success, the bigger the fall from grace when it is lost. If you didn't put anything into your business, you won't get anything out of it. Most great entrepreneurs created their empires on the ambers of businesses that went up in flames of failure.

The more you open yourself up to love, the more heartache you will feel when you lose it. I have dear friends who were hurt in love and vow to never to love again, but that is just when you need to love even harder. You felt the loss of love, and now you will value it and nurture it more than ever. This will expand and grow your Yin-Yang. Running from it will shrink your Yang-Yin like the Grinch's heart.

You get up at 4 am every day and run until the sun comes up. You train by chopping wood and dragging tires tied around your waist up hills. Yes, this is the story of Rocky. His triumph in the ring was built upon the pain from his losses and the discomfort he put his body through in his training. It may be a fictional story (don't tell that to the fine residents walking the streets of Philadelphia. They still think he is real), but there are thousands of real stories like his being created everyday. The more uncomfortable you make your body, the more it adapts. The harder you work, the more you enjoy the restful times. The better you sleep, the better you can perform in your workout the next day. Yin fucking Yang.

During the COVID-19 pandemic, I was speaking to my Nana, who was 99 years old at the time. The conversation was so impactful that I asked her if I could quickly hook up my podcast equipment and record the rest of our conversation. This is a woman who lived through World Wars, the decade-long Dust Bowl drought while living on her family farm on the Canadian prairie, the death of her husband, the births of her three children, grandchildren, great-grandchildren, and now great-great-grandchildren. She saw the first car in her community drive by while she rode her horse home from school. She witnessed the radio replaced by the TV and the computer replaced by the smartphone that she was speaking to me through that day. She has seen it all.

Here is a summary of our conversation: The pain people feel today is a pain based on life not meeting their expectations. When you are in a drought on the prairie with no food, no water, no heat, and no entertainment for a decade, you expect nothing other than life being hard. Then you spend the rest of your life with life meeting your expectations of it being exactly that.

I asked her, "If you could freeze life in one decade, which one would you choose? Pre- or post-industrial revolution? Before technology or after?" Her answer was the late 1960s and early 1970s. It was a special time when people lived free and enjoyed a life of abundance. This was just before technology changed everything. She said that technology made life easier for everyone. The easier life gets, the less enjoyment you get out of it. People seek hobbies like baking and gardening, but in the 1930s, you did those things to survive. You didn't need to exercise because life was exercise. You ate for fuel, not flavor.

The Yin-Yang of life was *big*: big love and big heartache, big joy and bigger pain. Technology made phone calls easier but mean less. A beautiful, handwritten letter was replaced with an emoji in a text. People replaced face-to-face time with screen time, which they named FaceTime.

So what does this mean to current generations that think this is the human experience? Know that life will be hard, but it gets better. "You need faith in a higher power and believe it will get better," she proclaimed. There will be incredible, new advances that will make it easier to live, but those same advances will take away what it means to be alive.

Every great leader, athlete, or artist came from a life of struggle. When my kids were young, I pondered this. If I want my kids to be great, they must learn lessons through hardship. But you can't manufacture hardship, can you? No, that would be child abuse. But they do need to experience hardship and struggle in their lives. You need to get cut from the team to learn how bad you want to be on the team. You need to lose love to learn how precious love is.

When I would share with my friends that I hoped my daughter would experience puke in her hair at a party, have her heart broken, and fail at something she loves before she finishes high school, they all thought I was crazy. You never want to wish pain and hardship on someone. Life does a good enough job of that by itself. But you also don't want to candy-coat life and protect them from living.

Life is a Yin-Yang. The bigger your Yin, the bigger your Yang, and the bigger your Yang, the bigger your Yin. The Yang starts an action, and Yin receives it. A life worth living demands you push the boundaries of both.

CHAPTER FORTY:

TIME TO RECONNECT

It's easy to get caught up in the external world. We are constantly being bombarded with news stories from faraway lands, stories about celebrities and sports stars we admire, and sensationalized drama about the world and how we fit in it. The media try to get you to take sides on issues that you never even knew existed. "Hell, yeah, I want to protect the nasal passages of the sea turtle." Meanwhile, your toddler is choking on a grape that wasn't cut in half.

Humans have med- itated for centuries. Meditation is going internal and blocking out all the external distractions and getting in touch with your inner self. Journaling and writing what you are grateful for each day are rituals that again bring you back internally to recognize what really matters in your immediate world. These techniques have been around long before your two feet touched the earth.

The Stoic writings of Seneca and Marcus Aurelius were passages about what they saw in their daily struggles, sharing lessons on how to live a life worth living. They didn't write gossip or obsess over the rumours that gladiator Tim may play both sides of the fence. They stayed internal, focussing on what is tangibly right in front of them and how it fit in the ethereal world of the cosmos. But then again, they weren't force-fed photoshopped images, sensationalized stories, and fake news through social media and 24-hour news outlets. It's the one thing you can't change, and most people focus 90% of their attention on it.

Turn off your TV and pick up a book, sign off from your Instagram and Twitter for a month or a week, and write in a journal. It's not going anywhere, and you can pick it up right where you left off at any time. You are not going to miss anything. If a comet is hurling toward the earth, you will hear about it. You won't miss anything. Ben and Jen are back together again? Who cares? Don't focus on them. Focus on your relationship with your significant other or your children.

You won't miss anything by not paying attention to the noise. But you will reconnect with what is really important. You will re-establish relationships with those around you, become more productive, and, once again, get to know the most important person in the world: *you*.

I haven't watched the news or subscribed to a newspaper for the past ten years. Every time I am in the States, I am bombarded with either CNN or Fox News, depending on what city or state I am in. I am blown away by the idea that every restaurant, lounge, coffee shop, and 3x6-inch screen on the plane is pumping out this 24-hour news cycle. Fear, hate, and debate sprinkled with a touching story of a transgender 8-year-old who found an abandoned puppy and in doing so found a new best friend. Awwww.

If you get tired of the relentless stories about things you have no control over, you pop over to a morning show or *The View* and listen to celebrities on Prozac talk about the same stories with a coffee in their hands.

What's the alternative? Put your head in the sand and hope it goes away? No. Awareness and the ability to separate yourself from it is the key. If you were watching the 75th Marvel superhero movie that came out this year where Ironman was unable to stop the world from imploding from the weight of discarded water bottles that built up in the ocean, you wouldn't shed a tear. You need to look at the news the same way. Ask yourself the following:

Does it affect me or directly affect the people in my inner circle?

Can I change it?

Do I feel strongly enough about this issue or topic to put myself in a position that I can create change? And in doing so, what am I willing to give up to get involved in this cause. My DreamBIG?

Here is an example. I am a Canadian. I have a ton of friends and colleagues who live in the US. When I hear political stories about their president, I can only watch it from the outside like I was watching a movie. Can I change it? No. Can I vote? No. So, like a movie, I can turn it off and walk away from the TV without it taking up space in my mind.

361

Even if you live in the US, I highly recommend you do the same. Can *you* change it? Yes. How? Vote. When? In four years. Can't wait that long? You can quit your job and join a local political party and make a difference today. But at what cost? What are you willing to give up to make that happen? Close your small business, move your family, and get a Lego haircut so you can fit in with the other politicians?

We are all looking for a distraction. Social media was built on this very premise. We can't do anything without either putting a podcast on in the background or putting together the perfect lawn-mowing playlist. It takes me eight minutes to pick a YouTube video that I can watch for the three minutes it takes to make coffee. These distractions are a form or *The Resistance* that we covered in Chapter 9.

Attention spans are getting shorter, and movies and podcasts are getting longer. There is a feature on your iPhone that gives you a daily screen-time report. My phone said I average 4.5 hours a day of screen time. I justify that amount of time by convincing myself that I use my phone for work. When I looked deeper, it showed that 4 of those hours were on Pornhub, and I contemplated changing my profession. My new name is Sylvester Stabone. Seriously, though, how can I justify devoting 4.5 hours of 16 waking hours to social media and YouTube videos? How much could I accomplish if I put 4.5 hours into solid work toward my current project?

I get it: You need distractions or a break every once in a while. It is unrealistic to work for 16 hours a day and sleep a solid 8. You just need to be conscious of the time you spend on the distractions that control you.

I understand that some people will read this and take a side. You can agree or disagree, but I can assure you of the following: If you choose not to disconnect from the machine, you need to acknowledge that the space you give up in your mind to the drama it propagates is space that you could have allotted to your DreamBIG. It is one of the biggest obstacles you will face on your journey to accomplishing your DreamBIG. Think about all the momentum you have gained while reading this book. You are telling me that you will let all your dreams vanish because you need to check your Instagram, YouTube, and Netflix series for five hours a day? Save that for your vacation that you earned when your DreamBIG became a reality.

What is directly in front of you right now? What is on your checklist for today? If you focus 100% of your attention on that list, you will get one step closer to accomplishing your dream. It is all you have control over — that is a powerful thing.

Take action and start. Now.

PART V: YOU HAVE REACHED YOUR DESTINATION.

I know it can be scary to start. Once you commit to your DreamBIG, there is no looking back. What if you fail? What if it doesn't turn out the way you want it to? These are questions that will surface when you are about to put your first step forward toward your DreamBIG. I want you to replace those nagging questions with the following thoughts.

What is scarier? Starting your DreamBIG or continuing the journey that you are currently on? There is a reason why you started this book. You owe it to the person who picked it up, the person who dared to DreamBIG. "Maybe I need to read four more books, take three certifications, and then I'll be ready." No—you *are* ready. And it's time to get down to business.

Think about all the new skills and perspectives you have gained through this book, such as these:

The Box: You have identified how others currently see you and have decided what you want the outside of your box to look like so it matches the contents.

The Golden Nugget: You have identified your Golden Nugget, that one thing that makes you stand out amongst your peers, the thing that makes you unique. And you are ready to let it shine in everything you do.

Life Purpose: You have established your purpose that drives everything you do. Your purpose should be simple, making it easy for you to see when you have veered too far from that purpose in your daily actions.

The Currency: You are clear on what you value most in life. You know what type of currency you want in exchange for the hard work you put toward your DreamBIG.

The Resistance: You have removed things from your life that would create resistance or a potential obstacle on your DreamBIG quest.

DreamBIG: You have the ability to DreamBIG and break it into one-, three-, and five-year goals. You can dream so big that the thought of it becoming a reality sends a chill down your spine.

OverDelivering: Doing the job is not enough. You need to OverDeliver on it. It is the way you approach everything in life. Ask you for a dozen, and you give me a baker's dozen.

Intention: You approach tasks, relationships, conversations, and your dreams with clearly defined intention.

A Game Plan: You know how to make long-term plans with checkpoints to keep you on course. You plan for the inevitable obstacles and put contingency plans in place in the event that the shit really hits the fan.

Speaking and Sales: You can sell essential lavender oil to a homemaker, polish a turd into gold, and set up and punch your delivery to close the deal.

Creating the Problem and Being the Solution: You are the solution to the problem you created in the mind of your audience.

Being Undeniable: You have the blueprint for an Undeniable body and mind. You can travel like a pro, paddle out into the danger zone, and own the ABCs of closing.

Compartmentalization: You can break up your day, your week, and your life into manageable chunks that receive 100% of your focus before being put away until you meet again.

Yin-Yang: You accept that there is positive in every negative and darkness in every light, and wouldn't have it any other way.

Destination: You are here.

You have all the tools you need to transform your life. If you don't like what you created, you need to go back and rework your way through the process. Were you honest with yourself? Did you chase a dream that never truly had a chance of providing you with fulfillment?

Did you create exactly what you envisioned when you started this DreamBIG journey? I want you to feel accomplished, fulfilled, and proud of yourself. Use this energy to propel you into your next project. As I shared at the start of this book, I have a stack of DreamBIG notebooks that have all come to fruition. Each one built upon the confidence and momentum of the one before it. The dreams didn't always get bigger in scope, but they all got closer to satisfying my deepest desires.

I have had many Coach Glass Mentorship graduates who reached for the stars on their first DreamBIG and saved themselves a stack of test dreams. You may want to start with a few smaller DreamBIGs to refine your system. The important thing is that you never stop dreaming.

AFTERWORD:

A LETTER FROM ME TO YOU

You made it. Your DreamBIG is right here. What seemed like a pipedream when you first started this book is now a tangible destination that you have laser focus on. You will now fill that dark hole inside you that you use to store all your fears of starting something big and the regrets from opportunities unrealized.

The dark hole is glowing with a beacon of light that fills it with hope, Undeniable determination, a plan of action, and a need to OverDeliver. You have opened the parts of your mind that allow you to accept that anything is possible. You have the ingredients and recipe to quench your insatiable desire to DreamBIG. You have learned the skills and practiced the foundations that drive you to OverDeliver.

You put your best work forward time and time again, opening new opportunities in your life and blazing trails for others to follow. You unleash the inner strength you possess and fortitude to be Undeniable. The tasks you have checked off in each chapter and the lessons you have learned from the stories you have read have transformed your brain into a lean mean DreamBIG machine.

Many of you have already reached the goal you initially set at the start of this book, and you are now ready to dream bigger. Others set a goal that now has traction for the first time in your life, and you are now ready to take the steps needed to see it through. Regardless of where you are, together we have created a spark.

This book is a catalyst for change. Once it is set in motion, there is no turning back. You can't stop what has now been put in motion. You gave yourself an opportunity to DreamBIG, and now there is no other option than to OverDeliver on it. When others get in your way or you hit the inevitable roadblocks along your path, you will be Undeniable. You are ready.

DreamBIG, OverDeliver, be Undeniable, and—

Cheers, everybody.

Manufactured by Amazon.ca
Acheson, AB